Regis College Library
15 ST. MARY STREET
TORONTO, ONTARIO, CANADA
M4Y 2R5

WITHDRAWN

Sage
Priest
Prophet

LIBRARY OF ANCIENT ISRAEL

Douglas A. Knight, *General Editor*

Sage
Priest
Prophet

Religious and Intellectual Leadership in Ancient Israel

JOSEPH BLENKINSOPP

BS
1199
L4
B58
1995

Regis College Library
15 ST. MARY STREET
TORONTO, ONTARIO, CANADA
M4Y 2R5

WESTMINSTER JOHN KNOX PRESS
LOUISVILLE, KENTUCKY

© 1995 Joseph Blenkinsopp

All rights reserved. No part of this book may be reproduced or transmitted in any form or by any means, electronic or mechanical, including photocopying, recording, or by any information storage or retrieval system, without permission in writing from the publisher. For information, address Westminster John Knox Press, 100 Witherspoon Street, Louisville, Kentucky 40202-1396.

Scripture quotations from the Revised Standard Version of the Bible are copyright 1946, 1952, © 1971, 1973 by the Division of Christian Education of the National Council of the Churches of Christ in the U.S.A. and are used by permission.

Book design by Publishers' WorkGroup
Cover design by Kim Wohlenhaus

First edition

Published by Westminster John Knox Press
Louisville, Kentucky

This book is printed on acid-free paper that meets the American National Standards Institute Z39.48 standard. ♾

PRINTED IN THE UNITED STATES OF AMERICA

95 96 97 98 99 00 01 02 03 04 — 10 9 8 7 6 5 4 3 2 1

Library of Congress Cataloging-in-Publication Data

Blenkinsopp, Joseph, date.
    Sage, priest, prophet : intellectual and religious leadership in ancient Israel / Joseph Blenkinsopp.
        p.   cm. — (Library of ancient Israel)
    Includes bibliographical references and indexes..
    ISBN 0-664-21954-3 (alk. paper)
    1. Leadership in the Bible.   2. Priests, Jewish.   3. Prophets.   4. Bible. O.T. — Criticism, interpretation, etc.   I. Title.   II. Series.
BS1199.L4B58   1995
296.6'1'0933—dc20   95-1792

Contents

Foreword

The historical and literary questions preoccupying biblical scholars since the Enlightenment have primarily focused on the events and leaders of ancient Israel, the practices and beliefs of Yahwistic religion, and the oral and written stages in the development of the people's literature. Considering how little was known about Israel and indeed the whole ancient Near East just three centuries ago, the gains achieved to date have been extraordinary, due in no small part to the unanticipated discovery of innumerable texts and artifacts.

Recent years have witnessed a new turn in biblical studies, occasioned in large part by a growing lack of confidence in the "assured results" of past generations of scholars. At the same time, an increased openness to the methods and issues of other disciplines such as anthropology, sociology, linguistics, and literary criticism has allowed new questions to be posed regarding the old materials. Social history, a well-established area within the field of historical studies, has proved especially fruitful as a means of analyzing specific segments of the society. Instead of concentrating predominantly on national events, leading individuals, political institutions, and "high culture," social historians attend to broader, and more basic issues such as social organization, conditions in cities and villages, life stages, environmental context, power distribution according to class and status, and social stability and instability. To ask such questions of ancient Israel shifts the focus away from those with power and the events they instigated and onto the everyday realities and social subtleties experienced by the vast majority of the population. Such inquiry has now gained new force with the application of various forms of ideological criticism and other methods designed to ferret out the political, economic, and social interests concealed in the sources.

This series represents a collaborative effort to investigate several specific topics—politics, economics, religion, literature, material culture, law, intellectual leadership, ethnic identity, social marginalization, the international context, and canon formation—each in terms of its social dimensions and processes within ancient Israel. Some of these subjects have not been explored in depth until now; others are familiar areas currently in need of reexamination. While the sociohistorical approach provides the general perspective for all volumes of the series, each author has the latitude to determine the most appropriate means for dealing with the topic at hand. Individually and collectively, the volumes aim to expand our vision of the culture and society of ancient Israel and thereby generate new appreciation for its impact on subsequent history.

The sages, priests, and prophets of Israel are rightly credited with crucial contributions to the religious life of the community and to the eventual canon of the Hebrew Bible. Yet as Joseph Blenkinsopp so clearly indicates, the dynamics of the leadership roles played by these figures in Israelite society are not fully appreciated simply by considering these contributions. Drawing on the sociological investigation of role performance and audience expectation, he shows how these intellectual leaders were able to relate effectively with each other and with the public. The general context of social interaction can thus go far toward revealing the character of their work, for they relied on continuity with their predecessors while at the same time responding to the various political and professional pressures of their own day. In the end their contributions coalesced to form a vital religious and intellectual tradition during the period of emergent Judaism. To reveal these processes, the author ranges over a vast amount of ancient and modern materials, and the result represents a significant advance in our understanding of these celebrated figures and in the social settings.

Douglas A. Knight
General Editor

Preface

Except where indicated, translations of biblical texts are my own. However, translations of Sirach (Ben Sira) are taken, with permission, from the Oxford Annotated Apocrypha, Revised Standard Version. Where the Hebrew and the English verse numberings differ, an unfortunately frequent occurrence, the English numbering is added in parentheses or brackets.

I wish to thank the administration of the University of Notre Dame and my chairman Lawrence Cunningham for granting me a leave of absence in the spring semester of 1992, during which most of the first draft was written. Thanks are also due to Douglas Knight of Vanderbilt University Divinity School, for inviting me to contribute to the Library of Ancient Israel series, and to my editors at Westminster John Knox Press, with whom I have enjoyed a long and agreeable relationship.

I offer this book as a small token of gratitude and appreciation to my wife, Jean Porter, who has enriched my life in ways too many to tell.

Abbreviations

ABD	*The Anchor Bible Dictionary*
AJSL	*American Journal of Semitic Languages and Literature*
ANET	James B. Pritchard, ed., *Ancient Near Eastern Texts Relating to the Old Testament*
Ant.	Josephus, *Antiquities of the Jews*
AP	A. Cowley, ed., *Aramaic Papyri of the Fifth Century B.C.*
ARS	*Annual Review of Sociology*
ASR	*American Sociological Review*
b.	Babylonian Talmud
Bib	*Biblica*
BN	*Biblische Notizen*
C	Chronicler
C.Ap.	Josephus, *Contra Apion*
CBQ	*Catholic Biblical Quarterly*
Dtr	Deuteronomic historian
EJ	*Encyclopaedia Judaica*
HS	*Hebrew Studies*
HUCA	*Hebrew Union College Annual*
IDB	*Interpreter's Dictionary of the Bible*
IEJ	*Israel Exploration Journal*
JBL	*Journal of Biblical Literature*
JEA	*Journal of Egyptian Archaeology*
JJS	*Journal of Jewish Studies*
JNES	*Journal of Near Eastern Studies*
JQR	*Jewish Quarterly Review*
JRAI	*Journal of the Royal Anthropological Institute*
JRE	*Journal of Religious Ethics*
JSOT	*Journal for the Study of the Old Testament*
JSS	*Journal of Semitic Studies*
JTS	*Journal of Theological Studies*

LXX	Septuagint
NEAEHL	*The New Encyclopedia of Archaeological Excavations in the Holy Land*
NEB	New English Bible
P	Priestly school
PEQ	*Palestine Exploration Quarterly*
RA	*Revue d'assyriologie et d'archéologie orientale*
RB	*Revue biblique*
RevQ	*Revue de Qumran*
RSV	Revised Standard Version
TDOT	*Theological Dictionary of the Old Testament*
TLZ	*Theologische Literaturzeitung*
Vita Mos.	Philo, *Vita Moysis*
VT	*Vetus Testamentum*
VTSup	Vetus Testamentum Supplements
Vulg.	Vulgate
ZA	*Zeitschrift für Assyriologie*
ZAW	*Zeitschrift für die alttestamentliche Wissenschaft*

DEAD SEA SCROLLS AND RELATED TEXTS

CD	*Damascus Document*
1QS	Manual of Discipline

Introduction

LABELS AND ROLES

Our subject is intellectual leadership in Israel and specifically the intellectual leadership exercised by sage, priest, and prophet. We are therefore not concerned with leadership in the political sphere—the monarchy together with its dependents and, in the later period, the local representatives of the Persian and Hellenistic empires. Since our principal and often our only source is the biblical text, religious aspects tend to predominate. In the context of ancient thought, however, it is not easy to make a clean separation between the religious and the intellectual spheres. We therefore feel justified in speaking of intellectual leadership and of the maintenance and transmission of intellectual traditions in both lay and clerical circles.

Let us note at the outset that not one of the three designations—sage, priest, prophet—is free of ambiguity. As a descriptive label, the term *sage* is not much in use in contemporary English, and its usage, when not facetious, is generally restricted to putatively wise individuals or groups in the past—as when we speak of Thomas Carlyle as the sage of Chelsea or of the rabbis as the sages. We shall see shortly that the corresponding Hebrew term (*ḥākām*), designating an individual or a class, is equally restricted. Our inquiry into sagedom in Israel therefore has to include a wide range of phenomena in accounts where other designations (e.g., scribe, counselor) are used or, in some cases, where none is used at all. We nevertheless persist with the term *sage* as a *faute de mieux* in view of the difficulty of coming up with an acceptable alternative. *Philosopher* is hardly appropriate, except perhaps with reference to the authors of Job and Ecclesiastes. If only because it is broader in connotation, *intellectual* might do, especially if it could be shown that a distinctly lay intellectual tradition existed in Israel during the biblical period. The more problematic term *dissident intellectual,* applied to certain prophets, will call for explanation and justification in due course.

The office and function of the priest (*kōhēn*) in Israel are more fully described and more easily identified in our sources, more so than in Mesopotamia and Egypt, where in each region the corresponding term covers a broader range of activities and functions. But even in Israel, the priest discharged tasks outside the cultic sphere, serving, for example, as scribe and magistrate. The main difficulty is in tracing the history of the priesthood, a principal feature of which was competition for power, both spiritual and temporal, that ended with the ascendancy of one branch, the Aaronites, in the Persian period.

In several respects the prophetic label is the most problematic. Its contemporary usage in our vernaculars is very fluid, covering such things as prediction, emotional preaching, social protest, and, within the sociological community, millennarian movements and their founders. The standard Hebrew term (*nābî'*) in the course of time came to acquire a very broad spectrum of meanings, to the point where it could apply to almost any significant figure in the tradition—Abraham and Moses, for example. An additional complication is that the prophetic office was the object of a deliberate process of redefinition within the Deuteronomic school, the effects of which lasted into the rabbinic period and beyond. When used to describe the fifteen "authors" of prophetic "books" and several persons in the historical record, it is therefore not a sure guide to their social identities and roles. In addition, *nābî'* is only one of several labels for intermediaries of different kinds who functioned in different social contexts, including sanctuaries and royal courts. Others again seem to have operated more or less as free agents, and of those there were some who, explicitly or implicitly, eschewed the prophetic label. In the section of this study dealing with the prophet, I venture to use the term *dissident intellectual* for members of this last group. The designation is admittedly subject to misunderstanding but has the advantage of highlighting aspects that are often overlooked and of being no more problematic than descriptions in more common use, for example, *charismatic* or *social critic*.

We note, too, that specific individuals could and did fill more than one of the three roles under consideration. A prophet could also be a priest (Ezekiel, perhaps Jeremiah); a priest could be a scribe and, to that extent, a sage (Ezra); a sage could be a prophet, or at least claim prophetic inspiration (Ben Sira). The boundaries between the roles are therefore fluid— not an unusual situation in role performance.

We should also anticipate the question: Why these three in particular? At the most obvious level, they are the classes that in their different ways were responsible for the biblical texts and therefore for the symbolic-conceptual world from which the texts derive, which gives the texts their distinctive character. We take it for granted that that world is *religious* in character, but in the present context the term is not self-explanatory. Biblical Hebrew had no word corresponding to our term *religion,* and contemporary Hebrew consequently has to make do with a Persian loanword, *dāt,* which originally referred to law rather than to religion. The religious dimension, therefore, enters into the performance of the roles in different ways, often obliquely. The world of the sages was, in the course of time, assimilated into the national cult of Yahweh and the religion of law, but its original impulse derived from the observation of nature—nonhuman and human—and experience. The concerns of the priesthood were, of course, primarily religious (i.e., cultic) but did not exclude attempts at systematic thought in cosmology and astronomy. Akkadian scholars speak without apology of the intellectual world of ancient Mesopotamia, but the scholarly interests pursued by Babylonian and Assyrian literati, including mathematics and astronomy, were dictated by religious concerns, for example, fixing the liturgical calendar on the basis of astronomical observation and predicting the future by means of a highly developed omen lore. Prophecy, finally, is not unambiguously religious in nature, especially if we pay due regard to those prophets who functioned as social critics. There is also the not irrelevant fact that some of these prophets directed their fiercest invective against contemporary religious practice.

Since we are embarked on a study in social history, we have to take account of the ways in which sage, priest, and prophet interacted with society and with one another at different stages in the social and political evolution of Israel. We are therefore concerned with how these classes of people filled their social roles. The sociological literature on role theory and role performance to which we turn for help is extensive, somewhat daunting for the nonspecialist, and by no means unanimous in defining social roles or even in concluding that the concept of role theory is either useful or necessary.[1] What gives role theory a certain allure is the theatrical analogy, which draws our attention to performance in accordance with, or occasionally at variance with, a script written by society; the interactions between different assumed roles (acting on cue); and an audience whose expectations and anticipated reaction in a real sense make the acting of the role possible. The existence of multiple kinds of dramatic production—from medieval mystery plays and Noh drama at one end of the spectrum to extempore street theater at the other—serves also to highlight different degrees of role identification on the larger stage of social interaction.[2]

A role may be defined as a more or less standardized social position corresponding to the expectations of the society, or a segment of the society, in which the role player is situated. It therefore involves certain rights and obligations and calls for the kind of performance that the society in question has come to expect from the position in question and which to that extent can be considered normative and prescriptive. Not all roles, clearly, are equally significant. If we are concerned with sage, priest, and prophet rather than, say, day laborer, potter, and temple gatekeeper, it is because the former embody in an important way intellectual, religious, and moral constructs in the society in which they function. According to Alasdair MacIntyre, they would belong to a category of role identified as *character,* with the corollary that in addition to providing a culture with its moral definitions, they can serve as focal points of dispute and debate.[3]

The term *role set* is used to describe the diverse expectations of different segments of society that have come to converge on a particular position or function. The same person can, and usually does, fill more than one role (e.g., Ezra was both priest and scribe), and this situation can create tension, misunderstanding, and conflict. It is also possible for the individual filling the role to identify with it more or less closely or to deviate from it. Amos was perceived by the priest Amaziah, and no doubt by many others, to be a *nābîʾ,* but he himself denied it, at least according to a probable reading of Amos 7:14 ("I am not a prophet nor am I a member of a prophetic group").

Our use of role theory does not, by itself, solve any problems, but it has the advantage of suggesting questions that might otherwise go unasked. Were the roles in question ascribed or achieved? What skills were required for their performance, and how did one go about acquiring them? How was the individual recruited to fill the role? What part did such important variables as gender and class play? What resources and sanctions did the society have to discourage role deviance? Leadership-role performance, whether of the charismatic or the managerial type, calls for a degree of recognition and acquiescence on the part of an at least significant segment of the population. We therefore have to look into the relationship between role bearer and public, performer and audience, taking account of changing social and political situations as they affect these relationships—principally the changes from lineage to state system and from state system to colonial dependency. We also want to determine, as closely as our sources permit, the more specific social location that helps to generate the role, at which point we link up with the form critics in their attempt to identify the *Sitz im Leben* of the literary genres in our sources.

Before taking a closer look at these sources, it may be useful to refer to Max Weber's concept of the *ideal type* as a way of assessing how the three roles in question actually functioned in Israelite society. In dependence on and, in part, reaction to the neo-Kantianism of the Baden school of social thought, Weber held that investigation must proceed on the basis of elaborated concepts or analytic abstractions drawn from concrete social facts that can serve as a theoretical model or a template against which the data, with their distinctive and possibly unique features, can be measured and assessed. Weber did not suppose that these abstractions were either value-free or normative; on the contrary, he was quite explicit that the features of the ideal type deemed to be significant would be affected by the value judgments of the investigator. The usefulness of ideal types is that they can serve to bring out in relief, against the background of the model, the distinctive features of the phenomenon under consideration and also stimulate the elaboration of explanatory hypotheses. A relevant example would be Weber's delineation of the essential features of the prophet as type of *persona religiosa,* to which we return in the last section of our study.[4]

THE PROBLEM OF SOURCES

An anthropologist who sets out to gather information on a society different from his or her own will, we assume, formulate the questions to be asked, interrogate available informants, and then process the information received in the light of what is known about comparable societies and guided by the theoretical assumptions of the discipline. Having formulated our questions at least provisionally, we must follow suit and put them to our informants, namely, the sources at our disposal: the relevant biblical texts, a few later works covering the same ground (e.g., Josephus), and whatever material, inscribed or artifactual, is in the archaeological record. The most obvious problem here is that we are dealing with *ancient* sources, written in languages different from our own, with their own distinctive conventions and thought patterns. We can therefore anticipate a fair amount of static between the incoding text and the decrypting interpreter, and we soon become aware that these sources are not really designed to provide the kind of information we need as social historians. Most of these texts are also heavily edited, and more often than not, date and authorship are uncertain, especially now that the standard documentary hypothesis on the formation of the Pentateuch is in terminal disarray. The major narrative corpora, ascribed to the Deuteronomic historian (hereafter Dtr), the Priestly school (hereafter P) and the Chronicler (Chronicles–Ezra–Nehemiah; hereafter C), present intractable problems because they reconstruct the past according to their own ideological and interested perspectives. The information provided is therefore likely to bear as much on circumstances obtaining at the time of writing as on the events or situations of the narrated past.

We are also dealing with a *canonical* collection, implying that both what is included or omitted and how what is included is presented are dictated by the ideology of the collectors and the constraints under which they worked, on neither of which we are well informed.

Dissatisfaction with this situation is understandable, and it has of late led several biblical scholars and historians of ancient Israel to transfer their allegiance to the archaeological record, in some cases excluding the biblical sources from consideration altogether. Archaeological data are certainly less removed from the situations or events to which they refer than are biblical texts. But the Palestinian climate, unlike that of Egypt, does not favor the survival of records on perishable writing surfaces, papyrus in particular. The result is that inscriptions useful to the social historian are few and far between. To this we must add the tendency of archaeologists working in that area, until recently at any rate, to concentrate on architectural features, public buildings in particular, with the result that we are poorly informed on how the mass of the population lived at any given time.

Enthusiasm for archaeology can also entail the illusion that artifacts are exempt from the uncertainties and vagaries of interpretation to which biblical texts are notoriously subject. It should be obvious that this is not the case. In one respect at least, archaeological data are less secure, since current interpretations are always under threat of revision or subversion as a result of new discoveries. To excavate is to destroy—archaeology has been defined as controlled vandalism—so that a great mass of potentially valuable information, for example, with respect to private housing and diet, can easily be lost forever. At least the biblical texts are still there after being worked over by the interpreter.

Comparativist or proxy data from other societies can be illuminating; they can even be essential, if they come from neighboring lands with close cultural and political ties to Israel. But the problem with sociological data of this kind is to know whether the society in question is, in fact, comparable with ancient Israel and, if so, in what respects. Comparison with preindustrial, traditional societies that have survived into the modern world is notoriously deceptive. The Israel of the biblical period was not a "primitive" or, in Lévi-Strauss's language, a "cold" society, its high antiquity notwithstanding. More promising, though not unproblematic, is comparison with social and institutional features in Near Eastern and Levantine societies contemporary with Iron Age Israel. The most obvious problem here is scale: Mesopotamian urban centers, for example, are up to ten times the size of those in Israel. Also, we cannot simply assume that institutions in pristine or primary societies such as Babylonia, Assyria, or Egypt functioned in the same way as those in Israel, which emerged within the social world of Canaan and, in addition, was for most of its history a client or dependent of one or another of the great empires.

All this seems very daunting, as indeed it is, but I believe it possible nevertheless to make some headway by dint of a careful screening of our sources, reading between as well as on the lines, and making use of whatever analogies may be available. Source material relevant to each of the three categories is dealt with in the corresponding sections of the study. The reader can then decide whether a reasonable degree of probability has been attained.

THE GOAL AND POINT OF THE STUDY

The question may be asked how a study of this kind can be of interest to the intellectually and religiously serious man or woman of the twentieth century. At the most obvious level, it purports to be a contribution to the social history of Israel and early Judaism, and one dealing with the categories that embodied and helped to mold the values and ideals to which many Jews, Christians, and others still in some measure adhere. (It would not be captious to add that these categories also contributed to the problems with which the same people have to cope). The discussion herein is at the interface of social and intellectual history. The history of ideas is still often studied independently of the social realities in which ideas are grounded and without which they are not fully intelligible, and the distinction is now firmly embedded in the curricular structures of higher education. We therefore pursue the laudable aim of overcoming this kind of academic apartheid.

We also hope to get a better idea of how traditions originate, how and by whom they are sustained and transmitted, how different and often competing traditions interact with each other, and what pressures, internal and external, can lead to their transformation or disintegration. We are particularly interested in investigating how the leadership roles under consideration shaped and were shaped by the traditions within which they functioned.

A study of the social roles of sage, priest, and prophet should also bring into view competing claims to authority in the religious sphere, an issue that is hardly a matter of indifference to religious people today. The basic claim is to control what have been called "the redemptive media" in Israelite

society, whether by means of cultic enactment, the drafting and interpret-
ing of laws, or direct access to the mind and will of God through prophetic
inspiration; and incorporated in this is the further claim to determine the
shape and ethos of the society in general. We cannot, therefore, avoid dealing with the ideological character of the literary productions associated with
our three categories. In the vocabulary of Marxism, *ideology* is a pejorative
term, denoting a doctrine consciously adopted to legitimate a dominative
political or economic system or unconsciously assumed in furtherance of
the interests of a particular elite. There is undoubtedly much that is ideological, in this sense, encrypted in biblical texts, and we shall see something
of the attitudes of elites toward those deprived of power—the poor, women,
certain ethnic groups, the physically disabled (for this last, see Lev. 21:16–24
and Deut. 23:1). But it is also permissible to understand ideology in a more
neutral sense, with reference to a conceptual scheme proper to a particular
class that informs the class's self-understanding and legitimates its social
role. The interplay among the different conceptual systems or ideologies
embodied in the roles of sage, priest, and prophet adds up to a significant
chapter in the social and religious history of Israel and early Judaism.

CHAPTER 1

The Sage

THE INTELLECTUAL TRADITION IN ISRAEL
AND ITS REPRESENTATIVES

We deal with the sage first, since the literary productions of Israel's sages are more easily seen to represent an intellectual tradition recognizable as such today than are the writings of priest or prophet. The profile of the sage also approximates more closely that of the intellectual than do the profiles of other categories.

Hebrew Bible scholars are in the habit of referring to certain compositions in the third part of the canon as "wisdom writings" and to their authors as "wisdom writers" or "the wise." The core group comprises Proverbs, Job, and Ecclesiastes (Qoheleth), to which may be added the Canticle (Song of Songs) and, among the Apocrypha, Ecclesiasticus (Ben Sira) and the Wisdom of Solomon, preserved in the Greek Bible, though we now know that Ecclesiasticus was written in Hebrew. Those literary and thematic features common to this core group that account for the designation *wisdom writings* are not, however, confined to these writings. Similar expressions, turns of phrase, genres, and themes have been identified in other compositions, for example, in prophetic books and psalms. This has led some scholars to speak of a "wisdom movement" or "wisdom tradition" of broad, indefinite, and sometimes practically limitless scope or of "wisdom influence" on prophets, psalm writers, and others. But the term *wisdom* (Hebrew, ḥokmâ) has too broad a range of meanings to be serviceable in this context. There is also the problem that a movement or tradition requires embodiment in institutions and roles if it is to achieve social visibility.

It therefore seems advisable to avoid this kind of language and begin our inquiry by asking whether there existed in the Israel of the biblical period an *intellectual tradition* outside of the priestly-cultic sphere, one that might bear comparison in some respects with the intellectual traditions of the great Near Eastern and Levantine centers, including Greek-speaking lands. In pursuing this inquiry, we have to attempt to identify those institutions and social roles with which the tradition was associated, which sustained and transmitted it, which elaborated its agenda, and which were therefore responsible for the distinctive character of the writings referred to above.

The short answer to this inquiry is encapsulated in the designation *sage* (*ḥākām*), but we have seen that this term is rather unsatisfactory, not least because biblical usage is generally either pejorative, especially when referring to foreign sages, or retrospective. In his monograph *The Intellectual Tradition in the Old Testament,* R. Norman Whybray provided a useful point of departure for our investigation of this term.[1] Whybray's survey of biblical usage led him to the conclusion that a professional class of *ḥăkāmîm* is not attested in the biblical literature, not even in Proverbs, Job, and Ecclesiastes. He accepted that the authors of these compositions wrote within a tradition, but a tradition requiring no institutional vehicle or professional class for its transmission. He found support for this conclusion in the absence of allusion to educational establishments before the second century B.C.E., when Jesus Ben Sira invited young males from well-to-do families into his school or academy (*bēt midrāš,* literally, "house of study"; Sir. 51:23).

Whybray went on to elaborate criteria for identifying the literary tradition within which the authors of the core compositions worked. Literary forms or genres have some criteriological value but are not entirely reliable, since they also occur in compositions (e.g., prophetic books) not within the tradition so defined. We must therefore rely on subject matter, defined broadly by Whybray as the human situation and the conduct of human life. What he took to be the most useful criterion, however, is the incidence of terminology characteristic of the three key compositions (Proverbs, Job, Ecclesiastes). On this basis he drew up a list of words and expressions either exclusive to or of frequent occurrence within the intellectual tradition, together with a list of passages in which the words and expressions occur and that he therefore took to be expressive of the tradition. The passages in question are Genesis 2—3 and 37—50; Deuteronomy 1—4 and 32; 2 Samuel 9—20, continued in 1 Kings 1—2; 1 Kings 3—11; some parts of Isaiah 1—39 and of Jeremiah; Ezekiel 28; Daniel; Hos. 14:10 and Micah 6:9; and several psalms.

Whybray performed a useful service in raising the issue of an intellectual tradition in Israel as a more profitable point of departure than the commonly accepted idea embodied in such expressions as "wisdom literature" and "wisdom influence." He did not, however, go on to identify the social and institutional settings of the passages identified as expressive of the tradition.

It is not, of course, always possible to establish the social coordinates of literary texts, but Whybray was surely mistaken in supposing that a tradition can be sustained and transmitted without institutional grounding. What is also lacking, here and in the discipline of biblical studies in general, is a theoretical account of traditions and of the role of the intellectual in their formation, maintenance, and transmission.

Something should also be said about Whybray's contention that, unlike *sōpēr* (scribe) and *yô'ēṣ* (counselor), *ḥākām* (plural, *ḥăkāmîm*) never stands for a distinctly identifiable class of specialists. In the great majority of occurrences this is evidently the case; the term refers to a person or persons endowed with a particular skill or insight or just low cunning. Even in the frequent and invariably pejorative allusions to foreign sages (e.g., Gen. 41:8; Ex. 7:11; Isa. 19:11–12), it is not always clear that a definite profession is intended. In the later period, however, it does seem that the word begins to be used as a substantive to designate a class of intellectuals, usually teachers. An appendix to Ecclesiastes describes the author as a *ḥākām* who instructed the public (Eccl. 12:9), and the title *dibrê ḥăkāmîm* (sayings of the sages), attached to one of the compilations in Proverbs (22:17; cf. 25:1), points in the same direction in spite of the missing definite article. (We might compare the title of the Mishnaic treatise *pirqê 'ābôt*, also lacking the definite article.) Furthermore, the same genre, "sayings of the sages" (*logoi sophōn*), is attested in the Roman period, inclusive of early Christianity, and it is a reasonable supposition that late biblical usage prepared for the identification of the rabbis as *the ḥăkāmîm*.[2]

We can, at any rate, be sure that writings have survived from the period in question which require us to postulate a literary and intellectual tradition. With the exception of Ben Sira and possibly two small segments of Proverbs attributed to Agur and Lemuel respectively (Prov. 30:1–4 and 31:1–9), none of the authors is known by name, not surprising since anonymity was normal in antiquity. The main point is that these writings can serve to identify and characterize an intellectual tradition, and their authors can be taken to belong to a particular type of intellectual leadership within that tradition. But before proceeding further, we need to clarify what, in the present context, we take this term *tradition* to mean.

THE IDEA OF TRADITION

Judaism and Christianity are traditionalist in the Weberian sense that their institutions, mores, and leadership are legitimated by appeal to the past. By the same token, both religions as a general rule seek, not always successfully, to exclude novelty on the principle that "valid is that which has always been."[3] The standard Christian approach can be summed up in the dictum *quod semper, quod ubique, quod ab omnibus* (what has always been believed everywhere and by all), attributed to Vincent of Lerin, while the Jewish idea of tradition with respect to the oral law is stated in lapidary fashion in the opening paragraph of the Mishnaic treatise *pirqê 'ābôt:*

> Moses received Torah from Sinai and delivered it to Joshua; Joshua [delivered it] to the elders, the elders to the prophets, and the prophets delivered it to the men of the Great Assembly.

These aphorisms illustrate the two aspects of usage, respectively the substance of tradition, or the *traditum,* and the process by which the substance is transmitted. All religions tend to be traditionalist once firmly established, but the particular forms traditionalism assumes in Judaism and Christianity reflect a more complex historical reality, emerging as they did out of conflict among competing traditions. This implies that we must begin by emphasizing the particular and specific and be careful in speaking of tradition in general.

In the critical study of the Old Testament, the concept of tradition could emerge only after the link between divine inspiration and authorship had been severed—Moses as author of the Pentateuch; David of Psalms; Solomon of Proverbs, the Canticle, and other compositions—for only then was it possible to think in terms of a process of formation and the contribution of a plurality of authors and tradents in the production of the texts. This is not the place to review this chapter of biblical scholarship, but we may note as particularly significant an early contribution, that of the French Oratorian priest Richard Simon, whose *Histoire critique du Vieux Testament* appeared in 1678. Simon argued that the Pentateuch was the outcome of a long process of formation and therefore could not have been authored by Moses or indeed by any other one person; and it is interesting to note that he appealed to the prominent place of tradition in Roman Catholic theology to justify according tradition equal prominence throughout the biblical period. This eminently reasonable appeal notwithstanding, the book was banned and he was expelled from the Oratory, but the point had been made and would not be forgotten. Subsequently, however, the single-minded concentration on identifying written sources or documents (the JEDP—Yahwist, Elohist, Deuteronomic, Priestly—of the classical documentary theory) led in a different direction. The romanticism of the late eighteenth and early nineteenth century provided something of a counterbalance, producing at least one distinguished contribution to the discipline, Johann Gottfried

Herder's *Vom Geist der Hebräischen Poesie* (1782–1783).[4] Interest in the creative role of the community and oral tradition as generative of traditional narrative is apparent in the *Kinder- und Hausmärchen* of the Brothers Grimm (1812–1815), but a century would pass before these ideas made a significant impact on the study of biblical texts.

There would be general agreement that the traditio-historical study of biblical narrative first began to show results in the work of Hermann Gunkel, whose commentary on Genesis, the first edition of which appeared in 1901, signaled a genuinely new departure. In the lengthy introduction to this commentary, surprisingly the only part translated into English,[5] Gunkel used the term *Sage* for the Genesis narratives in a quite nonspecific way, in keeping with German, but not English, usage. Concentrating on the prehistory of this narrative material, he argued that the individual stories and story cycles had been molded into the form in which we find them in the course of a long period of oral transmission. The concept of author therefore cedes pride of place to the creative genius of the *Volk,* the *Gemeinde,* so that Genesis can be described as the literary deposit of a popular oral and ethnic tradition ("die Niederschrift mündlicher, volkstümlicher Überlieferung."[6] Gunkel went on to classify the different literary types, or *Gattungen,* of the Genesis narrative, analyzing the dynamics of the oral process by which they reached their final form and proposing different social settings (*Sitze im Leben*), including the role of professional storyteller.[7]

While Gunkel's contribution has been justly ranked among the most significant of this century, more recent studies have considerably reduced the odds in favor of the staying power of oral transmission taken by itself. We are also in a better position than Gunkel to appreciate the difficulty of distinguishing between narrative generated by oral composition, performance, and transmission, on the one hand, and a literary work that incorporates elements of oral tradition, on the other. But for our present purpose, the main problem with traditio-historical study as generally understood is that it has been restricted almost entirely to *oral* tradition. Oral transmission certainly played a part in the production of some of the literature, often in tandem with writing—the two are by no means mutually exclusive—but the idea of tradition *in general* has never, to my knowledge, been the subject of sustained reflection within the discipline. It may therefore be useful to state briefly how the term is used in the present study.

We begin by putting aside the common pejorative connotation, according to which tradition stands for an unreflective or a superstitious attachment to the past, a resistance to progress, a disinclination to adapt when faced with changing situations, or even a willful choosing to live in the past.

While not presented in such starkly negative terms, traditional authority as understood by Max Weber contains a strong element of irrationality, in that it legitimates itself by appeal to antiquity, and sooner or later must give way before the bureaucratic type of authority based on efficiency and rationality.[8] In the broader, more general, and more benign sense, tradition may be defined as the aggregate of assumptions, beliefs, practices, and ethos that combine to sustain a sense of continuity in a society. On this provisional basis, we can proceed to an examination of specific traditions, in particular, those with an explicitly intellectual content.

In this more specific sense, a tradition has been described as "a sequence of variations on received and transmitted themes."[9] We could fill out and gloss this definition by speaking of a body of knowledge or a cluster of themes transmitted orally or in writing over several generations and subject to adaptation, modification, reinterpretation, and possibly refutation in the course of transmission. We therefore speak of scientific and philosophical traditions (Aristotelian, Newtonian, etc.), and in fact, all branches of knowledge taught in universities develop traditions of this kind. Traditions seem to have a special connaturality with religious doctrine and practice, though this is probably due to the innate conservative tendency of established religions. A well-known lyric from *Fiddler on the Roof* extols the Jewish kabbala; some Christian denominations insist on church tradition as an authoritative source of doctrine together with scripture; and Islam assigns importance to its *haddith* alongside the canonical Qur'an.

In addition to a body of doctrine, religious or secular, traditions often entail ethical and ritual practice. In the tradition represented by Israel's sages, ethical and practical concerns are much in evidence, but we shall argue that they presuppose a more or less coherent, if seldom articulated, worldview. At a certain point in the development of the tradition, we find that morality is grounded in the ethical character of God as the ultimate guarantor that justice will prevail in the world which God created. This tradition is therefore both speculative and practical. In Aristotelian terms, it combines *sophia* and *phronēsis,* speculative and practical wisdom, with the emphasis on the latter.

A tradition of this kind, partially embodied in the role of the sage and expressed in the literary productions of sagedom, entails a shared perception of certain issues as of central importance and a broad understanding as to how they are to be addressed. This does not imply that uniformity is essential to the well-being of a tradition; on the contrary, as Alasdair MacIntyre puts it, "when a tradition is in good order it is always partially constituted by an argument about the goods the pursuit of which gives to that tradition its particular point and purpose."[10] So understood, then, tradition does not rule out innovation or even the possibility of arriving at a critical juncture where internal contradictions, encounter with unassimilable situations or with a different and more powerful tradition, or a combination of these can undermine the foundations on which the particular tradition rests. We shall go on to test this very general and abstract characterization of traditions against the conceptual world of Israel's sages as our sources permit us to grasp it. Before embarking on this task, however, it may be helpful to take a retrospective view from the vantage point of the late biblical period.

BEN SIRA: PROFILE OF A JEWISH INTELLECTUAL IN THE HELLENISTIC PERIOD

Ben Sira, more fully Yeshua (Jesus) ben Eleazar ben Sira (50:27), was active in the early decades of the second century B.C.E., a few years before the persecution of Antiochus IV broke over the Jewish community in the Seleucid realm. The rather pedestrian prologue to the Greek translation from the author's grandson identifies the book (Ecclesiasticus) as a work combining *paideia* (education) and *sophia* (wisdom), in other words, as a didactic work, which it evidently is. He also places the book squarely within the religious and intellectual tradition of Israel, adding that it was addressed to those who love learning (*boulomenois philomathein*), but learning inseparable from piety. This combination of the intellectual and the practical does not by any means set the book apart from contemporary Greek philosophy, especially the Stoic variety with its strong emphasis on ethics. The form it assumes in Ben Sira is nevertheless unmistakably Jewish, as we shall see.

Ben Sira was a scribe, perhaps also an inactive priest, to judge by his uncritical reverence for everything priestly. He conducted an academy (*bēt midrāš*; Greek, *oikos paideias*, 51:23), presumably in Jerusalem, for upperclass youth who aspired to public service. From the scraps of autobiographical information he provides, we gather that he was getting on in years (8:6); that he had knocked around the world quite a bit (34:9–13; 51:13), perhaps in the capacity of government official with judicial functions (38:33); that he had dedicated himself to a life of piety and learning from his youth (51:13–28); and that the core of that learning consisted in the Jewish law. Even this minimum must, however, be treated with caution, since it is always possible that the author, who does not come through as particularly self-critical, may have incorporated familiar biographical topoi, not unlike Flavius Josephus in his *Bios*.

Ben Sira locates himself in relation to the tradition, but without undue modesty, as one of the epigoni:

> Now I was the last to keep vigil;
>   I was like a gleaner following the grape-pickers;
> by the blessing of the Lord I arrived first,
>   and like a grape-picker I filled my wine press.
> Consider that I have not labored for myself alone,
>   but for all who seek instruction.
> Hear me, you who are great among the people,
>   and you leaders of the congregation, pay heed!
>   (33:16–19)

As such, he seems to have proposed to himself to distill and synthesize the essence of the Jewish literary tradition in a form both acceptable to observant Jews and intelligible to readers acclimatized to the Hellenistic culture of the Ptolemies and Seleucids. The reader will, at any rate, observe that (1) the theme of law observance as the true wisdom is fully developed as the centerpiece of the book (24:1–34) and also occurs at the beginning (1:1–30) and end (50:27–29, probably the original *excipit* to the work); (2) the book is modeled on Proverbs, beginning as it does with a female personification of wisdom (1:1–27) and ending with an acrostic poem (51:13–30) equal in length to the acrostic composition about the *'ēšet ḥayil* (valiant woman? woman of substance?) in Prov. 31:10–31; (3) the "Praise of the Ancestors" (44—50) rather skillfully telescopes the biblical history into a form compatible with the contemporary Greek biographical genre (*diadochai tōn philosophōn;* Latin, *de viris illustribus);* (4) the author inherits the idea that prophecy has survived into the present only to the extent that it is encapsulated in the roles of priest and sage (24:30–34). Prophecy can therefore be dealt with summarily under the rubric of biography (46:13–47:1; 48:1–14; 49:6–10).

Ben Sira speaks of the scribal profession as a skill (*technē*) for which leisure—and therefore, financial independence—is an absolute prerequisite:

> The wisdom of the scribe depends on the opportunity of leisure;
>   only the one who has little business can become wise.
> How can one become wise who handles the plow, and who glories in
>   the shaft of a goad?
> who drives oxen and is occupied with their work,
>   and whose talk is about bulls?
>   (38:24–25)

The idea that wisdom is restricted to a particular social class may have been directed against the more universalist views of contemporary Stoicism. Ben Sira goes on to describe, at inordinate length, a range of more or less me-nial occupations, in the manner of the Egyptian *Satire of the Trades*,[11] contrasting them with what he himself does for a living. The sage's agenda is then laid out as follows:

> How different the one who devotes himself
>> to the study of the law of the Most High!
> He seeks out the wisdom of all the ancients,
>> and is concerned with prophecies;
> he preserves the sayings of the famous and
>> penetrates the subtleties of parables;
> he seeks out the hidden meanings of proverbs
>> and is at home with the obscurities of parables.
> He serves among the great
>> and appears before rulers;
> he travels in foreign lands
>> and learns what is good and evil in the human lot.
> He sets his heart to rise early
>> to seek the Lord who made him,
>> and to petition the Most High;
> he opens his mouth in prayer
>> and asks pardon for his sins.
>
>   (38:34–39:5)

It is apparent that scribes of this kind belonged socially and economically to the upper strata of Jerusalemite society. Ben Sira was a landowner (7:3, 15, 22) and slave owner (7:20–21; 33:25–33; 42:5), and his profession was his passport to the highest circles, perhaps including the Ptolemaic court in Alexandria. In contrast to Qoheleth, who belonged to the same social class without identifying so completely with it, Ben Sira manifests a love of wealth and a snobbish disregard for those less favored. He is concerned with the preservation and protection of property (28:24; 33:20), subscribes to the view that good fences make good neighbors (36:30), and counsels caution in such important matters as recording financial transactions (42:7), borrowing and lending (8:12; 29:1–7), and standing surety for the debts of others (8:13; 29:14–20). While issuing the occasional, routine warning against the dangers of wealth (e.g., 5:1), he urges those who have it to enjoy it while they can (14:3–19; 30:21–25).

Much the greater part of the book consists in instruction in ethics and etiquette, often tediously prolonged and not significantly different from the common stock of high-minded moral exhortation in older compilations, including Proverbs. What he has to pass on to his students on such matters as family values and education reflects, not surprisingly, his own and their socioeconomic situation. Parents are to be respected and obeyed (3:1–16);

children are to be treated on the "spare the rod, spoil the child" principle ("he who loves his son will whip him often"; 30:1); daughters are to be kept under wraps until suitable and sensible husbands are found for them (7:24–25; 22:3–6; 26:10–12); wives are to be cherished as long as they are obedient, silent, and modest, but the recalcitrant wife is to be divorced (25:26); slaves should be treated humanely, but the idle slave is to be flogged without compunction (7:20–21; 33:25–33; 42:5); prostitutes are to be avoided, since they rob you blind (9:6); and so on. We also find in Ben Sira depressingly familiar railings against women in general, sometimes to the point of utter irrationality; consider, for example, "Better is the wickedness of a man than a woman who does good" (42:14). These and similar injunctions addressed to the socially privileged, young adult male preparing for a public career exhibit Ben Sira's dependence on a long-established literary tradition of moral exhortation, one by no means confined to Israel.

Our first reaction may well be that this does not look much like an intellectual tradition, and this impression is strengthened when we go on to note indications in the book of a deliberate distancing from contemporary Hellenistic ideas of wisdom in favor of the traditional Israelite view, first clearly enunciated in Deuteronomy, that all wisdom derives from the God of Israel and finds its supreme expression in the observance of God's laws (Sir. 1:1, 14–20). At a later point, we come upon what looks like a deliberate distancing from and repudiation of philosophical speculation:

> Neither seek what is too difficult for you,
>   nor investigate what is beyond your power.
> Reflect upon what you have been commanded,
>   for what is hidden is not your concern.
> Do not meddle in matters that are beyond you,
>   for more than you can understand has been shown you.
> For their conceit has led many astray,
>   and wrong opinion has impaired their judgment.
>
>   (3:21–24)

This looks almost like a paraphrase of or gloss on certain passages in Deuteronomy:

> The hidden things are for Yahweh our God, and the revealed things are for us and our children forever, fulfilling all the stipulations of this law.
>   (29:29)

> For this commandment which I command you this day is not too difficult for you nor is it far off; it is not in heaven that you should say, "Who will go up to heaven for us to bring it to us that we may hear it and fulfill it?"; nor is it beyond the sea that you should say, "Who will cross

over the sea for us to bring it to us that we may hear it and fulfill it?";
but the word is very near you; it is in your mouth and in your heart, so
that you are able to fulfill it.

(30:11–14)

In referring to wrongheaded people whose conceit has led them astray, Ben
Sira may have had in mind contemporary Jewish apologists for Greek learning and the Greek way of life, whose efforts would facilitate the fateful intervention of Antiochus IV in Jewish affairs two or three decades later. Another possibility is that he was taking aim at the circles within which the
speculative theology and theosophy associated with Enoch originated, the
earliest parts of which antedate Ben Sira's work. Antipathy to what has been
called "mantic wisdom" would explain his warnings against astrological
speculation, dreams, omens, and the like (1:1–10; 3:21–24; 34:1–8).

In the main, however, we may read Ben Sira as an early example of conscious distancing from the Greek intellectual tradition, manifested not least
in his writing in Hebrew. (While it cannot be proved beyond a doubt, he
probably knew Greek, the language of choice for a number of more or less
contemporary Jewish writers—the historians Demetrius and Eupolemus, the
apologist Aristobulus, the epic poets Philo and Theodotus.) We find something similar in Josephus, who tendentiously and illogically contrasts the
"myriads of inconsistent books" of the Greeks, produced without quality
control, with the twenty-two "justly accredited" books of the Jews (*C.Ap.*
1.38–40). Something of this suspicion of "Greek wisdom" (*ḥokmâ yavanît*)
persisted into the Tannaitic and Amoraic periods (*b. Baba Qamma* 82b; *b.
Soṭa* 49b; *b. Menaḥ.* 64b, 99b), though it did not entail an absolute prohibition of learning the Greek language or studying Greek philosophy.[12] In
contrast, however, it seems that Ben Sira had done some reading over and
above "the law, the prophets, and the other books of our fathers" (Prologue). It has been suggested, for example, that the central chapter identifying wisdom with the law (24:1–29) draws on aretalogical texts from the
Isis cult, one of the most popular in the Ptolemaic Empire.[13] Commentators
have also claimed to have found echoes of Homer (14:18; cf. *Iliad*
6.146–49), the gnomic poetry of Theognis, and Stoic philosophy, this last in
the description of the deity as "the All" (*hakkōl;* Greek, *to pan,* 43:27).[14] We
note too that his use of the aphorism "Call no man happy before his death,"
which he applies to the well-being or otherwise of the descendants of the
deceased (11:28), is curiously similar to Aristotle's discussion of the same
aphorism in the *Nicomachean Ethics* (1100a10–30).

Ben Sira was active at a time when the Judean literary tradition was already, in essence, fixed as the basis for further reflection and study and,

especially, as a resource for the good life, defined as a life lived according to the traditional laws. The Prologue is often taken as evidence that the tripartite canon was in place at the time it was written, around 130 B.C.E. But the translator's allusions to "the law, the prophets, and the others that followed them" and "the law, the prophecies, and the rest of the books" suggest rather an open-ended corpus to which other compositions could, in theory, be aggregated; indeed, the translator seems to be hinting that his grandfather's work merits co-option into the collection. In any event, both the Prologue and the work itself take for granted that the written tradition determines the direction future developments will take.

In defining his place within this predominantly nomistic and didactic tradition, Ben Sira uses the apt metaphor of a river flowing out of Eden with its several tributaries, of which his own teaching is one (24:25–34; cf. Gen. 2:10–14). The identification of the law with wisdom, and so with the principle of cosmic order, comparable to the Greek *logos* or *dikē,* also entails the claim that this uniquely Jewish construct is no less intellectual than the Greek philosophical tradition. We can see the point of the claim, even though Ben Sira, who was hardly a thinker or writer of the first rank, may not have been the best person to advance it.

A reading of Ben Sira suggests that the consolidation of the tradition to which his book attests went in tandem with a certain blurring of the distinction between the traditional roles that embodied and sustained it. Ben Sira sees himself primarily as a scribe (*sōpēr;* Greek, *grammateus,* 38:24) and his principal function as that of teacher, especially teacher of morals (39:8; 51:23). The translator obviously shares this view and makes much of his grandfather's *paideia,* communicated both orally and in writing. But teaching did not preclude a wide range of other functions, including counselor, magistrate, and diplomat. We also note that several of the tasks the author felt called upon to perform overlapped significantly with priestly assignments. Prophecy, in contrast, was regarded basically as a thing of the past, but the study of prophecy was an important component of the scribal curriculum (39:1). In one way or another, therefore, the traditional roles had begun to coalesce, to collapse in on one another. We must now retrace our steps to discover how this situation came about and, specifically, what the sage contributed to bringing it about. As always, the first question is whether we have the resources (i.e., the sources) to address this issue.

ONCE AGAIN, THE QUESTION OF SOURCES

The study of any aspect of an ancient culture calls for a careful assessment of the possibilities and limitations of the source material at our disposal. Biblical texts are obviously a major source for Israel during the Iron Age and beyond, but they hardly comprise the sum total of writing produced during that long period. For one thing, we do not know how much had or had not survived to the time of the redaction of the major components of the Hebrew Bible. Practically all of the inscribed material that has come to light in the modern period was written on either stone (e.g., the Gezer calendar, the Siloam inscription) or pottery (e.g., ostraca from Samaria, Arad, Lachish, Jerusalem), neither of which is a suitable writing surface for literary compositions of the kind associated with sages. For such compositions papyrus would have been used, and we have seen that the Palestinian climate does not favor the survival of this material. (Apart from a clump of papyrus fibers discovered at Lachish, sticking to the seal of a certain Gedaliah, the only survivor from the Iron Age is an eighth-century papyrus discovered in the Wadi Murabba'at.)

Then there is the question how much of the writing that did survive to that time the final editors would have been interested in preserving. We can only speculate as to who these people were and in what social setting and under what constraints the final shaping of the material took place. We can at least be sure that the provision of sociological information—for example, on education—was not a high priority. The fact that most of the occurrences of the verbal stem *lmd*—"to learn" in Qal, "to teach" in Piel—have to do with the learning and teaching of law indicates clearly an important aspect of the selective process at work in the final redaction.

We assume, then, that the extant biblical sources represent a selection from a larger body of material. In the later period, for example, it became customary to put together compilations of sayings of prominent teachers (*dibrê ḥăkāmîm*), but few such compilations found their way into the canon. It seems unlikely that Prov. 30:1–4 and 31:1–9 represent the entire literary production of the sages Agur and Lemuel, respectively, or that Prov. 22:17–24:22, modeled on the Egyptian instruction of Amen-em-opet, was a unique case of borrowing from the massive corpus of Egyptian instructional literature.[15]

Something should be said about one peculiar feature of these biblical sources for the role and character of the sage, one noted above in our discussion of Ben Sira. In his discussion of the social psychology of the prophets, Max Weber commented on the "culture hostility" that characterized their attitude toward contemporary life.[16] In a later chapter of *Ancient Judaism* (the one with the unfortunate title "The Pariah Community"), he argued that this attitude carried over into the period of the second commonwealth, reinforced by ritual self-closure and a certain ressentiment induced by historical disaster and political subjection.[17] Weber exaggerated and misrepresented the particularism of early Judaism, but the need to preserve some semblance of historical identity and continuity did result in a rather consistently negative attitude toward the intellectual traditions of neighboring lands. It comes through in the many disparaging allusions to foreign sages (Gen. 41:8; Ex. 7:11; Isa. 19:11–12; Jer. 10:7) and in the dismissive attitude toward the intellectual tradition of Babylon in the later section of Isaiah (44:25; 47:8–13). Its clearest and most explicit expression is in Deuteronomy, which, in effect, identifies study and observance of the law as the Israelite equivalent of the intellectual traditions of other lands:

> See, I have taught you statutes and ordinances . . . you are to observe them and put them into practice, for this is your wisdom and understanding in the sight of the peoples who, when they hear all these statutes, will say, "Truly, this great nation is a wise and discerning people."
>
> (Deut. 4:5–6)

Throughout the book, the Deuteronomic homilist, speaking in the name of Moses, urges this *practical* wisdom of law observance on his hearers, a wisdom that is not to be sought in heaven—that is, in arcane speculation—or overseas—that is, in the intellectual achievements of other countries (Deut. 30:11–14). As we saw, this view of "the true wisdom" finds a sympathetic echo in Ben Sira.

As a source of information on the identity and role of the sage and on the nature of the intellectual tradition in Israel, the biblical sources must therefore be used with caution. What, then, can we hope to gain by consulting the archaeological record? The problems involved in doing so are easily stated. In the first place, the data pool is limited and its interpretation particularly vulnerable to revision as a result of subsequent finds. The paucity of inscriptional material, noted earlier, also invites the temptation to overinterpret, to squeeze out of the data more than they can be fairly expected to offer, and to propose dubious alignments with biblical texts. These problems are exemplified in the epigraphical data bearing on writing and education assembled by André Lemaire.[18] What it amounts to is the chance discovery in a few sites—'Izbet Sartah, Gezer, Lachish, Khirbet el-Qom, Arad, Aroer, Kadesh, Kuntillet 'Ajrud—of a few lines of writing, many of them letters of the alphabet in sequence (abecedaries). On the basis of these samples, Lemaire argued for the existence of schools in Israel from as early as the prestate period. In view of the lack of evidence for the physical environment of a school, however, this conclusion remains in the realm of speculation. Lemaire suggested that the room with benches in which the much-discussed 'Ajrud graffiti were discovered looks like a classroom, but the excavator of the site, Zeev Meshel, has more plausibly suggested that the benches were used for storage.[19] Moreover, the elementary skill required to write the alphabet or a list of months in the agrarian year could easily be imparted on a one-to-one basis, for example, in the domestic household.

A somewhat broader approach to the archaeological data bearing on literacy has been taken more recently by D. W. Jamieson-Drake.[20] Using what he calls a socioarchaeological approach, he synthesizes the results of surface surveys and excavations with a view to identifying evidence for settlement patterns, public works, and the incidence of luxury items. The aim is to trace the development of urbanization together with administrative and economic centralization in general, in the belief that these would have to entail a fairly high level of scribal skill. He concludes that there is little indication that Judah functioned fully as a state before the eighth century B.C.E., and that therefore scribal skill was little developed before that time. Most of the indications of administrative control, and therefore of scribal activity, are concentrated in the eighth and seventh centuries—say, from Hezekiah to Josiah—after which there is a sharp falloff. His inquiry does not extend beyond the fall of the Judean state.

Jamieson-Drake's methods are interesting and potentially important, but experience suggests that broad conclusions from a very thinly spread and uneven archaeological data base, and especially from the absence of data, are extremely fragile. A clearer picture would no doubt emerge if the same method and criteria were applied to the more extensive and prosperous kingdom of Samaria during the two centuries of its existence.

BEGINNINGS: CREATING A
MORAL CONSENSUS

Since hardly anything one could say at the present time about Israelite origins would pass unchallenged, we shall make a detour around this mined terrain and content ourselves with the statement that Israel first appears on the screen of history as a society based on kinship. All that this is taken to mean is that the principal organizing feature was the bond of real or fictive kinship; principal though not unique, since social bonding also came about by virtue of simple topographical vicinity, living in the same settlement and sharing in the same economic activities. As in other peasant cultures around the Mediterranean rim, these activities consisted in farming the land for cereal crops, olives, grapes, and other produce and perhaps also in raising livestock in a basically subsistence economy. It goes without saying that this kind of society is nonliterate and neither requires nor allows for much by way of occupational diversification or formal education.

A great deal has been written on the kinship network in preindustrial societies, including Israel, that need not detain us. Whatever their historical value, several episodes from the early history of Israel may serve to illustrate the basic structure. The violator of the ban during the conquest of Canaan was discovered by casting lots, which identified first the tribe (*šēbeṭ*), then the clan (*mišpāḥâ*), then the household (*bayit*), and finally the individual, the hapless Achan (Josh. 7:16–18). The procedure therefore corresponds to the tripartite breakdown of the kinship structure elaborated by Emile Durkheim.[21] Gideon explains to an angel that he cannot be expected to save Israel since his clan or phratry (*'elep*) is the poorest in the (tribe of) Manasseh and he is the youngest member of his ancestral household (*bêt 'āb*) (Judg. 6:15). The usurper Abimelech, supported by the *mišpāḥâ* to which his mother's *bêt 'āb* belonged, exterminated his father's household (Judg. 9:1–6). Saul was chosen by lot, beginning with the tribe, then the *mišpāḥâ,* then Saul himself, skipping the household (1 Sam. 10:21).

The ancestral household (*bayit, bêt 'āb*[22]) typically included three generations in unilinear descent and, depending on its economic assets, some or all of the following dependents or codependents: unmarried relatives, the families of grown children, a divorced adult daughter who had returned to the paternal homestead, an adopted child or adopted children, servants, and slaves. The larger households would also have employed day laborers as the occasion arose. The economic survival of these units depended on replenishing the work force by exogamous marriage and therefore on the observance of sex taboos, as listed in Lev. 18:6–18. The *bêt 'āb* was therefore the basic unit of social interaction. The *mišpāḥâ* was a cluster of households not all adjacent, but since the term is not used in connection with leadership roles, it does not call for discussion. The tribe (*šēbeṭ, maṭṭeh*), finally, is the macro-unit, claiming descent from a real or fictitious eponym.

The kinship network served to determine the role, social location, and social space of the individual, even for those who were not biologically part of the lineage system. The system was both patrilineal and patriarchal. While we cannot assume that biblical texts have faithfully recorded social situations and practices from remote antiquity, they present a range of leadership roles that merit consideration. Some (e.g., *rō'š,* "head") are too imprecise to be useful, others (e.g., *qāṣîn,* "chieftain") are predominantly military, and most came in the course of time to be used in several different ways, for example, *nāśî',* variously translated "prince," "king," "patriarch," depending on the context. For our purpose, the most important of these is the role of elder or patriarch (*zāqēn*), the prestige of which allowed it to service the breakup of the lineage system and continue into the Persian period and beyond.[23]

Tribal elders functioned as a deliberative body in matters concerning the tribe as a whole, especially in emergency situations. At the local level, the elder exercised authority in the individual household or village settlement, a situation somewhat analogous to the role of the *mukhtar* in Palestinian Arab villages today. Patriarchs or elders exercised a judicial function, both individually and collectively, in such matters as undetected homicide (Deut. 21:1–9), ungovernable sons (Deut. 21:18–21), sanctuary (Josh. 20:1–6), charges of sexual misconduct directed against wives (Deut. 22:13–21), and disputes concerning marriage and property in general (Deut. 25:5–10; 1 Kings 21:8–14; Ruth 4:2). The elders were also the depositaries, custodians, and transmitters of the group ethos and the shared traditions that helped to constitute the group's identity. They would also have presided over family rituals, especially concerning the ancestors, that did not call for the presence of a cultic specialist.[24]

As the one primarily involved in childrearing, the mother played an important role in the internalization and transmission of moral values and therefore in education, understood in the broad sense of equipping the child for survival in that kind of society. While the formative influence of mothers is not a major theme in the writings of the sages, Proverbs does occasionally refer to maternal teaching and has preserved at least one example of maternal instruction, albeit an exceptional one (Prov. 31:1–9).

As the encroaching state system gradually undermined the lineage network as the determinant of social identity, traditional roles were either curtailed or eliminated and new roles created. The earliest of these new roles to be mentioned in our sources is the type of ad hoc military leadership described and exemplified in Judges. Eventually, of course, a state bureaucracy came into existence, including a great number of cult personnel functioning in the state sanctuaries. But quite apart from these large-scale political changes, internal and external pressures on the subsistence agrarian economy would have impelled the more enterprising into new roles. It may have been in this way that Levites acquired the role of cultic specialists, after losing title to patrimonial domain, though the question of Levite origins is impenetrably obscure. We do, however, hear of one Levite of no fixed location finding gainful employment as a priest with a well-to-do family (Judg. 17:7–18:31). Indigent families could also place orphans as oblates in one or another of the local sanctuaries, a practice also attested in the Middle Ages. In due course, some of these might discover that they possessed special talents which could enhance the prestige and income of the holy place. The story of the early years of Samuel may be a case in point (1 Samuel 1—3). We might also speculate that the "sons of the prophets," bands of dervishlike ecstatics associated with the local sanctuaries, were recruited from the ranks of the landless—younger sons who had to make their own way, landowners evicted for nonpayment of debts, day laborers who could find no work.

Most precarious of all was the situation of women, whether unmarried, widowed, or divorced, who were left without the protection of a household. Apart from prostitution (Gen. 38:1–26), their options were severely limited. They might get into the witchcraft business (e.g., the witch of Endor, 1 Sam. 28:3–25; Ezek. 13:17–23) or, at a somewhat higher level, assume the role of the "wise woman," who could set up the ancient equivalent of a counseling service (2 Sam. 14:1–20; 20:14–22). It is not surprising that talents of this kind are discovered, activated, or even simulated in response to extreme economic distress.

We return now to the role of the *zāqēn* in this earliest stage of Israel's social evolution and go on to ask: What was the ethos with the maintenance and transmission of which the elder or paterfamilias was entrusted? This was a nonliterate society, one that had recourse to writing only in exceptional situations, for example, the drawing up of a contract, for which the services of a scribe trained in one of the larger urban centers would have to be secured.[25] It was also a society without educational institutions. What education there was consisted in imparting, within the nuclear family units, traditional standards of behavior and whatever basic skills were required for participation in the collective economy. We have seen that in this educative process the mother played a role at least as significant as the male head of the household. In addition, the cluster of households forming a cohesive unit would have provided its own rewards and incentives for the socialization of the child and the internalization of the traditional ethos.

Apart from a few residues of ancient practice that have survived in legal and narrative texts from a much later time, we have little information on the specific content of this ethos and the ways in which it was maintained. The principle of corporate liability would have applied in some instances, especially with respect to criminal acts, the perpetrators of which were unknown (e.g., Deut. 21:1–9, the case of homicide). The much maligned *lex talionis,* an attempt to apply the principle of equity in nonnegotiable situations, would also have had a place. In addition, we hear of certain things "not done in Israel," and with one exception (violation of the ban in warfare, Josh. 7:15), the act in question is of a sexual nature—rape, including gang rape; incest; adultery; and sexual misconduct in general.[26] The word used to describe these acts is *něbālâ,* usually translated "folly," though "outrage" would be nearer the mark. The idea is that these are acts that pose a direct threat to the order on which the survival of the group as a whole depends.

It would be natural to conclude that the regulation of social life at this early stage of social evolution contributed to the development of the legal tradition in Israel, a tradition embodied in the so-called Covenant Code in Exodus 20—23, the quasi-legal material in Deuteronomy 12—26, and the mostly cultic legislation in Leviticus and Numbers. Old Testament scholars are wont to take Albrecht Alt's essay on the origins of Israelite law, published in 1934, as the point of departure for the critical discussion of this subject. [27] For Alt, the first step was the form-critical distinction between casuistic and apodictic legal formulations. Casuistic or common law is of a kind that states the facts of the case in the protasis ("when a person does X") and the legal consequences in the apodosis ("then Y follows"). It is therefore concerned exclusively with the legal status of the act in question as determined by precedent and not with moral evaluation. Apodictic law, in contrast, is unconditional and universal in application. Its typical formulation is the prohibitive, as in the Decalogue, but it can also be couched in the participial form, specifying acts subject to the death penalty ("Whoever strikes a man so that he dies shall be put to death," Ex. 21:12), or in the form of a curse ("Cursed be anyone who dishonors father or mother," Deut. 27:16).

In keeping with the Canaanite–Israelite polarity characteristic of Alt's account of Israelite origins in general, he went on to argue that the apodictic formulations are uniquely Israelite, as opposed to case law, which he took to be a local Canaanite adaptation of a long-standing Near Eastern legal tradition. Criticism of Alt's understanding of Israelite origins, including the idea of an amphictyonic or tribal center at which the apodictic formulations were periodically recited, has since led to this part of Alt's thesis being widely rejected. It has also been noticed that the negative command formulation is attested in the didactic literature of Near Eastern countries, including Israel (e.g., Prov. 3:27–32; 22:22–28), which raises a question about the cultic origin of such injunctions as are found in the Decalogue. But it is worth noting that the first part of the (evidently composite) Covenant Code, presented under the rubric of legal stipulations (*mišpāṭîm;* Ex. 21:1–22:18[19]), contains both casuistic and apodictic formulations, in neither of which is there anything specifically Israelite or any reference to political institutions.[28] I take this as confirmation of the view that elements of both customary law and didactic teaching from this early period have contributed to the legal system that came into force some time after the rise of the state.

In common with other traditional societies, the Israel of the prestate period had resources beyond the sphere of customary law for regulating conduct, maintaining the common ethos, and discouraging deviance. Some of the traditional sayings recorded here and there in biblical narrative have distinct contextual features indicating origin in a particular event or situation (e.g., "Is Saul also among the prophets?" 1 Sam. 10:12; 19:24). Others, however, are of general applicability and must have been in circulation for a long time (e.g., Judg. 8:21; 1 Sam. 24:13).[29] Proverbial sayings generally play a significant role in regulating social relations, in sustaining common values, and even in establishing points of law in traditional societies. The reader disinclined to consult the relevant anthropological studies will find excellent examples, with respect to the Ibo of Nigeria, in the novels of Chinua Achebe. Early Israel must also have had its stock of traditional sayings and traditional narrative, including parables and cautionary tales, and these too would have contributed to maintaining the cohesion and ethos of the group. Residues of such traditional lore, in gnomic or narrative form, can still be found in societies resistant to the inroads of mass culture—rural Ireland or Yiddish-speaking communities, for example.

In sum, we have good reason to believe that elements of this common ethos in earliest Israel survived the transition to the state, and that the survivals can be detected in the legal system, in prophetic protest against the corrosive effect of state institutions on a traditional way of life, and, as we now go on to see, in the teachings of the sages.

WRITING IN THE SERVICE OF
THE STATE SYSTEM

We are not concerned to trace in detail the long and complex process by which the tribal and village culture of early Israel was absorbed into the state system. According to the biblical record, the earliest stage was the sporadic emergence of warlords, in response to external and internal pressures, culminating in the offer of kingship to Jerubbaal/Gideon, a warrior of the Abiezer clan. Though he appears to reject the offer, his subsequent conduct suggests that he accepted it for himself while rejecting the idea of a dynasty (Judg. 8:22–28). His son Abimelech nevertheless succeeded in seizing power and ruling for a short time in the Ephraim hill country, until he came to a predictably violent end (Judges 9). Equally fortuitous in its origins, though covering rather more territory, was the rule of the Benjaminite Saul.

Though all three are referred to as *kings,* the term is anachronistic, since the apparatus of kingship was almost entirely lacking. A more appropriate term would be *chieftain,* which is perhaps the meaning of the Hebrew *nāgîd,* used of Saul (1 Sam. 9:16; 10:1; 13:14), David (1 Sam. 25:30; 2 Sam. 5:2; 6:1; 7:8), and even some who came later (1 Kings 1:35; 14:17; 16:2; 2 Kings 20:5).

With the ascendancy of David, a brigand chieftain from the Judean highlands, we see the first rudimentary indications of statehood and the founding of a dynasty that was to prove remarkably durable.[30] According to the biblical record (1 Kings 3—11), this process was consolidated by Solomon. A temple and royal palace were built in Jerusalem, and the major cities, including Hazor, Megiddo, Gezer, and of course Jerusalem itself, were expanded and fortified. These operations called for forced labor on a large scale, requiring supervision by 550 foremen. We also hear of extensive trade with the Phoenician cities, the Arabian peninsula, and perhaps even East Africa. Solomon also divided the kingdom into twelve districts, each with its provincial governor, no doubt primarily for fiscal purposes (1 Kings 4:7–19). Measures such as these would, if historically plausible, have required the services of a considerable corps of educated and literate civil servants and would therefore signify important progress toward a society capable of generating a literary and intellectual tradition.

It has to be added, however, that in recent years historians have been increasingly disturbed by the fact that the United Monarchy—according to biblical tradition, the center of an empire stretching from the Euphrates to the Egyptian border—has left practically no mark on the archaeological record. Also, nothing written has survived from that time, with the exception of the Gezer calendar (the date of which is, however, uncertain) and a few names and letters of the alphabet scratched on ostraca, bowls, and arrowheads.[31] Many, therefore, are now concluding that the apparatus of state control remained at a fairly rudimentary level before, say, the reigns of Omri in Israel and Jehoshaphat in Judah (ca. 875 B.C.E.). The sixty-five inscribed shards discovered in the royal enclave in Samaria by the Harvard expedition, dated to the reign of one or other ruler of the Jehu dynasty, provide a glimpse into the process by which the old clan districts were absorbed into the state system in the kingdom of Samaria. They record shipments of oil and wine from provincial centers to the court in the capital city. Seven of the points of origin mentioned on the ostraca, including Shechem, also appear in biblical lists of settlements of the tribe of Manasseh (Num. 26:29–34; Josh. 17:1–13), and the rest are towns or villages unattested in tribal lists.[32] Jehoshaphat, contemporary and perhaps also vassal of Omri and the first ruler of either kingdom to bear a name with the theophoric element YHWH, was also apparently the first to accept the division of the kingdoms as a reality. If the catalogue of Judean cities in Josh. 15:21–62 reflects his administrative reforms, as some have argued,[33] it seems that either he followed Solomon's example by dividing Judah into twelve districts or subdistricts or the administrative measures attributed to Solomon have been modeled on those of Jehoshaphat. The archaeological record also suggests that such important regional centers as Lachish, Beersheba, and Arad were expanded and fortified at that time and a chain of forts built in the Negev, presumably against Edomite encroachment. There may also be some truth in the report of a later source (2 Chron. 17:7–9; 19:4–11) about judicial reforms carried out during this reign.

The point of all this is that encroachment on the established regional and kinship structures by the state system brought about the transformation or elimination of old roles and the creation of new ones. Therefore, while we may have to reserve judgment about much of the biblical record on David and Solomon, especially in the absence of nonbiblical corroboration, there is no good reason to reject out of hand what appear to be genuine archival records, especially the lists of royal officials at the courts of both kings (2 Sam. 8:16–18; 20:23–26; 1 Kings 4:1–6). Of these, the ones of interest to us are the offices of *mazkîr* ("recorder" in RSV) and *sōpēr* (scribe). None of the nine biblical occurrences of the former designation provides much of a clue to the functions associated with the office except 2 Kings 18:26, which suggests that Hezekiah's *mazkîr* knew at least one language other than Hebrew. But the related terms *sēper hazzikrōnôt* ("the book of memorable deeds"; Esth. 6:1) and *dokrān* ("book of records"; Ezra 4:15, Aramaic), both containing the same stem as *mazkîr,* suggest the office of court chronicler or archivist. If this is so, the *mazkîr* may have been charged with the task of putting together the royal annals, of the kind to which the biblical historian often refers the reader (1 Kings 11:41; 14:19, 29; 15:7, 23; etc.).

The office of *sōpēr* or *sōpēr hammelek* (royal scribe) has been compared to that of secretary of state; in any case, it occupied a prominent place in the emerging royal bureaucracy. One of its functions was to draw up official edicts, as did, at a much later time, the scribes of King Ahasuerus (Esth. 3:12; 8:9). Other functions probably included supervision of the royal commissariat and tax returns. At a somewhat later time we hear of royal scribes, the most prominent of whom were Shebna, in the service of Hezekiah, and Shaphan, during Josiah's reign. Their responsibilities included supervising the temple treasury and taking part in diplomatic missions (2 Kings 18; Isaiah 36). The service of scribes of more humble station was also an essential adjunct of the provincial administrative system and, indeed, of any urban center where taxes were collected, provisions stored, business conducted, deals struck, and complaints filed. The Jerusalem temple would also have had its scribes, predecessors of the *hierogrammateis* (sacred scribes) of the Roman period (Josephus, *Ant.* 11.128). The army must also have employed scribes to take roll call, count prisoners and booty, and the like (Jer. 52:25; 2 Chron. 26:11).[34] Scribes serving as secretaries to individuals of means must have been quite rare, and in fact, only one is attested, none other than Baruch, amanuensis of Jeremiah (Jeremiah 36).

It is a moot point to what extent we can extrapolate from the bureaucratic use of writing in the service of the emerging state system to postulate a genuine literary tradition prior to the middle of the ninth century B.C.E. I suggested earlier that elements of customary law and scraps of traditional wisdom survived the transition to the state system and found their way into writing. Old collections of ballads and songs were also passed on and augmented, including the Book of Yashar (Josh. 10:12–13; 2 Sam. 1:18; 1 Kings 8:12–13, 53), the Book of Yahweh's Wars (Num. 21:14–18), and other compositions of ballad writers (*mōšĕlîm;* Num. 21:27) and rhapsodists. Some of the livelier and earlier prose—for example, concerning the adventures and misadventures of Samson (Judges 14–16)—may be paraphrases of epic poetic originals, but evidence for a lengthy epic work underlying the earliest biblical narrative sources is lacking.[35]

To what extent court annalists went beyond the kind of propagandistic recording familiar from Assyrian chronicles cannot be decided easily, if at all. In the present state of Pentateuchal studies, we can no longer take for granted the existence of continuous sources from the early period of the monarchy—the J and E of the documentarians. Doubts have also been raised about the early date assigned by many to the so-called succession history (2 Samuel 11—20; 1 Kings 1—2), and the whole idea of a "Solomonic renaissance," proposed by Gerhard von Rad in particular, is justifiably no longer in favor.[36]

On a minimalist view, then, we conclude that in this early, formative period there circulated a considerable amount of traditional material in oral and written form—songs, ballads, saga, legends of holy places and people, and the like. This popular culture, probably much richer than our sources suggest, did not call for much in the way of role specialization. Court chronographers also composed annals, which could have served as a source for some of the biblical narrative about the early monarchy. But the almost complete lack of supporting evidence from the archaeological record currently available suggests that social and political development had not yet reached the stage at which a substantial literary and intellectual tradition could be expected to emerge.

THE SOCIAL AND MORAL WORLD OF THE SAGES
AT THE TIME OF HEZEKIAH

With the reign of Hezekiah (ca. 715–687 B.C.E.), the first Judean king since Solomon without a counterpart in the kingdom to the north, we begin to see the emergence of a literary tradition and a class of literati with ambitions that went beyond the writing of royal annals or the hackwork inseparable from daily administrative tasks. Social and economic development reached its zenith in Judah in the late eighth and early seventh centuries. The population and size of Jerusalem increased notably, no doubt in part to accommodate refugees from the kingdom of Samaria, now incorporated into the Assyrian provincial system. A significant increase in luxury items and imported goods indicates a corresponding increase in trade, to the benefit of the upper classes in the metropolis and in provincial centers such as Lachish, Beersheba, and Arad. Since this increase in trade involved a great deal of scribal activity, it is no surprise that the greatest concentration of inscribed material dates to this time: ostraca from Arad, Hurvat Uza, Tell Qasile, Meṣad Hashavyahu, and Jerusalem; the Siloam inscription; seals, seal impressions (bullae), and about a thousand stamped jar handles.[37] None of these texts is of more than historical interest, but taken together they point to a social and economic infrastructure capable of generating, or at any rate, of supporting, a genuine literary tradition.

In view of the preponderant size of Jerusalem (about 150 acres, compared with Lachish, the second-largest city, at 20 acres) and the centralization of the administrative apparatus in a kingdom of relatively small size, it was inevitable that the royal court would function as the primary locus of literary activity. Biblical tradition attributes to Hezekiah the composition of a psalm (Isa. 38:9) and to "Hezekiah's men" the collecting, copying, and editing of proverbs (Prov. 25:1).[38] On the assumption that a nucleus of genuine sayings can be identified in prophetic books, the contemporary prophet Isaiah, who had close contacts with the court even if not himself at one time attached to it,[39] exhibits a high level of literary ability. Quite likely, he or his acolytes committed his sayings to writing, thus preserving them for posterity (Isa. 8:1, 16–18; 30:8). His frequent castigation of royal counselors (*yôʿăṣîm*) reflects the high level of diplomatic activity going on at that time, some of it by correspondence (Isa. 5:18–25; 29:14–16; 30:1–5;

37:14; 39:1). Much of that activity was brought on by the fall of Samaria (722 B.C.E.) and the consequent direct threat to Judean survival, a threat that almost, but not quite, proved terminal in Sennacherib's campaign of 701. One wonders whether Judah's remarkable survival at that crucial juncture, a survival later attributed to direct divine intervention, did not precipitate a burst of literary activity, not unlike what happened in Athens more than two centuries later after the retreat of the Persian land and sea forces.

The compendiums of proverbial wisdom put together by "Hezekiah's men" were intended to serve as educational manuals for aspirants to a career in the Judean state bureaucracy—whether as diplomat, administrator, magistrate, or just hanger-on at court. They therefore circulated among a numerically insignificant percentage of the population, specifically young males from landowning families with enough surplus wealth to launch their sons—especially younger sons who did not inherit the patrimonial domain—on lucrative careers in the service of the state. To achieve membership in that restricted group was to be part of the ruling elite, comparable to the English establishment in the nineteenth and early twentieth centuries recruited from families wealthy enough to send their sons to the public schools and the universities. The essential first step was literacy, a powerful means of political control even with the relatively easy-to-learn paleo-Hebrew script. (By contrast, the Egyptian hieroglyphic script, knowledge of which was restricted to less than 1 percent of the population, was notoriously difficult.) There is also some evidence that the scribal office and other state offices dependent on scribalism were hereditary, a circumstance that would have contributed to the concentration of political power in the hands of a few wealthy and influential families. A good example would be the family of Shaphan, the "scribe" of Josiah, members of which occupied positions of power and influence through three generations. One of them, Gedaliah, grandson of Shaphan, was assassinated shortly after being appointed governor of the conquered province of Judah by the Babylonians.[40]

A distinct social class such as the one that administered affairs of state under Hezekiah creates its own moral environment and defines the limits of acceptable behavior for those who belong to it. Our principal source of information on the ethos and etiquette into which aspirants to public office at that time were socialized consists in the two collections of "Solomonic" aphoristic material in Proverbs (10:1–22:16; 25:1–29:27). The elaborated, bicolon form in which these proverbs are cast gives them a self-consciously artistic character quite different from the folk proverb. They are, for the most part, secular in tone and substance, drawing on experience and observation and emphasizing order, stability, and social hierarchy, with a very definite line on conformity and deviance. Mention of the national deity, Yahweh, rather more frequent in the second collection attributed to Hezekiah's men (28:5, 25; 29:13, 25), may be due to an editorial theologizing of this kind of proverbial instruction. The adaptation of the Egyptian instruction of Amen-em-opet to Yahwistic faith (22:17–24:34) points in this direction, as does the presence of alternative versions of proverbs, one of which suggests a deliberate modification of the other from a Yahwistic perspective (compare, for example, 13:14 with 14:27, or 27:21 with 17:3). Most of the "Yahwistic" sayings are concentrated in Prov. 14:26–16:15, perhaps, as has been suggested, because this was originally an independent section linking chapters 10—15 and 16—22.[41] It is, at any rate, clear that moral evaluation is for the most part based on the observation of human behavior in society and its consequences, with an occasional appeal to social life in the animal world—all the way from ants to lions.

Leafing through these two small manuals (10:1–22:16 and 25:1–29:27) conveys to the reader a strong impression of the importance of *being in control:*

> Like a city breached, without walls,
> is one who lacks self-control.
> (25:28)

The "cool" man (17:27) will not give way to fits of temper and will ignore insults (12:16). He will confine himself to saying what he knows (20:15); will avoid slander, gossip, and quarreling (10:18; 11:12–13; 26:21); and will be a good listener (12:15; 18:13; 25:12). The fool, the "hot" man, is by definition the one who does not know when to keep quiet, who has no control over his tongue (10:8, 14; 12:23; etc.). Just knowing when to stay silent can work wonders, even for one of limited talent:

> Even fools who keep silent are considered wise,
> when they close their lips they are deemed intelligent.
> (17:28)

This recalls the Latin saying, *si tacuisses, philosophus mansisses* (if you had kept quiet, you might have passed for a philosopher). There is nothing specifically Israelite about all this. Similar injunctions appear frequently in the didactic literature of other lands, especially Egypt. The scribe Ani, for example, tells his son (meaning, his pupil), "Do not talk a lot; be silent and you will be happy; do not be garrulous"; Amen-em-opet, mentioned earlier, compares the silent man who holds himself aloof to a tree that flourishes in a garden.[42]

Conduct incompatible with this ideal of reserve and control in public is to be diligently avoided. An obvious case in point is public intoxication. This can be productive of unfortunate consequences (20:1; 21:17), such as are vividly described in the "Egyptian" instruction (23:29–33):

> Your eyes will see strange things,
> your mind will utter perverse things.
>
> (23:33)

One must also choose one's company with care, since

> whoever walks with the wise becomes wise,
> but the companion of fools suffers harm.
>
> (13:20)

Or, as Plutarch put it in his treatise *On the Education of Children,* "If you live with a lame man you will learn to limp." Experience has also amply demonstrated the often undesirable consequences of overintimacy with women, especially when away from home (e.g., 22:14), and the wisdom of avoiding prostitutes (23:26–28; 29:3). The severely limited scope of this kind of moral didactic is nowhere more in evidence than in its petulant and over-whelmingly negative attitude toward women in general; an attitude that, as we saw earlier, reaches its nadir in Ben Sira. Women are acceptable if they meet the high standards of this class ethic, which means that they must be wise, sensible, and virtuous (11:16, 22; 14:1). While the final section of Proverbs (31:10–31), dealing with the *'ēšet-ḥayil* (capable wife? woman of substance?), should probably be read as a kind of allegorical counterpart to the Woman Wisdom in the first nine chapters of the book, it also depicts an ideal or, more likely (as the initial rhetorical question suggests), an unattainable fantasy about the kind of woman who would make the perfect wife—a woman who pleases her husband in everything, is adored by her children, and displays a daunting range of managerial skills. The counterpart is the quarrelsome and contentious wife, the object of more attention than any other topic in the collections (19:13; 21:9, 19; 25:24; 27:15).

Most indicative of the group ethos is the attitude toward poverty and wealth in these didactic manuals. Charity toward the poor is recommended (14:31; 22:16; 29:7), but there is more than a hint of the depressingly familiar point that poverty is the result of laziness (19:15; 20:4; 21:25). Hard work is the royal road to wealth (12:27; 13:4; 14:23; 20:13). Wealth will not necessarily bring happiness (11:4; 16:16; 22:1–2), but it is good in itself, it is essential for security (10:15; 18:11), and its possession is proof of clean living and divine blessing (10:22; 13:21, 25; 15:6; 22:4). The manuals also offer advice on how to go about acquiring wealth. There is a remarkably strong emphasis on the advantages of a gradual accumulation and the dangers of a "get rich quick" approach (13:11; 20:21; 21:5; 28:20, 22). Due deference to authority is recommended, helped out by the occasional timely and discreet bribe (17:8; 21:14). The beginner is warned to avoid lending and borrowing, especially if the one requesting a loan is a stranger (11:15; 22:7), and whatever you do, don't stand surety for someone else's debts (17:18; 20:16 = 27:13).

The writers and teachers who compiled these collections of aphorisms for the benefit of young, upper-class males hardly merit the title of intellectual. Their teaching is, at best, sclerotic and pedestrian and, at worst, complaisant and ethically insensitive on a whole range of issues. Their vision is limited and their language constrained by the social class to which they belong, the ethos of which they are committed to uphold and perpetuate. The *Weltanschauung* (view of life) has much in common, in both positive and negative respects, with that of the nineteenth-century English upper class described in the novels of Anthony Trollope, Henry James, and Ford Madox Ford. In one respect, however, their teaching transcends these limitations. We note at several points significant overlap with the evolving legal tradition in Israel, namely, at those points where they urge the observance of important items of customary law (e.g., concerning murder, theft, false witnessing, dishonest trading, removing landmarks) and the maintenance of fair and impartial judicial procedures (e.g., 18:5, 17–18; 21:15). The overlap may be exemplified by a saying about judicial bribery:

> The wicked accept a concealed bribe
> to pervert the ways of justice.
> (Prov. 17:23)

This may be compared with a stipulation of the so-called Covenant Code:

> You shall take no bribe, for a bribe blinds officials
> and subverts due process for the innocent.
> (Ex. 23:8)

The more discursive way in which the same injunction is formulated in Deuteronomy, together with the substitution of "the wise" (*ḥăkāmîm*) for "officials," points to a certain convergence of the didactic and the legal genres:

> You must not distort justice; you must not show partiality; and you must not accept bribes, for a bribe blinds the eyes of the wise and subverts due process for the innocent. Justice, only justice, you shall pursue.
> (Deut. 16:19–20)

This contamination between the didactic and the legal at the literary level raises some interesting issues with respect to the social situations generative of this kind of text. The most obvious point of departure is to ask who drafted this kind of legal formulation and how, as a class, those who did so stood in relation to the scribal profession in general. In the following section we try to answer these questions.

SCRIBES AND LAWYERS

In addition to the many laws of a ritual nature in Exodus, Leviticus, and Numbers, the Hebrew Bible has preserved two compilations of civil and criminal law, the covenant law book handed to Moses at Sinai (Ex. 20:21–23:19) and the law promulgated by Moses on the last day of his life in Moab (Deuteronomy 12—26). When compared with other legal corpora from the Near East, of which the 282 laws promulgated by Hammurabi of Babylon in the late eighteenth century B.C.E. are the best known, certain features of Hebrew law stand out that raise some interesting questions. The first is that, in addition to the standard casuistic or common law formulation, the biblical collections contain many categoric or apodictic statements more characteristic of the didactic than the legal genre. Compare, for example, this stipulation from the covenant law book—

> You shall not pervert justice when you bear witness in a lawsuit by siding with the majority
>
> (Ex.23:2)

—with the following injunction from the previously mentioned *Instruction of Amen-em-opet:*

> Do not bear witness with false words,
> nor support another person [thus] with your tongue.

Or compare

> You shall not move your neighbor's boundary marker set up by former generations
>
> (Deut. 19:14)

with a similar prohibition of Amen-em-opet:

> Do not carry off the landmark at the boundaries of the arable land,
> Nor disturb the position of the measuring-cord.[43]

In addition, many of the stipulations in the biblical compilations provide motivation for their observance and are presented in a discursive way quite foreign to legal compilations in general. This is especially the case in Deuteronomy 12—26, to the extent that we would be inclined to describe these chapters more as a *program* than as a collection of laws. The same features appear in the section of the covenant law book that begins and ends with injunctions about the resident alien (*gēr*):

> You shall not wrong an alien or oppress him; for you were aliens in the land of Egypt.
>
> (Ex. 22:20 [22:21])

> You shall not oppress an alien; you know what it means to be an alien, for you were aliens in the land of Egypt.
>
> (Ex. 23:9)

Couched in this form, the law loses something of its peremptory character as a direct divine command; the emphasis shifts toward the preservation of the ethos peculiar to this community, based as it is on a shared memory.

These features of the Israelite laws raise the question of the purpose of the compilations. They hardly qualify as law codes, since they are in no way comprehensive. They contain, for example, no legislation on marriage and divorce, with the exception of Deut. 24:1–4, which presupposes divorce but says nothing about who may initiate it, under what circumstances, and with what consequences. The alternative view sometimes advanced, that they deal in cases of special difficulty for the use of magistrates, is not very persuasive either, since most of the cases dealt with are fairly unproblematic. A more plausible suggestion, and one consonant with the way in which many of the laws are formulated, is that their intent was primarily didactic; the collections were put together to serve the purpose of moral education. The point has been made persuasively by Moshe Weinfeld with respect to Deuteronomy, though to what extent that book can be described as "humanistic" may be left open.[44] There is, in any case, considerable overlap between didactic and legal formulations. The apodictic commands (of the "you shall not" type) are of frequent occurrence in the admonitions and instructions of Near Eastern sages, who are also at pains to motivate the hearer or reader. Case law is also comparable to the kind of aphorism found in Proverbs, in the sense that both draw on social experience to link act with consequence, the former in the legal sphere, the latter in that of moral behavior in general. Common to both case or common law and aphorism, therefore, is the association of specific behaviors with certain consequences, based on the accumulated experience of the social group.

Who drafted the laws in Exodus and Deuteronomy? They clearly had to belong to the class of scribes in some way, and if the proposal advanced above about the intent of the legal collections is correct, they must have stood in some relation with the sages whose teaching is represented in Proverbs. It is well known that the word *tôrâ,* generally translated "law," also has the broader connotation of "instruction"; it occurs with this meaning in Proverbs with reference to a mother's teaching (1:8; 6:20) and the teaching of the sage as a fountain of life (13:14). One could also speak of a prophet's *tôrâ* in this more inclusive sense (Isa. 8:16–22). The intent of the authors of Deuteronomy to *instruct* is no less clear than that of the compilers of the aphoristic literature in Proverbs. Moses is presented primarily as teacher (4:1, 5, 14; 6:1; 31:19, 22), and the importance of passing on his teaching is emphasized at numerous points (4:10; 5:1, 31; 11:19; etc.). But it is also in Deuteronomy that the word *tôrâ* is used for the first time to refer to a legal corpus rather than to an individual injunction, with the result that from that point on, individual stipulations of law had to be referred to as *dibrê hattôrâ* (literally, "the words of the law").[45] Numerous allusions in Deuteronomy and the Deuteronomistic history to *the* Torah indicate clearly that there is now in existence an authoritative, officially promulgated corpus of law, and one that has precedence over all other claims to provide moral guidance, including the often disconcerting claims advanced by prophets. The claim is also advanced that this Torah encapsulates in a comprehensive way the teaching of the sages, in that the true wisdom for Israel consists in its observance (Deut. 4:5–8).

We conclude, then, that the emergence of a legal tradition in the strict sense has close connections with the work of those scribes whose moral instruction has come down to us in Proverbs. But having said this, we have to add that moral instruction, *tôrâ,* was also the responsibility of priests. One of the clearest statements on role performance in the Hebrew Bible occurs in a brief remark attributed to Jeremiah's opponents: "Instruction [*tôrâ*] must not perish from the priest, nor counsel from the sages, nor the word from the prophet" (Jer. 18:18; cf. Ezek. 7:26, which substitutes "elders" for "sages"). In keeping with this role assignment, the Deuteronomic *tôrâ* is confided to Levitical priests who are charged with its public recital on stated occasions and must see that the ruler is familiar with it (Deut. 31:9–13, 24–26; 17:18). So the question arises: Was the drafting of an official, one might almost say canonical,[46] law book the work of scribes, or of priests?

Before attempting to answer the question, we must broaden the inquiry by taking in certain allusions to a class of legal specialists that occur in a collection of sayings from the early career of Jeremiah. In denouncing different categories of people for their religious infidelity, Jeremiah mentions one group, described as "handlers of the law" (*tōpĕśê hattôrâ;* Jer. 2:8), that seems to be distinct from the priesthood. The *tôrâ* in question is clearly a written collection of laws, and the verb refers, here as elsewhere,[47] to the deployment of a particular skill. In what precisely that skill consists is not clear from this passage but emerges somewhat more clearly in another diatribe:

> How can you say, "We are wise,
> we have the law of Yahweh,"
> when scribes with their lying pens
> have made it into a lie?
> The wise men are put to shame,
> they are dismayed and have lost their wits.
> They have spurned the word of Yahweh,
> and what sort of wisdom is theirs?
>   (Jer. 8:8–9)

That the saying reflects an ideological conflict involving different and inconsistent versions of *tôrâ*—prophetic teaching over against a written law as interpreted by legal specialists—seems tolerably clear and is supported by similar language in another Jeremian saying:

> They have not heeded my words,
> and as for my *tôrâ*, they have spurned it.
>   (Jer. 6:19)

The claim to be wise by virtue of possessing a written law refers not to law in general but to the Deuteronomic law promulgated during the early years of Jeremiah's career. The homiletic introduction to the law identifies its observance as the form of wisdom peculiar to Israel (Deut. 4:5–6), and it is clear that the Deuteronomic authors share the conviction of the sages that to be wise is also to be successful and prosperous (e.g., Josh. 1:7–8; 1 Kings 2:3). Jeremiah's opposition to this Deuteronomic idea of "legal wisdom" is matched by the generally deterrent view of prophecy in Deuteronomy and the evident intent to bring it under institutional control (Deut. 13:1–5; 18:15–22).[48] Ideological conflict of this kind is by no means uncommon. As Max Weber put it, "A state of tension . . . is characteristic of any stratum of learned men who are ritually oriented to a law book as against prophetic charismatics."[49]

Jeremiah's animus was not directed at the Deuteronomic laws in themselves but against the idea of a codified law understood as the ultimate source of authority in the religious sphere, to the exclusion of prophetic teaching, including, of course, his own. This implies opposition to the *sōpĕrîm* and *ḥăkāmîm* responsible for the drafting of the law book so understood. The charge of turning the law into something false (*šeqer*) would presumably imply what he took to be misplaced confidence in a written legal code. But it would also be aimed at the claim to exclusive control by issuing binding interpretations of the law, a claim that inevitably reduced, if it did not eliminate, the need for prophetic guidance.

The task of determining more precisely the identity of the legal scholars in question is complicated by what Deuteronomy itself has to say about the responsibility of the Levitical priests with respect to the law. They are the custodians of the official draft (17:18; 31:9) that is deposited beside the ark of the covenant in the Temple (31:24–26), and they are to read it in solemn assembly every sabbatical year at the feast of Sukkot (31:10–13). While the "handlers of the law" and the scribes castigated by Jeremiah cannot be identified with priests, to whom he refers as a distinct category, they probably constituted a specialized category of clergy; in which respect they would have anticipated the Levitical instructors in the law encountered frequently in Second Temple compositions (e.g., 2 Chron. 17:7–9; 19:8–11; 35:3; Neh. 8:7–8). In this sense, Deuteronomy represents a point of convergence between the tradition of the sages and that of the priests. This is as far as we need go for the moment, but the issue is further discussed in the second chapter of our study, dealing with the priesthood.

FEMININE WISDOM: THE RETURN OF THE REPRESSED

The individual aphorisms in the two Solomonic compilations in Proverbs (10:1–22:16; 25:1–29:27) show few signs of having originated in popular usage and little, if any, overlap with proverbial sayings occurring here and there in biblical narrative. The typical bicolon form (two parallel or related statements) in which they are couched indicates rather their literary origin. Taken as a whole, they reveal very little systematic coherence. The only consideration that gives them any unity is the idea that certain kinds of behavior generally entail certain consequences, beneficial or otherwise, but there is no evidence that the compilers elevated this cumulative experience into a theoretical ethical principle. Very seldom, moreover, do we catch a glimpse of the more baffling and paradoxical aspects of human existence beneath the smooth surface of prudence and common sense—as, for example:

> There is a way that seems right to a man,
> but its end is the way to death.

> Even in laughter the heart aches,
> and the end of joy is grief.
> (Prov. 14:12–13; cf. 16:25)

or

> Sheol and Abaddon are open to Yahweh,
> how much more human hearts!
> (15:11 = 27:20)

This last is one of those sayings, referred to earlier, that relate human conduct and the human situation in general to the deity. It has been suggested that these may represent an indigenization of an older secular wisdom, a bringing it into contact with the cult of the national god, Yahweh, resulting eventually in a theologically determined view of the moral life encapsulated in the phrase "the fear of Yahweh." Most commentators have detected a similar process at work in the final verse added to the poem on inaccessible wisdom in Job 28:

> He said to humanity:
> "Truly, the fear of Yahweh, that is wisdom,
> and to turn from evil is understanding."
> (v. 28)

It appears even more clearly, and at a rather later point in time, in the final editorial comment on Qoheleth's disconcerting reflections on human life:

> The end of the matter; all has been heard. Fear God and keep his commandments, for this is encumbent on all humanity. For God will bring all deeds into judgment, including every hidden thing, whether good or evil.
> (Eccl. 12:13–14)

Whether Qoheleth himself would have accepted this as an adequate summary of his teaching is, of course, another matter.

The insertion of the two Solomonic compilations into the book of Proverbs marks a further stage in the process of consolidating this scattershot aphoristic wisdom into a coherent schema. Recontextualizing them in this way was an invitation to read them in the light of the intellectual and religious postulates with which the final editors of the book worked, presumably in the Persian or early Hellenistic period. The addition of an extended preface (chapters 1—9) with which—as pointed out earlier—the acrostic poem on the capable woman in Prov. 31:10–31 forms an inclusion,[50] served to endow the aphorisms with greater depth and resonance.

The scattered bits of practical wisdom that they embody are now subsumed under and unified in a theoretical concept of wisdom expressed by means of a feminine personification. The process is taken even further in Prov. 8:22–36, in which wisdom is a transcendent principle, "the beginning of [God's] work," an entity belonging in some way to the divine sphere.

That wisdom is presented at the beginning and end of the book as a woman could hardly have been anticipated, in view of the negative attitude toward *real* women in the Solomonic compilations. (That this attitude was no worse than that of many other cultures in antiquity does not do much to reconcile most modern readers to it.) Why, then, did it happen? The most obvious explanation is that the Hebrew word for wisdom, *ḥokmâ,* is feminine, as is the Greek *sophia,* and it is well known that abstract qualities in Greek were often personified (e.g., *eris, nemesis, tyckē*). In Proverbs 1—9, both *ḥokmâ* and *bînâ* ("understanding"; 7:4) are personified, and feminine personifications were in any case well established in the literary tradition— virgin Israel, daughter Zion, for example. This usage permitted the introduction of a range of affective language into the common stock—the language of union, erotic desire, affection between spouses, and the like—that might otherwise have been excluded.

The gender of *ḥokmâ,* then, provided the occasion for granting the feminine persona hospitality in the world of the sages, but it does not explain the specific features of Wisdom as presented in Proverbs 1—9 or why she is juxtaposed with the mirror image of the *'iššâ zārâ,* the foreign or outsider woman. Some scholars suspected that a goddess figure must have served as a model for the Woman Wisdom. One of the earliest proposals along this line was that of W. F. Albright, whose candidate was a Canaanite-Hebrew goddess of wisdom called *ḥukmatu* (cf. *ḥokmôt;* Prov. 9:1), somewhat similar to the Ishtar/Siduri who makes a cameo appearance in the Gilgamesh epic. Similar proposals have been made more recently, but it must be said that to date there is absolutely no evidence for the existence of such a deity.[51]

A more promising line of inquiry, I believe, begins with the assumption that the Woman Wisdom of Proverbs 1—9 was conceived as a counter to the baleful influence of the Outsider Woman, who therefore is the primary symbolic persona in these chapters. The Outsider Woman represents alien cults, especially those with a strong sexual component, and the kind of behavior associated—in the writer's mind—with them. The association between the allure of alien deities (*'ĕlōhîm zārîm*) and sexual seduction ("whoring after foreign gods") was well established at the time of writing.

To this add the obvious fact that the Woman Wisdom personifies the sage's teaching and, as such, functions precisely to counter aberrant religious and moral conduct. If we take this route, we will have little difficulty in identifying the deity behind the Outsider Woman. Goddess cults, and the cult of the goddess Asherah in particular, are well attested throughout the history of Israel. They formed a normal component of popular religion and were, understandably, of special interest to women. They persisted into the Persian period, as is clear from some strongly worded denunciations in the last part of Isaiah and the very odd vision of the woman in the barrel in Zech. 5:5–11.[52] A careful reading of Proverbs 1—9 confirms the view that the character, attributes, and activities of the Woman Wisdom are presented as a reverse image of those of the Outsider Woman. Suffice it to note that both can be grasped and embraced (3:1, 8; 4:8; 5:20), but while contact with the one is life-enhancing, the other is death-dealing, literally a femme fatale.

I imagine it would not be difficult to conjure up a psychoanalytic hypothesis to explain the dissonance between wisdom as a feminine hypostasis and attitudes toward real women in the aphoristic literature. We find a somewhat analogous situation in those Gnostic systems that, while exalting feminine *sophia* as a divine entity, assigned women a low status on the chain of being. Only those women who make themselves male will enter the kingdom of heaven.[53] But without indulging in excessive speculation, we may suspect that idealization was another means of control, just as at the level of social realities the position of women in marriage was determined by the retention of male control over property. Proverbs 1—9 was certainly composed by a man or men; the personification of wisdom represents the teaching of the male sage, and the Woman Wisdom has an audience only by courtesy of the male author.[54] A further possibility is that personified wisdom is occupying the space vacated as a result of the (not entirely successful) delegitimation and proscription of the goddess cult by reformers, the results of whose zeal are enshrined in Deuteronomy and Dtr (Deut. 7:5; 12:3; 16:21; 2 Kings 18:4; 23:4–7, 14–15). The protest of the Judean women in Egypt *after* the fall of Jerusalem in favor of the cult of the Queen of Heaven, one of the few occasions on which the voices of women are heard speaking about religion, testifies to the strength and persistence of the goddess cult (Jer. 44:15–19).

It is generally agreed that where the Woman Wisdom speaks, she does so in the guise of a prophetic figure. Her admonitions, therefore, incorporate several prophetic forms of discourse. This feature is most clearly detectable in the invitation–response pattern in the first discourse (Prov. 1:24,

28), which is modeled on prophetic sayings datable to the Persian period—
for example:

> You will call and Yahweh will answer,
> You will cry and he will say, Here I am
> (Isa. 58:9)

There are also parallels between Proverbs 1—9 and the denunciations of
alien cults and their practitioners in the same part of Isaiah. The first of these
(Isa. 57:3–13) is of particular interest, since it is addressed to a woman who
is a sorceress, adulteress, and prostitute. Not everything in this passage is
clear, but the main accusation seems to be directed at participation in idol-
atrous rites of a sexual nature, together with child sacrifice and necromancy.
The description of this sorceress (*'ōněnâ*) runs parallel in important respects
with that of the *zārâ* in Proverbs 1—9. Both are addicted to adultery and
prostitution; they are wanton and shameless; their pitch is on the high places
(Isa. 57:7; Prov. 9:14); they have their own houses, in which the most important piece of furniture is the bed (Isa. 57:8; Prov. 2:18; 5:8; 7:16–17, 27;
9:14); and they both engage in sacrificial rituals (Isa. 57:6–7; Prov. 7:14).[55]
It seems, then, that the author of Proverbs 1—9 is in debt to late prophecy,
and therefore it is understandable that the public discourse of the Woman
Wisdom is modeled on that of the prophet. Her assumed role is another
pointer to a situation in which the sages are beginning to fill the vacuum
created by the disappearance of "classical" prophecy and to claim an authority for their teaching analogous to that of the prophet. We find the same
kind of claim advanced by Eliphaz, Job's learned interlocutor (Job 4:12–21),
and we have seen that Ben Sira compares his teaching to prophecy (Sir.
24:33). In due course this would lead to the rabbinic dictum that prophecy
has been taken from the prophets and given to the sages (e.g., *b. Baba Batra* 12a).

To the extent that we can reconstruct it, the editorial history of Proverbs
marks a trajectory along which the consolidation of the intellectual tradition
of the sages can be traced—let us say, from about the eighth century B.C.E.
to the Hellenistic period. In pace with the increasing ascendancy of Yahwistic orthodoxy, the unsystematic instruction in morals and manners of the
earliest stage, which had little to distinguish it from the didactic literature of
other Near Eastern lands, was gradually brought within the orbit of the national cult and given an explicitly religious reference, summed up in the
phrase "the fear of Yahweh." The female personification of this teaching
then conferred on it a semblance of unity and coherence that it had previ-

ously lacked. A further stage of rationalization, in the Weberian sense of "the coherent ordering of beliefs and actions in accordance with a unifying central criterion,"[56] was reached when this personified wisdom was brought into relation with a doctrine of universal and cosmic creation. The result opened the way for the unfolding of a speculative theology that would have far-reaching effects in both Judaism and Christianity.

Some of the principal points on this trajectory may be briefly noted. In the first instance, it was simply a matter of affirming that the divine attributes of wisdom, understanding, and knowledge were involved in the act of creation:

> By wisdom Yahweh founded the earth,
> establishing the heavens by [his] understanding;
> by his knowledge the abysses were cloven,
> and the clouds drop down [their] dew.
>
> (Prov. 3:19–20)

Proverbs 8:22–31, however, goes further in presenting personified wisdom as having a unique, if subordinate, relation to the Creator Deity. Little need be added to the great volume of commentary on this passage, except to note that the author makes three affirmations about Wisdom, dealing with her unique place in the divine sphere, her primordiality, and her role in the created order. On each of these a brief note is in order.

First, there is a studied ambiguity in the way Wisdom's relation to the deity is described at the beginning and the end of the passage (vv. 22–25, 30–31), especially as to whether ḥokmâ is simply first in the created order of things or the firstborn, daughter of Yahweh, "begotten not made." The ambiguity may well be due to taking over the formal features of a cosmogony that generally includes a theogony, the genealogy of the gods, a genre that would not sit well with orthodox Yahwism. A fairly close parallelism from Egypt is the birth of Maʻat, principle of cosmic order and identified with the goddess Isis born of the sun god Re. At any rate, the relation of Wisdom to the Deity is unique and of the most intimate kind. Second, the primordiality of Wisdom is stated by enumerating the elements of the cosmos to which she has priority. Since antiquity is the best warrant for authority, the authoritative status of Wisdom and therefore of the sages' teaching is second to none. Third, Wisdom's relation to the Creator Deity during creation suggests active participation, a co-creative role, a conclusion that would be beyond doubt if we translate the notoriously obscure 'āmôn (v. 30) as "artificer," a reading supported by most of the ancient versions and well represented in the Jewish exegetical tradition.[57] In any case, the point is made that both the natural order and humanity are permeable to the influence of divine wisdom, toward which the teaching of the sages directs attention.

A final step toward the conceptual integration of the tradition represented by the sages, and one that, in retrospect, was inevitable, was taken when the transcendent Wisdom whose voice is heard in Prov. 8:22–31 was identified with Torah, a move facilitated by the fact that *tôrâ*, like *ḥokmâ*, is feminine. We recall that the Deuteronomic homilist identifies *observance* of the official, written law as the wisdom proper to Israel (Deut. 4:5–8). By the time of Ben Sira, writing in the early second century B.C.E., cosmic and cocreative wisdom was represented as finding its social embodiment in *tôrâ*. In the much-quoted passage in question (Sir. 24:1–34), the author opens with an apostrophe of personified wisdom, addressed to the divine assembly, in which she relates how she proceeded from the mouth of the Deity as the first of creation, how she came down from her throne to wander through the world in search of a resting place, and how her search ended when she found accommodation in Israel (v. 1–12). The floral and arboreal language in which she goes on to describe herself (v. 13–17) is reminiscent of the courtly conceits of the Canticle, and the erotic undertones of the invitation issued to her protégés (desiring, possessing, eating, drinking, honey and the honeycomb, etc.) go considerably beyond what Wisdom said of herself in Proverbs 1—9. An interesting case, therefore, of intellectual passion expressed in the language of physical desire.

The thematic resemblance between this first-person account of Wisdom's descent and search for a resting place, on the one hand, and certain texts from the cult of Isis in which the goddess proclaims her attributes and status in the divine world, on the other, has long been noticed. In one of these pronouncements of virtue, copied from a stele in Memphis, Isis lists her titles and speaks of her place in creation:

> I divided the earth from the heaven;
> I showed the path of the stars;
> I ordered the course of the sun and moon.[58]

As the embodiment of Ma'at, principle of cosmic and social order, she also maintains justice, ordaining laws for humanity and filling the world with good order and righteousness. Indeed, one of her titles is "lawgiver" (*thesmophoros*). Ben Sira's poem indigenizes this theme by identifying *ḥokmâ/ sophia* with Israel's law, thus claiming for it a universal significance (24:23– 29) and at the same time responding to the charge of particularism and obscurantism leveled against contemporary Jewish traditionalists. Other

Jewish writers both at that time and later—for example, Aristobulus of Alexandria, Philo, Josephus—would argue in greater detail, and with the help of allegorical interpretation, that the Jewish law was equal or even superior to the best that Greek philosophy had to offer.

As the product of a particular social milieu and class, the thinking of the Jewish sages moves for the most part unreflectively on the father–son, teacher–disciple axis. Even when viewed benevolently, women are outsiders, part of the environment that must be controlled. A teaching of this kind, which gives so much attention to self-control, social maintenance, and property rights, has slight interest in affirming the erotic and expansive possibilities in human relations. We hear a little of it in the riddle about different mysterious forms of propulsion, including "the way of a man with a maid" (Prov. 30:18–19), followed closely, however, by the petit bourgeois portrait of the busy, prosperous, and productive wife (31:10–31). It comes through very clearly in the Canticle, a cycle of erotic lyrics in the courtly style, but it is unclear whether this composition relates in any way to the tradition of the sages, apart from the formal attribution to Solomon. A comment added near the end points, at any rate, in a rather different direction: "If a man offered for love all the wealth of his house, it would be utterly scorned" (Cant. 8:7).

Whatever the reason for the idealization of wisdom in feminine guise—whether the reason is to be sought in the collective unconscious or, as suggested earlier, in the need to counter the cult of the goddess, or in both of these—it persisted as a potentially subversive challenge to male dominance and as deconstructive of the rationality and rigidity of mainline orthodox systems, in both Judaism and Christianity. Speculation on the Shekinah, or divine radiance, a feminine principle connected with the personified wisdom of the sages, served in the medieval *Zohar* and in the teachings of the sixteenth-century kabbalist Isaac Luria as a corrective to the overwhelming masculinity of the Deity. Early Christian speculations on the Holy Spirit also drew extensively on the language and imagery of preexistent wisdom, as a result of which Christian thinking about godhead came to incorporate feminine elements, though never in entire accord with orthodox teaching. At this point, however, we have moved beyond the limits of the present study.

THE IMPACT OF EVENTS ON
THE TRADITION

One of the ways in which the aphoristic wisdom of the sages attempted to wrest order from the chaos of experience was to postulate a connection between act and consequence. The connection does not, of course, entail a strict theory of causality. It is based on what observation and experience teach can generally be expected to result from certain behaviors or attitudes. The banal statement that pride goes before a fall, or as Prov. 16:18 puts it,

> Pride goes before destruction,
> and a haughty spirit before a fall

derives partly from the occasional gratifying experience of the arrogant getting their come-uppance and partly from resentment, but it hardly amounts to a doctrine of retribution, still less to one admitting of no exceptions. But when the act–consequence nexus is given a religious qualification—when, that is, it is assimilated to belief in a deity who presides over and validates the moral order—exceptions pose more serious problems. In any society, a religion or its equivalent provides a basic orientation or cohesive worldview generally strong enough to survive the occasional discrepancy between theory and experience. But disconfirmation of the religiously sanctioned view of moral causality can also happen on a scale that, for either individual or society, raises fundamental questions about either the reality of the deity, meaning generally the deity's ability and will to act, or the deity's ethical character.

The causal links between moral probity and general well-being, on the one hand, and between sin and punishment, on the other, are affirmed constantly in those aphorisms in which the contrast between the righteous and the wicked has taken the place of the contrasting situations of the wise person and the fool:

> No harm befalls the righteous,
> but the wicked have their fill of trouble.
> (Prov. 12:21)

Such a link also comes up regularly in the language of prayer: Yahweh knows the way of the righteous, but the way of the wicked will perish (Ps. 1:6). A disturbing example in narrative context is the account of David's adultery with Bathsheba, since the sin results not in his own death, foreseen in Nathan's parable, but in the death of the unnamed child born of their liaison (2 Samuel 11—12). In those prophetic sayings that employ political language, especially the language of relations between suzerain and vassal, human action results in the direct *judicial* intervention of the Deity. In Deuteronomy and Dtr, however, the link between moral probity and general well being provides a theological explanation for the course of events and the evaluation of individuals, especially rulers, which comes close to being a doctrine.

One or two examples suffice to make the point. During the conquest of Canaan, military success is contingent on fidelity to a law presumed to be available and known (Josh. 1:8). The history of Israel's "heroic age," that of the "judges," is organized on the basis of the same principle, resulting in the sequence (1) apostasy (2) divine anger (3) military disaster (4) repentance (5) temporary salvation (6) renewed apostasy, and so on (Judg. 2:11–23). The success of rulers is in proportion to their religious fidelity, and the final disaster of the destruction of Jerusalem resulted from the wickedness of Manasseh, who lived more than half a century earlier (2 Kings 21:10–15; 23:26–27; 24:3–4). The persistence of this way of thinking is evident in the strongly theologizing history comprising Chronicles-Ezra-Nehemiah, written at least two centuries later. The author not only explains the success or failure of rulers by appeal to a moral criterion; he does not hesitate to invent in order to bring the history into line with the theory. Thus the aforementioned Manasseh had a long reign, so he must have repented (2 Chron. 33:15–16), while Josiah, who died young, even though entirely beyond reproach according to Dtr, must have done something wrong, such as disregarding a divine oracle (2 Chron. 35:21–22).

This interpretation of events in the life of society and the individual was not confined to Israel; it was part of the common theology of the ancient Near East and, with variations, of ancient Greece. So, for example, a prayer of the Hittite king Mursilis II from the fourteenth century B.C.E. laments a plague that is ravaging the land; the cause is finally discovered to be the violation of a treaty oath in the previous reign. The father of Pharaoh Merika-re admits to having destroyed tombs, a heinous offense, and speaks of retribution, though he does not say what form it took. A king of Moab in the ninth century B.C.E. attributes conquest by the Israelite king Omri to the anger of the native deity Kemosh, presumably consequent on some offense.[59] Even in Herodotus, an author of a much more secular mentality, the twin themes of human pride and retribution, hubris and nemesis, are rarely far below the surface.

Biblical texts that reflect the impact of political disaster from the death of Josiah in 609 to the fall of Jerusalem in 586 and subsequent deportations exhibit a broad spectrum of reaction, from outright rejection of conventional religious answers to attempts, some rather desperate, to come up with alternative explanations without entirely abandoning the tradition. Some took the line that the disaster was the result of the suppression of the goddess cult, perhaps with reference to the Josian reform (Jer. 44:15–19). Others denied either the ability or the will of the national deity to intervene ("Yahweh will do neither harm nor good"; Zeph. 1:12) or questioned Yahweh's knowledge of what was going on ("Yahweh does not see us"; Ezek. 8:12; 9:9). Others again attempted to maintain the causal link between sin and punishment by accusing the Deity of injustice in punishing the contemporary generation for the sins of their forebears, and this in spite of the fact that the statute of limitations—three or four generations, according to Ex. 34:7—had run out for most of them. Hence the saying "The ancestors have eaten sour grapes and the teeth of the children are set on edge" (Jer. 31:29–30; Ezek. 18:2). It is, of course, possible that these citations do not report verbatim what people were actually saying, but they convey a sense of what must have been the mood at that time.

One of the most interesting theodicies in ancient literature comes to expression in the dialogue between Abraham and Yahweh preceding the destruction of Sodom (Gen. 18:22–33). The peculiar literary character of this passage, quite unlike anything else in Genesis; the sobriquet "Sodom" often used of Jerusalem in prophetic diatribe (e.g., Isa. 1:9–10; Jer. 23:14); and coincidence with the issue of theodicy raised in prophetic texts from the sixth century (e.g., Ezek. 14:12–21) permit the suggestion that this midrash-like addition to the Sodom story actually reflects the destruction of Jerusalem and the grievous theological problems to which that event gave rise. The issue is whether God as judge of all the earth is prepared to distinguish between the righteous and the reprobate. The answer is in the affirmative, and the further point is made that the presence of the righteous can itself have a salvific effect, *but only at a certain critical mass.* As Abraham gets God down from fifty to ten by stages and then stops, it is apparent that the critical mass does not exist, and so the city is destroyed. The same issue arises in Ezekiel (14:12–21), but with a quite different solution. In a land threatened with destruction—Judah, for example—such ancient paradigms of righteousness as Noah, Daniel, and Job would, if present, save no one but themselves, not even their sons and daughters.[60]

THE JOB DEBATE: PROTAGONISTS, ISSUES, OUTCOME

The Book of Job presents a test case of the issue raised in Genesis 18 and Ezekiel 14. The lead character is one of the three worthies mentioned in the Ezekiel passage; the land is the land of Uz, known to the ancestors (Gen. 22:21); and disaster in the form of hostile raids and meteorological disturbances affects not only Job himself but also his sons and daughters and, indeed, the entire country. It is important to bear this in mind from the start, for Job's protest against the God of traditional religion is not limited to the disasters inflicted on his own person, grievous as they were (e.g., 21:1–34; 24:1–25). We might add that the prominent use of forensic language— bringing charges and countercharges, calling witnesses, making an oath of clearance (chapter 31)—is reminiscent of the making and breaking of covenants and therefore insinuates that Job in extremis also represents Israel.

Since there is no question of writing a commentary on the book, a whole range of questions dealing with language, structure, formation, and the like must be left aside. We are concerned primarily with the debate between Job, on the one side, and four interlocutors, on the other, which constitutes the body of the work (chapters 4—37). These four are not straw men, set up just to be knocked down by Job's arguments. On the contrary, they represent the best thinking available at that time within the intellectual tradition of the sages. Job himself is identified as a *ḥākām* and a teacher, and he also refers to himself as a counselor (4:3; 15:2; 29:21). He invites his opponents to instruct him (6:24) and, even while calling their wisdom in question and describing their maxims as proverbs of ashes (13:12), acknowledges that they too are sages, counselors, and recognized purveyors of wisdom (12:1–3; 13:5; 17:10; 26:3).

In keeping with the tradition in which they stand, all of the disputants appeal to the wonders of the natural world (e.g., 26:5–14; 36:24–37:24), acknowledge the possibility of learning lessons from animals and plants (12:7–9), and demonstrate at least a passing acquaintance with astronomy (e.g., 9:9). Even God intervenes in the guise of a sage, inviting Job to contemplate the awesome wonders of the natural world (chapters 38—41). The learned use of mythological figures is also in evidence throughout: the mythic monsters Yamm, Tannin, Rahab, Leviathan, and Abaddon surface from time to time to remind the reader of the threatening presence of moral chaos, and the disputants are familiar with such staples of ancient myth as rebellion in heaven (4:18), the defeat and binding of the forces of chaos (3:8; 7:12; 9:13; 26:12), and the first man (15:7). Noteworthy also is the absence of reference to such sacrosanct Israelite traditions as the wanderings of the ancestors, the sojourn in Egypt, exodus, the giving of the law, and the occupation of the land. The deity invoked, appealed to, or called to account is, significantly, never Yahweh, as in the prose prologue and epilogue, but Elohim or Shaddai.[61]

These features of the debate suggest that it has been set up to address and, possibly, resolve an issue of critical importance for the tradition of which the sages are representatives. While the issue was clearly of major concern in postdisaster Judah, its more universal incidence may be hinted at in the Arabic names of the sages Eliphaz, Bildad, and Zophar, names chosen, no doubt, on account of the reputation for wisdom enjoyed by Arabs and Edomites. (Elihu, who bears an Israelite name, may have been inserted by a later commentator to express a critique of the preceding debate from a putatively more "orthodox" point of view.) The arguments leveled against Job by all four reveal fairly clearly what counted as authoritative in the intellectual milieu of the sages. They appeal to the teaching of former representatives of the tradition (15:18) and to their own experience after a life spent in observation and reflection in concluding that *sooner or later* good moral behavior will be rewarded (4:7–11; 8:8–10; 15:9–10; etc). The accumulated experience of the past, moral consensus, personal observation and experience—these are the grounds on which the sages attempt to make good their claims. To these, however, Eliphaz adds another dimension in hinting at prophetic inspiration granted him and denied to Job (4:12–21; 15:8, 17). A similarly unverifiable and unfalsifiable claim is advanced by the long-winded Elihu (32:8; 33:15–18), which may be taken to confirm a point made earlier, that by that time the sages were beginning to usurp the prophetic role.

The basic point at issue in the book, and therefore in contemporary sagedom, is the possibility of maintaining the traditional theological rationale for suffering and misfortune in the face of experience that seems to disconfirm it on a massive scale. Theodicy is a social, not just a personal, issue; in a very real sense, the social order depended on keeping intact the linkage between conduct, divine blessing, and prosperity, or at least survival. Taking the book as a whole, the situation is, of course, rigged, since God has allowed Satan to set up a test, a kind of laboratory experiment—a theologically scandalous idea that demonstrates the desperate nature of the intellectual and religious crisis that the author was confronting. The point emerges more clearly as the dialogue proceeds. Job cannot make sense of a world in which evildoers prosper and even come out on top posthumously, their funerals well attended and their tombs well cared for (21:1–34). Later (24:1–25), he conjures up a terrible vision of a world in which moral chaos rules supreme, in which power is triumphant and the poor are beaten into the ground, a world presided over by a God who chooses not to intervene:

> From the city the dying groan,
> the throat of the wounded cries,
> but God sees nothing amiss.
> (24:12)

The problem defies solution and is not removed by the divine intervention, not even in the epilogue in which the health and fortunes of Job are restored (42:10–17). After all, those of Job's household and country who met a sudden and violent death in the prologue stay dead.

Job ends his peroration with a final declaration of innocence in the judicial form of an oath of clearance, followed by what is, in effect, a subpoena served on God, a call for him to appear and state the terms of his indictment (chapter 31). Once Elihu, an intruder in the debate, has said his say (chapters 32—37), at inordinate length, God does appear and answer, not once but three times (38—39; 40:1–2; 40:6–41:34). The answers do not, however, correspond to the expectations of either Job or the reader; in other words, there is nothing in the answers that has not already been said in the course of the debate. There is no theoretical solution, only a demonstration of the power of the Creator God, which confirms the existence of the problem rather than solving it. As this display of the splendid and often destructive forces of nature, including the animal world, unfolds, with no human being in sight, we might be tempted to read into it a bleak and disillusioning message: your afflictions, your complaints, your endless and futile self-justifications—all of these are of little account in the created order of things. Nature can get on very well without you; you are really not that important. So go and solve your problem as best you can.

Whatever kernel of truth there may be in this interpretation of the divine responses, it can hardly be the whole truth of what the author wishes to convey. Another line of interpretation could take into account Job's final reply:

> I have heard of you by hearsay,
> but now my eye sees you;
> therefore I despise myself,
> and repent in dust and ashes.
>   (42:5–6)

I take this to imply a contrast between knowledge of God and his ways available in the intellectual tradition of which both Job and his opponents are representatives, on the one hand, and a kind of direct experience of God's reality and presence that leads to existential humility, on the other. The appearance of God in the whirlwind (*sĕʿārâ;* 38:1; 40:6) points unmistakably to a theophany of the kind described elsewhere:

> You will be visited by Yahweh of the hosts
> with thunder, earthquake, and great noise,
> with *whirlwind,* tempest, and flame of devouring fire.
>   (Isa. 29:6)

> As I looked, a *whirlwind* came out of the north, and a great cloud with
> brightness round about it, and fire flashing out continually.
>
> (Ezek. 1:4)

A reading of certain psalms suggests further that this language of theophany
is rooted in cultic experience. One of those psalms generally classified as
sapiential, Psalm 73, exhibits some affinity with the situation described in
Job, in spite of obvious differences in genre and length. The poet begins by
affirming the traditional thesis that God is good to the upright but finds that
both his personal experience and his observation of the prosperity of evildoers contradict it. It is only when he enters the sanctuary, experiences the
divine presence, and acknowledges his ignorance and stupidity that he finds
a solution not unlike Job's:

> When my heart was embittered,
> when I was inwardly riven,
> I was stupid, I did not perceive,
> like a beast in your presence;
> but I am always with you,
> you hold me by the right hand.
>
> (Ps. 73:21–23)

Similar features occur in the lament psalms with which, as has often been
noted, Job's discourse with God has much in common.

Returning to the Joban theophany (an appearance or manifestation of
God), a further implication is that the God who reveals the divine self at last
is not a God who can be circumscribed by learned debate in the schools,
or about whose intentions and actions calculations can be made, or with
whom contractual arrangements can be drawn up. In this respect, the author reflects the move away from a national deity toward a more transcendent and universalist perspective. In this sense, the theophany implies a critique of the participants on both sides of the issue.

Do we have any way of establishing the social coordinates of this critical juncture in the developing intellectual tradition? Most scholars would
agree that the Book of Job is to be dated to the Persian period (sixth to
fourth centuries B.C.E.) and should therefore be read against the background
of what is known of conditions in the province of Judah (Yehud) at that
time. Among the indications favoring this epoch is the role of Satan, reminiscent of the Persian officials known as "the king's eye" or "the king's ear"
whose task was to tour the provinces, checking up on local officials. The
Arabic (i.e., Edomite, Kedarite, or Sabean) names of the three "friends" also
recall Arab opposition to Nehemiah in the person of the Kedarite ruler

Geshem, or Gashmu (Neh. 2:19; 4:7; 6:1, 6). The bleak view of social conditions, and especially the contrast between wealth and poverty, power and powerlessness, presented by both sides in the debate, also fits what little information can be extracted from writings dated to that time. The province took a long time to recover from the effects of the Babylonian conquest and from late disturbances on which we are poorly informed (see, for example, Neh. 1:3). Economic conditions were bad (Hag. 1:5–6, 9–11; 2:16–17; Zech. 8:10), the wealthy upper class showed no concern for the poor (Isa. 57:1; 58:3, 6–7; 59:4; Neh. 5:1–13), and their unconcern led to social unrest and occasional violence (Zech. 8:10; Isa. 58:4; 59:3, 7); a situation of anomie, therefore, calculated to induce questioning of traditional religious ideas. As one anonymous author from that time put it, "Now we count the arrogant happy; evildoers not only prosper, but when they put God to the test they escape" (Mal. 3:15).

If we have correctly identified the time and place of composition, the author of Job probably belonged to the upper-class lay intelligentsia, educated in the tradition of public morality and piety of which we have been speaking. The contestants on both sides of the debate clearly belonged to the same privileged class and subscribed to the same social code. Job himself is a wealthy landowner (1:2–5; 29:1–25; 31:25, 38–40) with a large and prosperous household (19:13–16) employing slaves and day laborers (7:2; 31:13–15). His wealth assures him prominence in the assembly, the *qāhāl* (30:28), the same body of which we hear so often in Ezra-Nehemiah. It also gives him access to public office, including that of magistrate (29:7–25; 31:21). The ethos of this social class entails a strong sense of public service and an enlightened concern for the poor (29:24; 30:25; 31:16–23). In these respects, then, Job and his interlocutors share the same background and outlook.

They are also unanimous in setting themselves apart from those of the same class—wealthy and influential landowners—who violate the accepted social norms. These are accused of oppressing the poor (5:12–16; 20:19; 24:4–12); distraining land, livestock, and the persons of the insolvent (20:19; 24:2–3, 9); corrupting the judicial process by bribery (6:22; 9:24; 17:5); removing landmarks (24:2); and the like, not to mention murder and adultery (24:13–17). And they get away with it. None of Job's disputants has a program to deal with this situation. Their concern is to understand the world, not change it. What they have to offer is an explanation, one that Job stubbornly refuses to accept. The vehemence of their assault on his refusal is an indication of the extent to which the postulates from which all of them start out and the tradition in which they all stand have begun to lose their hold.

QOHELETH: UNDERMINING THE TRADITION
FROM WITHIN

When we pass from Job to Ecclesiastes (Qoheleth), it would be natural to think that we have moved a step closer to the total breakdown of the intellectual tradition of the sages. It would be misleading, however, to position Job and Qoheleth as points on a descending trajectory. Both works are too isolated and decontextualized historically for that, and there is plenty of evidence that the traditional verities still held good for others both before and after Qoheleth. Also, aspects of Qoheleth's thinking are encountered in Near Eastern texts from a much earlier date. A fragmentary Mesopotamian tablet from no later than the seventh century B.C.E. counsels piety toward the gods and enjoyment of the pleasures of life as a counter to the thought of death.[62] One of the most remarkable texts from the same area is the so-called *Dialogue of Pessimism,* in which the issue is not suffering but ennui, terminal boredom, a sense of the pointlessness of life. Like Qoheleth (alias Solomon), a lord proposes to embark on certain courses of action and his servant encourages him to do so, providing what appear to be convincing reasons; whereupon the lord changes his mind and the servant comes up with even better reasons for not doing so. The conversation runs somewhat like this:

> "Slave, listen to me." "Here I am, sir, here I am."
> "I am going to love a woman." "So love, sir, love;
> the man who loves a woman forgets sorrow and fear."
> "No, slave, I will by no means love a woman."
> ["Do not] love, sir, do not love;
> woman is a pitfall—a pitfall, a hole, a ditch;
> woman is a sharp iron dagger that cuts a man's throat."[63]

These sentiments are not unlike Qoheleth's "I found more bitter than death the woman who is a trap, whose heart is snares and nets, whose hands are fetters" (Eccl. 7:26). Not without a certain cynical humor, the *Dialogue* makes short shrift of the "consolations of religion" and proceeds to its terminus in the decision to commit suicide. This remarkable text has often been compared with Ecclesiastes, but the resemblance is more apparent than real, as we shall see.

In the title and postscript (1:1; 12:9–14), both later additions, Qoheleth is taken to be a personal name, but in the body of the work it occurs with the article and therefore designates an office or function (7:27; 12:8). By connecting the name with *qābāl* (assembly), translated *ekklēsia,* the Old Greek version arrived at the title *ekklēsiastēs,* meaning an ecclesiastical office, the office in question being understood by Jerome and Martin Luther as that of preacher. But since there is very little of the ecclesiastical about our author, the title should probably be related to assembling students and therefore to teaching. The title also identifies him as "son of David, king in Jerusalem." Though the fiction of Solomonic authorship is maintained only through the first two chapters, it serves to locate the work within the sapiential tradition of which, by that time, Solomon was undisputed patron. It also made a good fit with the genre of royal testament, familiar in ancient Egypt, with which Qoheleth's lucubrations have much in common. Adoption of this genre would have been appropriate during the period of Ptolemaic rule (third century B.C.E.), when the book was probably written. The Ptolemaic court in Alexandria liked to think of itself as in line of succession from the ancient pharaohs, and the Ptolemies promoted a revival of pharaonic style in life and letters.

The author belonged to the ranks of the professional sages who were also teachers; in fact, the title suggests that he came to be referred to as *the* teacher, perhaps not in an unambiguously positive sense, meaning the one whose controversial views could hardly be ignored. After the inclusion rounding off the author's reflections ("emptiness, emptiness, all is empty"; 12:8), several comments have been added by at least two editors in the manner of a colophon:

> Not content with attaining wisdom himself [or, "In addition to being a sage"], Qoheleth gave instruction to the public.

> Qoheleth weighed, examined, and edited many aphorisms, seeking to identify appropriate sayings and recording truthful sayings plainly.

> The sayings of the sages are like goads, and like nails firmly fixed are the collections of sayings. . . . [64]

> My son, beware of anything beyond these; of making many books there is no end, and much study is a weariness of the flesh.

> The end of the matter: all has been heard. Fear God and keep his commandments, for this is the sum total of everyone's duty. For God will bring every deed into judgment, including every hidden thing, whether good or evil.

From these editorial comments we gather that Qoheleth was an intellectual and a teacher who collected and edited aphorisms, like so many of his predecessors. The third of the comments suggests that his sayings were meant to needle his students into thinking for themselves, to force them to take a critical view of the received wisdom. The last two, from a different hand, are much less positive. Their drift seems to be that this sort of speculative and skeptical approach to life is all right, but the best policy is to keep it simple. Pious injunctions of a similar nature, perhaps from the same hand, have been inserted into the book itself, most clearly where the fear of God and divine judgment are mentioned.[65]

That the author wrote within the intellectual tradition of the sages is also apparent from his insistence on inquiry and investigation (using the verbs *dāraš* and *tûr;* 1:13; 2:3; 7:25). What the sage is supposed to do is apply the wisdom supplied by the tradition to experience and observation: "I applied my mind to seek and search out by means of wisdom all that is done under heaven" (1:13)—a good description of the sage's agenda. But what is new, what is modern, in Qoheleth is the personal, the autobiographical element: I applied my mind, I saw, I said to myself, this is what I have seen to be good, this is what I have found, adding one thing to another to see what it all amounts to (1:12, 14, 16; 5:18; 7:27). What there is of speculation arises out of observation and experience. Correspondingly, the author's basic concern is not speculative but practical—to discover, if possible, "what is good for mortals to do under heaven for the brief span of their lives" (2:3).

A procedure followed by the author throughout the work, one that gives us the essential clue to his situation vis-à-vis the tradition, is to quote samples of traditional proverbial wisdom and comment on them, generally with a view to refuting them. So, for example, he cites the traditional proverb:

> The wise have eyes in their head,
> but fools walk in darkness

but then goes on to comment that it does not make any difference since the same fate befalls all, wise and fools alike (2:14). He also at times juxtaposes traditional sayings that contradict and cancel out each other, for example:

> Fools fold their hands,
> and consume their own flesh

followed by

> Better a handful with quiet
> than two handfuls with toil.
> (4:5–6)

In other instances, he applies a saying in a way never intended in common usage; thus

> What is crooked cannot be made straight,
> what is missing cannot be counted
>
> (1:15)

is given a meaning deliberately offensive to pious ears:

> Consider the work of God:
> who can make straight what he has made crooked?
>
> (7:13)

He follows a similar procedure in reflecting on the issue of divine gover-
nance of the world in 3:16–4:3, beginning with the observation that where,
according to the accepted theology, one would expect to find justice and
righteousness, what one finds is the opposite. Referring back to the poem
about the right time for different actions, he seeks for an answer in the assurance of divine judgment, and it is fairly clear from the context that he includes belief in a postmortem settling of accounts:

> I said to myself, God will judge the righteous and the wicked, for he
> has appointed a time for every matter and for every work.
>
> (3:17)

But then, he goes on: How can we be sure that this world is not all that
there is? How can we find comfort in current speculations about survival of
death and astral immortality?

> I said to myself with respect to human beings that God is testing them
> to show that they are just animals. For the fate of human beings and the
> fate of animals is the same. As one dies, so dies the other. They both
> draw the same breath, and the human being has no advantage over the
> animal; for all is futility. All go to the same place; all are from the same
> dust and all return to it. Who knows whether the spirit of the human
> being goes upward and the spirit of the animal goes downward to the
> earth?
>
> (3:18–21)

Working back from these somber reflections on injustice, oppression,
and impermanence, we come to the composition listing fourteen pairs of
opposite actions, each with its appropriate time—doubtless the best-known
passage in the book (3:1–8). Since there is nothing in it characteristic of Qoheleth's way of speaking or thinking, the indications are that it is an independent composition of different authorship, the longest of the samplings
of conventional wisdom that Qoheleth cites only to refute. It implies something the truth of which was by no means apparent to Qoheleth, namely,
that we have the resources and the knowledge to exercise control over our

lives on condition that we get the *timing* of our activity right (cf. Prov. 15:23, with respect to the right time for speaking and keeping silent). To this poem, if that is what it is, Qoheleth has added a title (3:1) and a brief commentary (3:9–15). In the latter he acknowledges the traditional teaching about the importance of timely action but adds that the ability to live in accordance with this principle is contingent on knowing the dispositions of God with regard to human existence. He seems to be saying that each of the moments listed in the poem has its place on the continuum of God's time, but since divine intention and the mode of divine activity are hidden from us, the traditional teaching does not translate into the ability to act appropriately, to exercise control over our lives. This ignorance of ours about "the work of God," what God is up to, is, for Qoheleth, the fundamental problem, one posing an unanswerable threat to the claims advanced by his learned colleagues:

> When I applied my mind to know wisdom and to observe the business that is done on earth . . . I concluded that no human being can fathom the work of God—what is going on under the sun. However much they may toil in seeking, they will not fathom it. Even if the sages claim to know, they cannot fathom it.
>
> (8:17)

It is therefore hardly surprising that Qoheleth was the first we know of to introduce the idea of *fate* into the tradition. The Hebrew term *miqreh* (2:14–15; 3:19; 9:2–3) has the connotation of something that happens by chance or as a result of some factor beyond our control, as opposed to something we intend (cf. 1 Sam. 6:9; 20:26). For Qoheleth, this is true in the first place of death, but there is much else outside of our control that the intellectual tradition of the sages cannot account for. We are adrift on the tide of the world, and we must cope as best we can.

Since we are almost completely in the dark with regard to Jewish intellectual life in the third century B.C.E., we can only speculate that the erosion of confidence in traditional dogmas and practices was fairly widespread in the social class to which Qoheleth belonged. I have taken the view that Qoheleth is addressing a radical critique to the tradition of the sages from the inside, but that is only part of the picture. Apart from assuming the persona of Solomon at the beginning, the author says nothing that would require us to identify him as Jewish. The fundamental problem of the book is religious—what we can know about God and what consequences follow from that knowledge—but he refers throughout to the Deity (*hā'ĕlōhîm* = *to theion*), never to Yahweh. On the subject of religious practices—sacrifice, prayer, vows, and the like—he speaks in a detached and guarded way. His God is not one who suffers fools gladly (5:4). This attitude may have been quite prevalent among the upper-class lay intelligentsia in third-century Jerusalem, especially in view of the availability by that time of powerful alternatives to traditional religion in the philosophical systems of Cynics, Stoics, and Epicureans.

On this last point we recall the long-standing discussion on the possible influence of the early Stoics on Qoheleth. If Ecclesiastes was written no earlier than the middle of the third century B.C.E., and maybe somewhat later, the writings of Zeno, Cleanthes, and probably also Chrysippus could have come to the author's attention. While these early Stoic teachers dealt with the big philosophical issues—fate, death, time, and so on—the fundamental issue was ethical, as it was for Qoheleth: What is good for human beings to do under heaven for the brief span of their lives (2:3)? According to Stoic ethics, an essential point is to know the right time to act or abstain from acting. Good timing (*eukairia*) is a matter of judgment, but it is also, to quote a recent writer on Stoic ethics, "the point at which the process of a man's actions meets and coincides with those events which are the result of a series of causes called Fate."[66] The true sage reveals himself (or herself, according to the Stoics but not Qoheleth) to be such by knowing the right time and the appropriate manner of acting (cf. Eccl. 8:5). In other words, the true sage must be *eukairos,* and all morally perfect acts (*katorthōmata*) must also be timely acts (*eukairēmata*).[67] We have seen that Qoheleth would agree with this in principle; the only problem for him was that the knowledge which would enable us to bring our actions into coincidence with what is preordained to happen is simply not available to us.

Ecclesiastes, therefore, wrote out of a situation in which the received wisdom of the schools was faced with formidable intellectual competition and a prevailing skepticism about traditional dogmas and practices. The situation in question cannot, however, be grasped exclusively at the level of competing ideas. A remarkable feature of the book is the prevalence of terminology and metaphor taken from economic activity. The author is obsessed with toil (*'āmāl*) as the defining characteristic of human activity; the substantive occurs twenty times in this short composition, and the corresponding verb twelve times. He refers often to trading ventures (5:13–14; 11:1–2) and to transacting business (*'inyan;* 1:13; 2:23; 3:10; 4:8; 5:13; 8:16), accruing interest (*tĕbû'â;* 5:9), making a profit (*yitrôn;* 1:3; 2:11, 13; 3:9; 5:15; 10:11), accumulating wealth (5:9), and the uncertain fate of wealth when left as a legacy to others (2:18–19, 21, 26; 6:1–2). He also comments more than once on the spectacle of economic exploitation and injustice. We cannot say that it leaves him unmoved, but he does not think anything can be done about it (3:16–4:5; 7:7; 8:14). It is simply a by-product of economic activity, a side effect of the working of the vast bureaucratic machinery of the Ptolemaic Empire:

> If you observe the oppression of the poor and the violation of justice and right order in the province, don't be surprised at this state of affairs; for one high official is watched over by another, and there are others yet more highly placed watching over them.
>
> (5:7)

And above all of them is the absolute monarch, the Ptolemaic pharaoh ruling in distant Alexandria, who can do whatever he pleases (8:3).

We get a rare glimpse of the workings of this bureaucracy and its impact on the poor by way of the archives of Zeno, estate agent to Apollonius, finance minister of Ptolemy Philadelphus. This batch of papyri, discovered in Egypt in 1915, is roughly contemporary with Qoheleth and fills out the author's somewhat laconic comments on the state of the poor. It testifies, inter alia, to a crippling burden of taxes collected by rapacious tax farmers: 50 percent rent and tax levied on peasants working crown lands; 33.5 percent tax on vineyards, orchards, and gardens; 10 percent sales tax; surtaxes on various commodities; duties on wool and linen; and so on. This was a world in which vast fortunes were quickly accumulated and just as quickly lost. The papyri deal primarily with Egypt, but the situation was not essentially different in Palestine where Apollonius had estates and considerable commercial interests.[68] Josephus (*Ant.* 12.154–236) records how a certain Joseph of the Tobiad family, also referred to in the Zeno papyri, undertook a mission to the Ptolemaic court in Alexandria, while there discovered that tax-farming rights were being auctioned to the highest bidder, and managed to obtain exclusive rights for Phoenicia, Syria, and Palestine. By this means he amassed a huge fortune and passed it on to his son Hyrcanus. Josephus goes on to tell how the latter built the fortress of Arak el-Emir in Transjordan, mentioned in the papyri (though in fact it was already in existence); eventually got in trouble with the Seleucid king Antiochus IV; and committed suicide.

The papyri and Josephus afford us a glimpse into a Jewish world very different from the world of priests, prophets, and pious sages, a world inhabited by Jews with very tenuous attachments to traditional values. In reflecting that world, Qoheleth demonstrates how problematic it had become for the literate upper class to which he belonged to reassert these values, to continue defending traditional beliefs about God and God's action on the world. This is by no means to imply that Qoheleth endorses the amorality of the Tobiads and their like. He does indeed reject much of the rationale for right living elaborated within the tradition of the sages, as well as many of its practical consequences—the work ethic, for example (4:4). But he also makes his own recommendations, which amount to a kind of stripped-down reactive or response ethic based on the acknowledgment of human limitations and the acceptance of death. But for him, and no doubt for many others at that time, the tradition as we have been describing it no longer provided an adequate account of reality in general and moral reality in particular.

SOME PROVISIONAL CONCLUSIONS

When we survey the writings that have survived from the time of the second commonwealth, we cannot help being struck by the contrast between the intellectual world of Judah and the contemporary Greek-speaking world. In the latter, the sixth to the fourth century B.C.E. was a time of intellectual ferment in metaphysics, cosmology, astronomy, mathematics, and geometry. It was the age of Xenophanes, Heraclitus, the Eleatics, and the Sophists, the age of Socrates, a contemporary of Ezra. The difference can be explained, in part, by the fact that mainland Greece never came under the rule of Persians. The latter tended to favor priesthoods and temple communities, which constituted an intellectually less challenging and open environment than the democratically organized polis. Economic conditions on the Greek mainland, in Ionia and Magna Graecia, also seem to have favored, or at least permitted, the emergence of a leisured class of lay intellectuals, unlike the situation of economic distress in Judah during the same period, a situation exacerbated by the harsh fiscal policies of the Persian imperial administration.

The situation in Judah was also the result of an intellectual and religious history very different from that of the early Greeks, marked at many points by what Weber called "culture hostility." In this first chapter of our study, we have traced that history in rough outline, taking account of the distinct contributions of different roles, especially that of the ḥākām. We have seen how completely speculative thinking and the acquisition of "scientific" knowledge (e.g., astronomy and the taxonomy of flora and fauna) were subordinated to the practical and the ethical. We have noted the socioeconomic and cultural limitations of the tradition represented by the sages—manifested with particular clarity in its attitude toward possessions and gender relations and its demotion of the erotic. And finally, we have traced the process by which a naturalistic ethic based on observation and experience was drawn into the orbit of the law, the *tôrâ,* understood as the fundamental religious principle.

There are other strands, not considered in this section, that contributed to the one, mainline biblical tradition that was in place by the last century of the Second Temple at the latest. In Genesis 1—11, for example, the frequent use in the non-Priestly sections of terminology and themes characteristic of the sapiential books has led an increasing number of commentators to suggest a postexilic date for this material. If this is so, it may even be suggested that the "Yahwistic" narrator in this section intended to balance the optimistic Priestly version with a more psychologically realistic and disillusioned diagnosis of the human condition, one composed after the manner of the later sages.[69] It was, notwithstanding, the priesthood that occupied the position of greatest power and influence as long as the Second Temple stood. We must now go on to see how this situation arose, how the role of the priest related to other and sometimes competing roles, and in what sense we can talk of an intellectual tradition proper to the priesthood.

CHAPTER 2

The Priest

THE BAD REPUTE OF THE ISRAELITE PRIESTHOOD
IN THE MODERN PERIOD

The Israelite priesthood and its literary productions have not had a good press in Christian Old Testament scholarship since the Enlightenment. For the theologically liberal biblical scholar, the priesthood's massive concentration on the detailed performance of ritual made a painful contrast with the spiritual and ethical religion of the prophets. Nor were the descriptions in unsparing detail of the sanctuary, its appointments, and its liturgies; the lists of clerical personnel; and the genealogies calculated to arouse the enthusiasm of the enlightened reader. "What sort of creative power is that," asked Julius Wellhausen rhetorically in his discussion of the Priestly source (P), "which brings forth nothing but numbers and names?"[1] At a later point in the same work, he stated more comprehensively his judgment on the religious worldview of the dominant priest class of the Second Temple period:

> The Creator of heaven and earth becomes the manager of a petty scheme of salvation; the living God descends from his throne to make way for the law. The law thrusts itself in everywhere; it commands and blocks up access to heaven; it regulates and sets limits to the understanding of the divine working on earth. As far as it can, it takes the soul out of religion and spoils morality. It demands a service of God which, though revealed, may well with truth be called a self-chosen and unnatural one, the sense and use of which are apparent neither to the understanding nor the heart. The labour is done for the sake of the exercize; it does no one any good and rejoices neither God nor man. It has no inner aim after which it spontaneously strives and which it hopes to attain by itself, but only an outward one, namely, the reward attached to it, which might as well be attached to other and possibly even more curious conditions.[2]

Wellhausen's indictment of the religion of the priests as legalistic, restrictive, and servile, as destructive of spontaneity and the religion of the heart, was widely shared and has often been expressed, though rarely with his eloquent and mordant wit. It would take us too far afield to reflect on the reasons for this extremely negative assessment, but it is at least worth noting that for many liberal Protestant theologians and commentators in the nineteenth and early twentieth century, and residually up to the present, the Israelite priesthood embodied all that they found distasteful in contemporary Roman Catholicism or Judaism or both. For some, the main grievance was concern for the externals of religion, for others a venal approach to divine worship, manifested especially in the sacrificial system (cf. the "sacrifice of the mass"), for others again the stifling of spontaneity. Whatever it happened to be, the priesthood and its principal literary product, the Priestly source (P), did not get high ratings in most theologies of the Old Testament and histories of the religion of Israel written over the last two centuries.[3]

That the Jerusalem priesthood formed a restrictive caste, jealously protective of its privileges and perquisites, also did little to endear it to the enlightened reader. No great acquaintance with the sociology of knowledge was needed to detect the self-interested nature of many priestly regulations, for example, those concerning tithes and the allocation of cuts from sacrificed livestock. Such self-protective measures, however, characterize practically all skilled professions to this day, whether medical, legal, or academic. Charges of legalism and ritualism also require reassessment in the light of our better understanding today of the societal roles of law and ritual. Further, the attentive reader of the historical narrative attributed to the priest-author will find a universalist perspective notably absent from other parts of the Pentateuch, especially Deuteronomy. Humanity as a whole receives a religious denomination expressed in the theme of creation in the image of God. The postdiluvian humanity is partner with God in a covenant long before Israel appears on the stage of history and is also the recipient of a first law, the nucleus of the Noachide laws of rabbinic tradition.

We also observe that the cultic and ritual prescriptions in the Pentateuch, the compilation of which we owe to the clergy of the Second Temple, can be construed as embodying a coherent system, a cosmology within which Israel's place in the world is to be understood. A positive view of the ritual law has been advanced in the work of the cultural anthropologist Mary Douglas, whose writings have had a notable impact on the study of the ritual law.[4] For the moment we mention only the correspondence between the taxonomy of clean and unclean in Leviticus and the created order as set out in Genesis 1, the homology between the physical body and the body politic, and the reverent attitude toward life that has gone into the dietary laws. It is therefore arguable that the ritual law is an essential ingredient of a total system created, maintained, and transmitted within a distinctively priestly tradition; also, that the strength and persistence of that tradition derived precisely from its incorporating the kind of institutional, ritual elements dismissed with contempt by Wellhausen.[5]

SOURCES

For our knowledge of the priesthood, we have to rely heavily on the considerable bulk of ritual law and narrative in Genesis through Joshua, attributed to priestly authorship and therefore designated by the siglum P. Psalms are of limited use as source material because of the difficult matter of dating. The P corpus is presented as a history of human and Israelite origins, from creation to the settlement in the land into which all the legal material, indeed, everything considered necessary for the life of the community, had to be inserted. The authors were aware that laws and rituals came into existence at different times throughout the history, some of them not long before the time of compilation, but placing them all together at the beginning was a way of affirming their foundational and authoritative character. For P, the choice of the historiographical genre was largely dictated by the need to ground the religious institutions in a well-thought-out series of divine revelations that punctuate the history.

That the history begins with creation is obvious, but opinions differ as to its *excipit*. According to some scholars, the finale is the death of Moses, recorded in a brief P addition to the end of Deuteronomy (Deut. 34:1, 7–9). Others, however, take it down to the setting up of the wilderness sanctuary at Shiloh in the Promised Land, as recorded in Joshua 18—19. This latter option is preferable, since language and themes characteristic of P are in evidence at least at the beginning and end of the Joshua passage in question, not least with respect to the role of Eleazar son of Aaron and the description of Israel as *'ēdâ* (congregation), a typical P term. If this is granted, the basic lines of the P history emerge as the creation of the cosmos as a temple for worship, the construction and dedication of the sanctuary in the wilderness (Exodus 25—31; 35—40, especially 40:1, 16–17), and the establishment of worship in the newly occupied land. This prominent structural feature, along with much else in the P history, reflects the situation obtaining in the early period of the second commonwealth, either shortly before or shortly after the rebuilding of the Jerusalem temple and the reestablishment of worship.

The death of Moses is, of course, an important turning point, but what is generally taken to be the P account of his death at the end of Deuteronomy corresponds to a later phase in the formation of the narrative tradition. I take this to be the stage at which Deuteronomy was taken up whole and entire into the P history, a move that was accomplished by the simple expedient of adding a date in the P style at the beginning of the book (1:3) and a revised version of the commissioning of Joshua as Moses' successor toward the end (32:48–52), followed by the brief notice about Moses' death and burial in the final chapter. Comparison with Num. 27:12–23, also unmistakably P, suggests that the account of the death of Moses originally stood at this point of the wilderness saga, following the commissioning of Joshua. The inclusion of Deuteronomy in the P history, however, meant that Moses could not be allowed to die until he had promulgated the Deuteronomic law on the last day of his life. No doubt this restructuring of the narrative was the last major move leading to the Pentateuch in its present form.[6]

Since the history inscribes important elements in the conceptual world of the priests, it will call for selective comment as we proceed. In the meantime, we note that it is punctuated by the orderly revelation of those ritual and cultic ordinances by means of which Israel had access to God and God made himself present to Israel. In the first phase, before the setting up of the cult and ordination of the priests at Sinai, only those ritual acts were revealed and enjoined that required neither sanctuary nor priest—first, circumcision as initiation rite and sign of the covenant (Gen. 17:1–14); then, Passover (Ex. 12:1–28, 43–49); and finally, Sabbath (Ex. 31:12–17; 35:1–3). Consistently, therefore, the P author does not allow the pre-Sinaitic ancestors, including Noah, to sacrifice, and no distinction is made between clean and unclean animals entering the ark.

The next and decisive phase takes place at Sinai. For P, however, Sinai consists not in the making of a covenant but in a vision, granted to Moses on the mountain, in which he receives detailed specifications together with a blueprint for the construction of the sanctuary. He also receives instructions for the ordination of the clergy and the carrying out of the cult (Ex. 19:1–2; 24:15b–18a; 25:1–31:17). The correspondingly detailed account of the implementation of these instructions after the golden-calf episode (Ex. 35:1–40:38) assures the reader that they retained their validity in spite of Aaron's involvement in the apostasy at the foot of the mountain. Aaron and his sons were ordained in a seven-day ceremony (Lev. 8:33), and the cult was inaugurated on the eighth day (9:1), one of several links with the work of creation. All of the essential cultic and ritual legislation was promulgated at Sinai, from which Israel departed after a stay of almost a year (Ex. 19:1; Num. 10:11). From that point on, the trek through the wilderness provided the occasion for promulgating supplementary legislation and presenting

narrative paradigms which offerred solutions to problems and conflicts
(e.g., the crushing of a Levitical revolt against the priesthood, Num. 16:1–50)
solutions of a kind congenial to the priesthood but not necessarily to their
critics and opponents. Roughly speaking, Leviticus deals with matters per-
taining to the priesthood (in Jewish tradition it is known as *tôrat kōhănîm,*
"the priestly law") and Numbers with the status and roles of Levites.

The entire P literary complex, with its schematic narrative, its many lists
and genealogies, its imposing bulk of cultic and ritual law, is therefore our
primary source for understanding the religious and intellectual world inhabited by the priesthood at the time of its ascendancy during the Second
Temple period, beginning in the sixth century B.C.E. The information it provides can occasionally be checked against other biblical texts, especially
postexilic prophecy and Chronicles-Ezra-Nehemiah. Postbiblical texts only
rarely provide additional information, though some have interesting perspectives of their own on priesthood and cult—the *Testament of Levi* and
the Epistle to the Hebrews, for example.

Source material for the history of priesthoods during and prior to the time
of the kingdoms is very patchy indeed. This is not the case for those who
follow the Israeli scholar Yehezkel Kaufmann in assigning a preexilic date
to P,[7] but the arguments they adduce have not convinced a majority of their
colleagues. Needless to say, a postexilic date does not exclude some degree
of continuity in liturgical and ritual practice, though in fact, practices alluded
to in texts generally thought to be preexilic rarely, if ever, confirm the antiquity of practices described in P and are often quite different. The prohibition concerning the eating of the sciatic sinew in Gen. 32:32 is not listed
in P, and there is nothing in the latter corresponding to the "lucky dip"
method by which the priest-sons of Eli secured their share of the sacrificial
meat (1 Sam. 2:13–17). Sacrificial material is sometimes the same, sometimes
different (e.g., Judg. 6:19–21,26; 13:16, 19–20; 1 Sam. 7:9; 2 Sam. 6:13), and
P makes no provision for such practices as ritual incubation (1 Sam. 3:3–9)
and sexual abstention in warfare (1 Sam. 21:5; 2 Sam. 11:11). None of this
disproves the antiquity of specific stipulations in P, but it may serve to highlight the very different social and cultural situations obtaining before and after the deportations of the sixth century.

In the earliest period of the history, there were as many priesthoods as
there were cult centers. With the emergence of the state system, the priesthoods of the state-sponsored cults—at Bethel and Dan in the north,
Jerusalem in the south—achieved dominance, though they were not entirely
successful in suppressing unofficial cult centers attested in both the biblical
and the archaeological records. Even the determined effort to create a

Jerusalemite and Yahwistic cult monopoly in the last decades of the kingdom of Judah was only partially successful (2 Kings 23:4–20; cf. Deut. 12:1–28). Several sanctuaries other than the three (Bethel, Dan, Jerusalem) mentioned appear, sometimes in passing, in narrative and prophetic texts—Shiloh (1 Samuel 1—3), Shechem (Judges 8—9), Beersheba (Amos 8:14), Gibeon (1 Kings 3:4), Gilgal (Amos 4:4; 5:5)—and there were also numerous open-air shrines or "high places" (*bāmôt*) that would have required the services of one or more priests. Regrettably, we can deduce little from these scattered allusions about how the role of the priest was understood and deployed.

Archaeological data would be particularly helpful to correct the not uncommon misconception that people were actually thinking and acting religiously in accordance with Priestly and Deuteronomic orthodoxy. The orthodox view insists, for example, that Yahweh is a celibate deity, but biblical narrative, prophetic denunciation, and archaeological data attest that the cult of Yahweh was often linked with that of a goddess as *parhedros*. The evidence is, in fact, abundant enough to allow the conclusion that the cult of the goddess was a normal part of popular religion, retaining its attraction even after it was officially proscribed. The material remains bearing on cult practice support this view of the matter, a point made by William G. Dever. After surveying the available evidence, he concluded that

> early Israelite religion developed gradually out of the Late Bronze and early Iron Age fertility cults of greater Canaan, and that despite the growth of a royal/priestly cultus and its theology in Jerusalem, local cults continued to flourish and some of them reflected a highly syncretistic blend of Yahwism and pagan practice until the end of the Monarchy. "Normative Judaism", as portrayed in the Deuteronomic and Priestly literature, is a construct of the late Judean Monarchy and in particular of the exilic period. Thus our only resource for religious practice in the early formative period lies in correlating the "minority view" reflected in scattered indirect references in the Pentateuch and the Former Prophets with actual material remains of local cults unearthed by archaeology.[8]

These material remains are not abundant. With regard to the state sanctuaries, nothing is known archaeologically about either Jerusalem or Bethel. When we realize how much information has come from the archives of other temples in the Near East (e.g., Uruk/Tell el-Warka), we can appreciate how much poorer we are for not having the Jerusalem temple archives and how much we do not know, and probably never will know, about the priesthood. A large cultic installation from Iron II has been excavated at

Dan, at the extreme northern point of the kingdom of Samaria. Small household shrines from the Iron Age have come to light at Megiddo and Taanach in the north and Lachish in the south. The discovery of a horned altar in Beersheba may be taken to confirm the biblical allusions to a cult center there (2 Kings 23:8; Amos 8:14). About thirty kilometers east-northeast of Beersheba, at Arad, the remains of a temple of the broad room type were uncovered, with inner sanctum, incense altars, *maṣṣēbôt* (sacred pillars), and a raised dais, or *bāmâ*. The more recent excavation of a cult installation (if that is what it is) at Kuntillet 'Ajrud on the caravan route in the eastern Sinai peninsula, probably from the ninth century B.C.E., has proved to be of particular interest on account of the graffiti on jars, with blessings in the name of Yahweh of Samaria (or Yahweh our protector) and his Asherah. Excavations on other sites associated with cults in biblical texts (e.g., Shiloh, Shechem, Gibeon, Samaria) have been less successful.[9]

We have already noted the sad fact that relatively little inscriptional material has survived from ancient Palestine, and there is none bearing directly on the priesthood. The Jewish colony established on the island of Elephantine (Jeb) on the Upper Nile during the Persian period had its own temple, and some of its priests are referred to in the papyri recovered from the site in the late nineteenth and early twentieth centuries. The somewhat unorthodox religious practices of the community may reflect origins in the Bethel region, but that is speculative.[10] Many cultic artifacts have come to light at numerous Palestinian sites, including altars, incense stands, incense shovels, lavers, votive offerings, and the like. These can help to fill in details of the work environment of the priest but contribute little to our understanding of the role itself.

EARLY STAGES

It is obvious that the level of complexity at which a cult and priesthood operate is correlative and coextensive with the stage of development of the society in general. As long as the kinship system remained functionally decisive, the paterfamilias would have represented the local unit in the performance of cult acts, often involving the ancestors of the group in question.[11] Something like this situation is re-created in the narrative cycles about the ancestors in Genesis 12—50. We read of one or another patriarch building an altar and calling on the name of Yahweh, that is, setting up the Yahweh cult at what was formerly a Canaanite holy place—Bethel (Gen. 12:8; 13:4; 28:18, 22; 35:7), Shechem (12:6–7; 33:20), and Beersheba (26:25) in particular. Of special interest is the sudden and unexpected appearance of the priest-king Melchizedek, who brings bread and wine out to Abraham—presumably for a sacrificial meal, though this is not said—blesses him in the name of El Elyon, maker of heaven and earth; and accepts tithes from him (Gen. 14:18–20). The origin and date of this text, behind which there must lie a distinct tradition, are unknown. But we can at least conclude that it would have provided ancient warrant for the practice of supporting the clergy by means of the tithe.

Other allusions to early priesthoods can be found here and there. A certain Ephraimite, Micah by name, installed one of his sons as shrine priest in his own house (Judg. 17:1–6). David also appointed his sons as priests alongside the official priesthood, represented by Zadok and Abiathar (2 Sam. 8:18). In such cases as these, it seems unlikely that much skill or training would be called for.

One of the most basic tasks of priests in antiquity in general was divination, the giving of oracles. In pre-Islamic Arab society, this was expected of the *kahin,* who combined the functions of *kōhēn* and *nābî'* (prophet) in ancient Israel, perhaps suggesting a stage at which the functions of these two classes were undifferentiated. In the Hebrew Bible the diviner (*qōsēm*) is more often linked with the *nābî'* than with the *kōhēn,*[12] but consultation with a view to receiving an oracle was also expected of the priest. The Levite hired as house priest by the aforementioned Micah gave the good word to the Danite scouts on their way to their new home at Laish/Dan (Judg. 18:5–6). In one of the many traditions that have clustered about Samuel, he received an oracle unfavorable to the local priesthood while engaged in an incubation ritual in the temple at Shiloh (1 Sam. 3:2–18). Samuel's status in this particular tradition is uncertain. While the context of Dtr suggests he is a prophet, and the night vision marks a new phase in the history of prophecy (1 Sam. 3:1b, 19–21), he also wears the priestly ephod and is described in cultic terms as *na'ar* and *mĕšārēt* (1 Sam. 2:11, 18; 3:1). The same terms, generally translated "youth" and "minister" respectively, are also used of Joshua in the poorly represented tradition in which he serves as cult functionary in the wilderness tent (Ex. 33:11).[13]

Divination as a priestly function is also indicated by the priestly manipulation of Urim and Thummim, generally thought to be a kind of dice giving a yes or no answer to inquiries. The oracle in Deut. 33:8 assigns this divinatory technique to Levi, eponymous ancestor of the priesthood; Aaron's son Eleazar makes use of it (Num. 27:21), and it is eventually incorporated into the priestly apparel (Ex. 28:30; Lev. 8:8). During the Persian period, the status of those who could not prove their priestly descent was to be decided by Urim and Thummim in the hands of a priest (Ezra 2:63; Neh. 7:65).

Before the establishment of state cults in both kingdoms, priests would have carried out a range of cultic acts, including sacrifice, at local sanctuaries. Perhaps the most important occasion would have been the annual sacrifice of the clan or phratry (*mišpāḥâ*) at which the cultic specialist of the kinship unit, perhaps a younger brother from one of the households, officiated (e.g., 1 Sam. 20:6, 29).

The widely held opinion that there was one central sanctuary in prestate Israel derived from the widely accepted hypothesis of a pan-Israelite league or amphictyony, associated especially with the scholars Albrecht Alt and Martin Noth. Now that the amphictyony theory is no longer in favor, we have less trouble acknowledging the multiplicity of cult centers in the early period, not all dedicated exclusively to the cult of Yahweh. (We may add the allusion to a Philistine temple dedicated to the Canaanite deity Dagan in 1 Sam. 5:1–5 and the archaeological evidence for Philistine cult centers at Tell Qasile near Tel Aviv and Miqne, perhaps the biblical Ekron.)[14] One of the most important of these early sanctuaries was Shiloh (Khirbet Seilun, about twenty miles north of Jerusalem), its prominence in the tradition due no doubt to its association with the early stages of the monarchy at the time of Saul and David. After its destruction by the Philistines, the descendants of the priest Eli established a new cult center—new, at least, for them—at a site named Nob just north of Jerusalem, perhaps identical with the prominent hill known as Nebi Samwil, at that early period within the Gibeonite enclave.[15] Following on the massacre of the Nob priesthood by Saul, the lone survivor, Abiathar, served David as priest together with Zadok (1 Samuel 22; 2 Sam. 8:17; 20:25). But Abiathar was unlucky or unwise enough to antagonize Solomon and was banished to Anathoth, a village north of Jerusalem where, according to the editor of Jeremiah (Jer. 1:1), there was still a colony of priests more than three centuries later.

The Shiloh priesthood clearly played an important part in the transition to the idea of an official priesthood as the religious aspect of the state apparatus. Biblical tradition traces the genealogy of this priest family through five generations: Eli, Phineas, Ahitub, Ahimelech (Ahijah), Abiathar (1 Sam. 14:3; 22:9, 11, 20; 23:6; 30:7; 2 Sam. 8:17). The extirpation of this dynasty with the banishment of Abiathar and the ascendancy of Zadok is predicted moralistically by a "man of God," who brings the bad news to Eli (1 Sam. 2:27–36). In this prophetic word of judgment, the origin of the Eli priesthood is traced back to a revelation and commissioning that took place in Egypt before the exodus. Wellhausen and, more recently, Frank Moore Cross, Jr., took "the house of your ancestor" (1 Sam. 2:27) to refer to Moses *qua* Levite, but the allusion to a collectivity, a "house," points to Levi as ancestor of the priesthood rather than to Moses (see especially Deut. 33:8–11). The threatened disasters, however, threaten only the Shiloh-Nob branch of the Levitical priesthood. We have a close parallel in the intervention of another "man of God" following on the establishment of Jeroboam's new cult center at Bethel (1 Kings 13:1–10). This equally anonymous prophetic figure comes from Judah to the Northern Kingdom, condemns the Bethel priesthood, predicts its extirpation, and gives a sign guaranteeing the fulfillment of the prediction. The two episodes therefore run parallel.

The comminations and dire predictions of these two men of God, directed against the priests of Shiloh and Bethel respectively, are free compositions of the Deuteronomic historian, writing no earlier than the reign of Josiah (640–609 B.C.E.) who is named in the second passage (1 Kings 13:2). They are meant to support the negative verdict of the historian on the (from the Judean point of view) religious schism of the kingdom of Israel. The second incident also fits in with the unfavorable view of Aaron in Deut. 9:20 and the golden-calf episode, edited, if not actually composed, by the Deuteronomists.[16] It also leads us to think of a possible association of the Aaronite priesthood in its early stage of development with the Canaanite sanctuary of Bethel. The parallels between the golden-calf episode, in which Aaron plays a dubious role, and the setting up of the separatist bull cult at Bethel by Jeroboam (1 Kings 12) are unmistakable and familiar. Inviting the same conclusion is the curious coincidence between the names of Aaron's sons (Nadab, Abihu) and those of Jeroboam (Nadab, Abijah). However, the origins of the Aaronite priesthood remain obscure, and other possibilities have been entertained.

The origins of Dan, the other official cult center of the Northern Kingdom, are even more obscure. In one of the appendices to the Book of Judges, a Bethlehemite Levite is employed as a priest by a certain Micah, whose house shrine was mentioned earlier. In due course both the Levite and the cult objects he tended were forcibly appropriated and installed by the Danites in their newly conquered city (Judg. 17:7–18:31). It seems that the report originally stated only that they set up Micah's graven image and it remained in place as long as the Shiloh temple stood. But in that case an editor must have inserted the additional information that Jonathan, son of Gershom and grandson of Moses, was first in line of the priests who continued serving the Danite sanctuary down to the Assyrian conquest (733/32 B.C.E.).

This tradition of a priesthood in direct descent from Moses, serving a graven image (*pesel*), the making of which is expressly forbidden in the Decalogue (Ex. 20:4; Deut. 5:8), is disconcerting to say the least, so much so that the Masoretes changed the name Moses to that of the evil king Manasseh by the simple expedient of adding a suspended *nun* (*m[n]šh;* Judg. 18:30). Together with the equally surprising information about Nehushtan, the bronze replica of a serpent deity made by Moses and destroyed by Hezekiah (Num. 21:8–9; 2 Kings 18:4), it seems to point to a partially submerged tradition about Moses' Midianite connections. His father-in-law was a Midianite priest (Ex. 3:1; 18:1); if his wife, Zipporah, was not also a priest, she is presented as performing a ritual action (Ex. 4:24–26); and Moses himself at times acted in a priestly role, for example, in performing the blood ritual at Sinai (Ex. 24:3–8) and in officiating in the oracle tent (Ex. 33:7–11). The Mosaic connections of the Danite cult may well be historical, therefore, especially since it is difficult to imagine why anyone would want to invent them.[17]

Turning now to the early stages of the Jerusalem cult and its personnel: an excerpt from the Judean royal archives has come down to us in two versions (2 Sam. 8:17; 20:25–26). It lists Zadok, Abiathar, and a certain Ira the Jairite as David's priests, in addition to certain of David's sons. In view of the understanding of the ruler's function in the culture area at that time, it is hardly surprising that David himself officiated as priest and passed on the priestly function to his sons. But with the beginnings of a state system, however rudimentary, a more formal cultic apparatus would be called for. Abiathar, we have seen, was the surviving representative of the Shiloh priesthood. His appointment was a logical corollary to David's transfer of the ark-shrine, originally lodged at Shiloh, to Jerusalem. Zadok, a rather more enigmatic figure, was eventually, and inevitably, provided with a Levitical pedigree, being listed in the genealogies as descended from Aaron in the tenth generation through Eleazar, Aaron's son (1 Chron. 5:27–42; Ezra 7:2). The name of his father, Ahitub, has caused problems since an Ahitub is also named as grandfather of Abiathar, which would make Zadok Abiathar's uncle and a descendant of the Eli priestly line. But this is highly unlikely, especially since Zadok is the one destined to replace the Eli priesthood (1 Sam. 2:27–36). Either the paternal reference is to a different Ahitub or, more likely, the text (2 Sam. 8:17) is corrupt.

Together with Abiathar, Zadok functioned as David's priest and is described as playing a leading role in the political history of the reign, including the palace intrigues leading to the accession of Solomon (2 Samuel 15—20; 1 Kings 1—2). It is generally assumed that the Zadok line continued to occupy the office of chief priest during the Judean monarchy. This may be correct, but the name never occurs again in Dtr after the reign of Solomon, and there is no hard evidence even that the preexilic priestly leadership in Jerusalem was hereditary.[18] The next mention of Zadok and Zadokites occurs in Ezekiel's "law of the temple" in chapters 40—48, or, more probably, in contentious additions made to it (Ezek. 40:46; 43:19; 44:15; 48:11). From these we gather that some time in the late exilic or early postexilic period, a priestly faction claiming descent from a real or putative Zadok, priest of David and Solomon, arrogated to itself exclusive rights to the office, privileges, and perquisites of the Jerusalem priesthood. The claim was not, in the event, sustained, since after the reestablishment of the temple cult in the early Persian period the priesthood was open to all who could prove descent from Aaron, including Zadokites.

The sudden appearance of Zadok as David's priest has given rise to a great deal of inconclusive speculation about his origins. Frank Moore Cross, Jr., is one of the few scholars to accept Zadok's Aaronite descent, which permits him to postulate an Aaronite and a Mushite priesthood in both kingdoms, the former represented by the Bethel priests in the north and by Zadok in the south, the latter by the priesthood of Dan and by Abiathar in Jerusalem.[19] The Norwegian scholar Sigmund Mowinckel was the first to propose that Zadok had served the Jebusite sanctuary in Jerusalem before being employed by David, and the same hypothesis was argued at length by Harold H. Rowley. One of the main supporting arguments was, and is, the occurrence of Jerusalemite names with the theophoric element *zdk* (as in Melchizedek and Adonizedek), the deity in question deemed to have been worshiped in Jerusalem both before and after the conquest of the city by David.[20] Yet another line of argument associates Zadok with Gibeon (el Jib), described as "the great[est] high place" at the time of Solomon (1 Kings 3:4); this argument, however, rests on the rather shaky foundation of the Chronicler, who tells us that David posted Zadok to Gibeon as sacrificing priest (1 Chron. 16:39). The Gibeonite sanctuary does seem to have achieved prominence at the time of Saul and for a time must have been a serious rival to Jerusalem. But if there was a Gibeonite connection in David's cult establishment, it was more likely through Ira the Jairite, on the assumption that this priest hailed from Kiriath-jearim, one of the four Gibeonite cities.[21] In that case, the sacerdotal triumvirate would represent the ark-priesthood of Shiloh (Abiathar), the Canaanite-Jebusite element in the Jerusalem region (Zadok), and the superseded but still powerful rival cult center of the Gibeonite enclave (Ira).

Pulling together these scattered bits of information in our sources about early priesthoods, and making due allowance for the ideological bias of the same sources, we will try to draw out some conclusions of a general nature. First and most obvious of these is that all the priests mentioned in the sources are male. If we assume some correlation between the gender of the deity and gender roles among the deity's devotees, this may not seem surprising, given the official view of Yahweh as a male, celibate deity. But there is quite a difference, then as now, between an official view, an orthodoxy, and what people are actually thinking and doing in the religious sphere of their lives. We have had occasion to note that the cult of the goddess, generally Asherah, either alone or as the consort of Yahweh, was widespread under the monarchy and continued thereafter in defiance of Deuteronomic orthodoxy. Since, in other societies, including some Mesopotamian societies,[22] the gender of cultic personnel often corresponded to the gender of the deity, we should leave open the possibility that women played a more significant role in the cult than our sources are prepared to admit. As it is, no female cult personnel are mentioned, with the exception of cultic prostitutes (*qĕdēšôt*) and perhaps temple singers (*šārôt*), but even here the male cultic servants occur more frequently than the female.[23]

Taboos concerning ritual cleanness would also have militated against female participation in cult, as they did in other cultures. According to Levitical law, menstruation rendered the woman ritually unclean for seven days (Lev. 15:19), and childbearing put her out of commission for a much longer period of time—a total of eighty days in the case of a female child (Lev. 12:1–5). While we cannot be certain that these precise regulations were in force from early times, fear of pollution from the female on the part of males had deep roots in Israelite culture, as in most others, and would certainly have influenced who participated in worship and in what capacity. Indeed, it continues to do so in both Judaism and Christianity, conspicuously in debates over the ordination of women to the priesthood.

It is generally assumed that the Israelite priesthood was not only male but hereditary. The hereditary principle seems to go back to family cults in which the paterfamilias as chief officiant passed on the office to a son, a custom reflecting the great (and generally neglected) importance of ancestor cult in ancient Israel. Thus Micah in Ephraim installed a son in the priestly office (Judg. 17:5), Abinadab appointed his son Eleazar as priest of the ark-shrine after the Philistines returned the ark (1 Sam. 7:1), and David's sons officiated as priests alongside Zadok and Abiathar (2 Sam. 8:18). The priesthoods of both Dan and Shiloh were also hereditary, the latter attested for five generations. Lists of Jerusalem temple priests compiled in the Second Temple period present an unbroken genealogical chain from Aaron to Jehozadak, whose son Joshua (Jeshua) was the first to officiate in the rebuilt Temple (1 Chron. 6:1–15; Ezra 7:1–5). This was to be expected, given the importance of establishing a continous linkage with origins, an unbroken list of twelve legitimating the present occupants of the office. Its accuracy, however, cannot be taken for granted.

If, in fact, we check these genealogical lists against the few references in Dtr to the Jerusalem priesthood, we find the names of only the first and the last few in the genealogies, namely, Zadok and Azariah at the beginning and Hilkiah and Seraiah at the end. The only other two priests referred to by name in 1–2 Kings—Jehoiada, who engineered the coup against Queen Athaliah (2 Kings 11), and Uriah, priest of King Ahaz (2 Kings 16:10–16)—do not occur in the lists. This seems to correspond to what we know about such genealogies, which tend to concentrate on the beginning and the end, filling in as best they can in the middle. The function of the priest genealogies is transparently to legitimate the contemporary holders of the office and to do so by establishing an unbroken line with the normative past, like the apostolic succession in early Christianity. More specifically, they aimed to underpin the claim of one branch, the Aaronites, to exclusive control of the office.

With the consolidation of the state apparatus, the role of the priests officiating at the state sanctuaries would have become more complex, though in no way comparable in scale to the great temples of Egypt and Mesopotamia. The Jerusalem temple had its head priest (*kōhēn gādôl* or *kōhēn rōʾš;* 2 Kings 12:11; 22:4; 23:4; 25:18) and its second-in-command (*kōhēn mišneh;* 2 Kings 23:4; 25:18). In the administration of the Temple and its considerable economic assets, the head priest was assisted by a panel of senior priests (*ziqnê hakkōhănîm;* 2 Kings 19:2; Isa. 37:2; Jer. 19:1), and we also hear of what is presumably a lower class known as "keepers of the threshhold" (2 Kings 12:10; 22:4; 23:4; 25:18). All of these were state employees, since the temple of Jerusalem, like that of Bethel, was "a royal sanctuary, a national shrine" (Amos 7:13). The head priest, consequently, had a special relationship with the monarch. It was natural, therefore, that Amaziah, priest of Bethel, should report inflammatory and seditious prophetic utterances to Jeroboam (Amos 7:10–17), or that the chief priest Hilkiah should hand over the law book found in the Temple to state officials (2 Kings 22:8–9).

As Weber pointed out, the crucial difference between prophet and priest is that the former is called while the latter is appointed to office and therefore dispenses salvation by virtue of the office, rather than through personal charismatic endowment.[24] From the strictly religious point of view, installation in the priestly office is described as an act of consecration (with the verb *qiddēš;* 1 Sam. 7:1; Ex. 28:3; 30:30), but the expression "filling the hand" is also used (Judg. 17:5, 12; 1 Kings 13:33), suggesting the conferring of the benefice that went with the office. Anointing was added only in the postexilic period, being one indication that the priesthood had acquired some of the aura and trappings of the monarchy, now a thing of the past. (Exodus 28:41 uses all three terms—*consecrating, filling the hand,* and *anointing*—with respect to Aaron and his sons.)

The economic status of the clergy was no doubt as diverse as that of the laity, much depending on the prestige and popularity of the sanctuary at which they served or the generosity of the patron who had appointed them. The Bethlehemite Levite mentioned earlier was offered a regular salary, a clothing allowance, and living expenses when employed as Micah's personal chaplain (Judg. 17:10). The standard means of support, however, were tithes, income from sacrifices (2 Kings 12:17), sacrificial portions, and offerings of the faithful, not all of them voluntary. In addition, the clergy of the official cults under the monarchy were almost certainly exempt from taxation, as were the cult personnel of the Second Temple (Ezra 7:24).

THE ROLES OF THE PRIEST

Since roles exist to satisfy expectations within a particular society, we go on to ask what the expectations were to which the role of priest corresponded and which determined how it functioned. The question is inseparable from the social, psychological, and religious functions of cultic acts, which in principle can be carried out without a priesthood, even in advanced religions (e.g., Buddhism). The priest therefore exists in the first place to *facilitate* the carrying out of ritual. The increasing complexity of society and societal needs produced a correspondingly more complex and specialized set of cultic acts, thereby rendering the services of priests increasingly indispensable and enhancing the prestige of the office. The prestige and rewards of the role must therefore be assessed in relationship to the social and political situation in which the role functions. Since, for example, Achaemenid imperial policy favored local priesthoods as compliant instruments of control and pacification, the Jerusalem priesthood reached its apogee of power, if not popularity, during the late Persian period, that is, in the fifth and fourth centuries B.C.E.

It would be widely agreed that the most basic social function of cult, priesthood, and religion in general is to assure survival and material well-being. Thus far, we may accept Weber's thesis of the this-worldly orientation of religious phenomena. Whatever the authenticity of the passage below, the point was made clearly by those Judean refugees in Egypt after the Babylonian conquest who rejected Jeremiah's explanation of the disaster:

As for the word you have spoken to us in the name of Yahweh, we will not listen to you. We are determined to do everything we have vowed, burning incense for the Queen of Heaven and pouring out libations to her, as we have been doing, and as our ancestors, our kings and princes did in the cities of Judah and the open places of Jerusalem; for then we had plenty of food, we fared well and experienced no evil. But since we stopped burning incense for the Queen of Heaven and pouring out libations to her, we have lacked everything and been consumed by the sword and by famine.

(Jer. 44:16–18)

A candid admission, this, that the cult of the goddess Asherah was a normal part of worship under the monarchy and that, in terms of responding to basic needs, it worked. But cult is meant to assure well-being in the fullest sense, with respect to not just material but also psychological and spiritual needs. Cultic acts serve to meet these needs, and the priest exists to facilitate the carrying out of such acts. The emphasis is consequently on the *act*, not the person as the mediating agent, a fundamental distinction between priest and prophet. In this sense we may accept Weber's definition of the priesthood as "the specialization of a particular group in the continuous operation of a cultic enterprise, permanently associated with particular norms, places and times, and related to specific social groups."[25]

One of the principal means for ensuring well-being, in Israel as elsewhere, was sacrifice. The tendency for this practice to become increasingly complex with the passage of time is to be expected, but increasing specialization implied increasing control by sacrificial specialists, namely, priests. Since sacrifice, the priestly doctrine for which is set out in Leviticus 1—7, came to be considered essential for the removal of certain involuntary offenses ("sins") that disqualified one from membership or at least good standing in the cultic-civil community, the exclusive control of sacrifice by the priesthood translated very readily into a fair degree of social control. The sacrificial system also had a considerable economic impact, especially where livestock were involved, and this, too, worked to the advantage of the officiating priesthood. In this kind of society the allocation of cuts of sacrificial meat is one way of denoting and confirming social status. The listing of portions reserved for the priests (Ex. 29:26–28; Lev. 7:31–36; 10:14–15; Num. 18:18–19) provides a valuable indicator of their economic and social standing.

As was noted earlier, priests were also involved in divination, though not nearly to the extent or with the sophistication attained in Mesopotamia.[26] In Israel, the technical side of the practice does not seem to have been well developed, and divination tended to shade off into consultation of a more general nature. The priest was also a teacher, and in the first place a teacher of law (Jer. 18:18; Ezek. 7:26). The responsibility of priests for the maintenance, transmission, and teaching of the laws comes through most clearly in Deut. 31:9–13, 24–26, including the edited oracle on Levi in which instruction in the law is mentioned before sacrifice:

> They shall teach your statutes to Jacob,
> your law to Israel;
> they shall place incense before you,
> and a whole burnt offering on your altar.
>   (Deut. 33:10)

What level of training and skill this involved can only be conjectured. Priests would have had to be literate, would themselves have received instruction in ritual law, and were supposed to be available to answer queries and solve problems. The priest Jehoiada instructed King Joash during his minority (2 Kings 12:2), and the historian notes that the Assyrians brought back one of the priests deported from the kingdom of Samaria to teach the new settlers "the law of the god of the land" (2 Kings 17:24–28). In the course of the last century of the kingdom of Judah, priests were beginning to serve as magistrates (Deut. 17:9; 21:5), which presumably implied a more than casual acquaintance with the law. We recall a point made earlier, that the legal scholars referred to by Jeremiah as "handlers of the law" (Jer. 2:8) probably represented a specialization originally within the priesthood that evolved into an independent lay class of experts in jurisprudence.

One function that, as far as we know, priests in Israel did not perform was preaching. The biblical origins of this practice, of such importance today, especially in Protestant churches, are very obscure, and the subject as a whole has suffered neglect in biblical scholarship. It seems that the sermon, as a distinct art form, came into its own only after the Babylonian conquest, in either the Diaspora or the homeland or both, perhaps in connection with a rudimentary synagogue service. The examples closest to our understanding of the genre are the "Mosaic" homilies in Deuteronomy and the short sermons attributed to Levites (as distinct from priests) in Chronicles. In the latter, in particular, we detect frequent interpretative allusions to existing "scriptural" texts, foreshadowing what was to become a standard feature of the homily in both Jewish and Christian worship, namely, preaching from a text. Getting at the origins of this practice is complicated by the absence of clear terminology. The terms used in postbiblical Hebrew (*dāraš*, "preach"; *daršān*, "preacher") connote the investigation and elucidation of biblical texts in keeping with the important aspect of preaching just noted. The closest we come in Biblical Hebrew is the verb *hetîp* (Hiphil of *ntp*), meaning, literally, "to drip" but used metaphorically, without the unflattering associations we might be tempted to make today.[27] Interestingly, this verb is used of the public discourse of prophets (Amos 7:16; Micah 2:6, 11; Ezek. 21:2, 7), never of priests. But prophetic discourse is still—fortunately, we might add—some distance removed from what we would consider a typical homily. We conclude, then, that the homily as a distinct genre emerged only in the late biblical period, perhaps in circumstances in which sacrifice, the cultic act exclusive to the priest, had either declined in prestige or was in abeyance.

Priests have so often been the target of suspicion and abuse that it is no surprise to find something of the same in the Hebrew Bible, especially in prophetic texts. A battery of accusations is leveled at them, including venality (Micah 3:11; Jer. 6:13; 8:10), drunkenness (Isa. 28:7; Jer. 13:13), negligence and ignorance (Zeph. 3:4; Jer. 14:18; Ezek. 22:26), and even murder (Hos. 6:9). Much of this can be safely dismissed as the standard rhetoric of abuse, comparable to what others had to say about prophets. On the positive side, it can at least be said that priests played an important role in social maintenance, emotional unburdening, and the satisfaction of some basic religious needs and aspirations. With the end of national independence, the eclipse of the native dynasty, and the eventual creation of a temple community in the Persian province of Judah, the scope for the exercise of the priestly roles was greatly expanded. We must now go on to see what the priesthood of the Second Temple made of this opportunity.

ZADOK, AARON, LEVI

Some form of worship, including sacrifice, may have continued on the site of the Jerusalem temple, burned by the Babylonian commander Nebuzaradan in the summer of 586 B.C.E. How thoroughly Nebuzaradan did his job we do not know, but we hear of a delegation from the central hill country coming to Jerusalem a few years later to offer cereal and incense at the site of the Temple (Jer. 41:5). The idea that the land, including Jerusalem, was depopulated after the Babylonian conquest is a transparent ideological postulate of a later age (2 Chron. 36:17–21; cf. Lev. 26:27–39).[28] At the same time, there must have been many civilian casualties, including priests, during the conquest and occupation. The chief priest Seraiah; his second-in-command, Zephaniah; and three keepers of the threshold were among those executed (2 Kings 25:18), and many more ended up in Babylon following deportations both before and after the fall of Jerusalem (2 Kings 24:14–16; 25:11–12; Jer. 39:9–10). Priests were among the deportees to whom Jeremiah addressed a letter (Jer. 29:1), Ezekiel the priest was among the deported, and Ezra-Nehemiah, our chief source for the early Persian period, reports a steady stream of Babylonian-Jewish priests, including Ezra himself, returning to Judah at that time (Ezra 2:36–63 = Neh. 7:39–65; Ezra 7:1–6; 8:1–36).

One of the purposes that the Chronicler's genealogical list of chief priests (1 Chron. 6:1–15) was meant to serve was to establish continuity between the priesthoods of the First and Second Temple. This was accomplished by taking the series down to Jehozadak, son of the executed chief priest Seraiah. Jehozadak was taken into exile and his son, Joshua, was the first to officiate in the rebuilt Temple (Hag. 1:1, 12; 2:2, etc.). The Chronicler's list also proclaims that, during the time of the Judean monarchy, the chief priesthood was a hereditary office occupied by the descendants of Zadok, priest of David and Solomon. This conclusion has been generally accepted in the modern period,[29] but there is room to doubt, and further room to suspect that the list is basically fictive and schematic. Note, in the first place, how it has been constructed in such a way as to assign Zadok the central position, preceded and followed by twelve generations. This should arouse our suspicions, especially since, on the assumption of the conventional 40-year generation, the list would fit the overall chronological schema of the Hebrew Bible with 480 years from the exodus to the building of Solomon's temple (1 Kings 6:1) and 480 from that point to the rebuilding of the Temple at the time of the high priest Joshua.[30] While there is nothing inherently improbable about a Zadokite dynasty of priests in control of the Temple under the monarchy, it is poorly supported and may be another example of the tendency to construct the past in the light of contemporary realities. We cannot, in other words, exclude the possibility that a branch of the priesthood named for Zadok, priest of David and Solomon, created the genealogical link as a way of claiming continuity with the past, thereby establishing its own legitimacy.

A similar situation confronts us when we consider the figure of Aaron. Traditions about this person were apparently in circulation, in either oral or written form, from a fairly early date. He is linked on one occasion with Hur, one of the more obscure dramatis personae in the Pentateuch (Ex. 17:10–12), on other occasions with Miriam (Ex. 4:14; 15:20; Num. 12:1–6; Micah 6:4), but most often with Moses, sometimes in opposition to him (Ex. 32:1–35; Num. 12:1–16). The origin and development of these traditions are obscure and for our present purpose may remain so. The only point that needs to be made is that in early tradition Aaron is represented as spokesman for Moses, as his adjutant, as closely associated with the elders, *but not as priest*. He and Moses are Levites, and at one point Aaron's Levitical status is emphasized (Ex. 4:14), but in none of these early traditions does he actually discharge priestly functions. Deuteronomy likewise says nothing about Aaron *qua* priest and nothing about Aaronite priests ("sons of Aaron"). Leaving aside incidental allusions to his death (Deut. 10:6; 32:50), acknowledged to be P additions, the book speaks of him only once, in an uncomplimentary reference to his role in the golden-calf episode (Deut. 9:20).

In brief, there is no mention of Aaron the priest or of Aaronite priests in any preexilic text or, for that matter, in any postexilic text, with the exception of the Priestly matter in Genesis through Joshua and Chronicles-Ezra-Nehemiah. It is particularly significant that in Deuteronomy, first issued (as is generally assumed) toward the end of the kingdom of Judah, priests are neither Zadokite nor Aaronite but Levitical. The standard designation in the book is, in fact, "Levitical priests" (*kōhănîm halĕwiyyîm;* Deut. 17:9, 18 etc.). If we take this together with the derogatory reference to Aaron at Deut. 9:20, it might suggest that the Deuteronomic author chose this title to designate an ideal priesthood, that is, one according to ancient tradition, and did so in opposition to Aaronite claims then being pressed for the first time. But in the present state of our ignorance this is hardly more than a possibility.

At this point we encounter Levi, the most basic of the priestly eponyms. The assumption that priests are ideally descendants of Levi, or at least should be able to stake a claim to Levitical descent that is not demonstrably false, may well be quite ancient. After hiring the Levite from Bethlehem, the Micah considered earlier was confident of future prosperity "because I have a Levite as priest" (Judg. 17:13). The historian accuses Jeroboam, founder of the Northern Kingdom, of introducing an unwarranted innovation by appointing non-Levitical priests to operate the state cult in Bethel and Dan (1 Kings 12:31). It remains unclear how claims on behalf of Levi as prototypical priest, and corresponding Levitical claims to a cultic monopoly, could have arisen. Some scholars still accept what seems to be the simplest solution, that the members of the secular tribe of Levi, belonging to the Leah group, lost out in the struggle for tribal lebensraum, perhaps because of the events recorded in Genesis 34 (see also Gen. 49:5–7). As a result, it is claimed, they took over the role of cultic specialists as a *faute de mieux*. Others, however, deny any necessary connection between the tribe of Levi and Levites as cultic specialists, arguing that there were from the beginning Levites, perhaps of both sexes, who filled this role. At this point, appeal is sometimes made to the inscriptions in the Minaean script discovered at El-Ela (ancient Dedan) in northern Arabia, in which occurs the word *lw'*, with the feminine *lw't*, taken by some to be identical with Levite.[31] The warlike propensities of Levites, exemplified in the golden-calf incident (Ex. 32:25–29), have suggested a variation of this position, namely, that the earliest Levites, like the Nazirites and Rechabites, formed a distinct cult association connected with warfare under the banner of Yahweh. Discussion will no doubt continue, with little prospect of a definite outcome in the absence of additional information. A close parallel is the problem, long familiar to historians of ancient Iran, of the identity of the Magi. According to Herodotus (1.101), they were one of the six tribes of the Medes; according to later Zoroastrian tradition, however, they constituted a distinct priestly caste. With respect to both Levites and Magi, we are unlikely to know for certain whether there was an evolution or devolution from one status to another, or whether our sources have misled us into making a connection where in fact none existed.

The earliest clear distinction in biblical texts between different classes of priests is the notice that Jeroboam appointed non-Levitical priests to staff his state sanctuaries at Bethel and Dan (1 Kings 12:31–32). We are not told who these non-Levitical priests were or where they came from. A possibility suggested earlier is that they belonged to the priestly caste that came to be known as "the sons of Aaron," and since the Deuteronomists take a very dim view of Jeroboam's cult "reforms," the hypothesis would be consistent with the disparaging reference to Aaron in Deut. 9:20. The question then would be how they came eventually to a position of prominence in the Jerusalem cult. Perhaps the devastation of Judah and deportation of priests from Jerusalem provided them with their opportunity. The notice in Jer. 41:5 about Yahweh worshipers coming to Jerusalem *after* the catastrophe from cities in the former kingdom of Samaria may be significant in this connection. Another effect of Jeroboam's cultic innovations was that priests claiming Levitical descent, those excluded from employment by his measures, migrated south and created an oversupply of clergy in Judah (2 Chron. 11:13–17). Many of those who survived the Assyrian conquest about two centuries later no doubt followed their example.

From Dtr we learn that the attempt to establish a cult monopoly in Jerusalem by closing rival sanctuaries began with Hezekiah, the first Judean king to reign without a counterpart to the north (2 Kings 18:4, 22), and was repeated by Josiah in the following century (2 Kings 23:5, 8). To the extent that this move was successful, it would have added to the number of unemployed clergy, thus producing the situation in which many of them sur-

vived only on charity and because of the economic safety net of the triennial tithe (Deut. 12:19; 14:27–29; 26:11–13). Deuteronomy justifies the attempt to establish a cult monopoly on the theological ground of the divine
election of Jerusalem, a recurring refrain in the book (12:5, 11, 14, etc.). But
it is also possible to view it as a measure designed to put rivals out of business and thus protect the privileges and perquisites of the clergy employed
at the state sanctuary. The historian wishes us to understand that the measure was successful and informs us that the clergy of the "high places" were
unable to exercise their right to officiate in the state sanctuary (2 Kings 23:9;
cf. Deut. 18:6–8). As it turned out, however, the Jerusalem priests had little
time to enjoy their success before the Babylonian conquest in the early years
of the sixth century B.C.E.

THE PRIESTHOOD OF THE SECOND TEMPLE

After the fall of Babylon in 539 B.C.E. to the forces of Cyrus and his allies,
the Neo-Babylonian Empire, including the province of Judah (Yehud), came
under Iranian control. In the next year Cyrus issued his famous edict, justifying his conquests as carried out under the mandate of the Babylonian god
Marduk and proclaiming a policy of reconciliation and the repatriation of
deportees and their deities.[32] Ezra 1:1–4 (cf. 2 Chron. 36:22–23 and Ezra
6:3–5) reproduces what purports to be a similar firman addressed specifically to the Jewish ethnic minority in Babylon, permitting a return to the
homeland with a view to rebuilding the Temple of Yahweh, God of heaven.
We hear that the decree met with an immediate and enthusiastic response,
with the return of some fifty thousand Babylonian Jews, priests and laity, to
Jerusalem. An altar was set up, sacrifices offered, and the feast of Sukkot
celebrated. In the next year the foundations of the Temple were laid, but
nothing further was done until the sixth year of Darius I, therefore 516/15
B.C.E., when the task was completed (Ezra 6:15).

In taking stock of this information on the founding of the second commonwealth provided by the biblical sources, we need to bear in mind the
convictions that drive the narrative. First, those who came from Babylon,
the diaspora community (*běnê haggôlâ*), are the true heirs of the old Israel.
Before their arrival, either the land was empty of its former inhabitants or
those who were there were ritually unclean—though mutually incompatible, both views are represented. With respect to the cult, there is no hint
that anything was there to replace. The Babylonian immigrants can start
with a tabula rasa. The Temple is built from the foundations up, and a new
high priest fresh from Babylon, Joshua ben Jehozadak, officiates in it. But

newness is combined with continuity. Jehozadak was himself deported to Babylon after the execution of his father, Seraiah. The sacred vessels confiscated by Nebuchadnezzar are returned (2 Chron. 36:10, 18; Ezra 1:7–11; 5:14–15; 6:5), though the forging of this particular link with the past involves ignoring the fact, reported in 2 Kings 24:13, that the cult vessels, or at least the ones made with gold, were deliberately destroyed by the same monarch.

Prophetic texts from the early Persian period often mention priests but provide few clues to their origin or particular affiliation. Moving back into the late monarchy, the superscription to Jeremiah identifies him as one of the priests in Anathoth (Anata, about four kilometers north of Jerusalem), the village to which Abiathar had been confined by Solomon. Jeremiah is therefore linked, if somewhat tenuously, with the Shiloh priesthood; and the link may help to explain his hostility to the clergy of the Jerusalem temple and his prediction that it would share the same fate as the Shiloh sanctuary (Jer. 7:14).[33] But apart from the reference to Levitical priests in 33:21, belonging to the well-attested Deuteronomic editorial strand, the book provides no information on the connections of the temple priesthood.

Ezekiel, a younger contemporary of Jeremiah, is also critical of the temple priesthood, to which he himself had belonged before his deportation to Babylon (Ezek. 7:26; 22:26). The various "abominations" shown to him during his visionary tour of the Temple no more than six years prior to its destruction could not have happened without the knowledge and connivance of the official priesthood (8:1–18). Only in the "law of the Temple" (chapters 40—48), or, more precisely, in additions made to it, do we find anything specific bearing on the status and identity of the priests. These Zadokite additions (40:45–46; 43:19; 44:10–16; 48:11) distinguish between altar clergy and temple clergy. The quintessentially priestly task of sacrificing is restricted to the "sons of Zadok," while all others, now simply referred to as "Levites," are responsible for the upkeep and running of the Temple in general but are debarred from the privileges of the Zadokite inner circle.

Class distinction within the priesthood is justified on the grounds of a history of religious infidelity involving priests and people, during which time only the "sons of Zadok" remained faithful (Ezek. 44:10–15; 48:11). In the modern period, most commentary on these passages has followed Wellhausen in locating the "time of straying" as prior to the Josian reform and the unfaithful priests as those who had staffed the "high places" at that time. The Zadokites could then be simply equated with the Jerusalem temple clergy who, as we learn from 2 Kings 23:9, succeeded in preserving their cult monopoly by excluding the now unemployed priests of the *bāmôt* (high places) from employment at the state sanctuary.

Wellhausen's hypothesis provided a gratifyingly simple solution to the problem of Levitical origins, but it is not without its own problems. As noted earlier, we cannot simply assume that the Jerusalem priesthood under the monarchy was Zadokite. The Jerusalem priesthood was, moreover, itself capable of quite a bit of straying, including such aberrations as the cults of the god Tammuz and the goddess Asherah carried out in the Temple itself (Ezek. 8:1–18; 2 Kings 23:4–14). An alternative explanation would be that some time after the sack of Jerusalem, probably in the Babylonian Diaspora, ideological conflict between rival branches of the priesthood generated denunciations and anathemas, claims and counterclaims, involving appeals to real or fictive priestly eponyms of the remote past. One of these branches, we may surmise, was named for Zadok, perhaps motivated by attachment to the exiled Davidic ruler Jehoiachin. The claims of this faction found expression in the Zadokite additions to Ezekiel 40—48,[34] and the Zadokites may have succeeded in making good on their claims from the beginning of the "return to Zion." The name of Jehozadak, son of Seraiah and father of Joshua, first priest of the restored Temple cult, is formed with the element ṣdq, and he is the essential link between the old order and the new. Joshua, or Jeshua, is invariably referred to as son of Jehozadak, or Jozadak, and is generally associated with Zerubbabel, grandson of Jehoiachin and the focus of messianic fervor early in the reign of Darius I. While no source earlier than Chronicles, with the exception of Ezekiel 40—48, refers to Zadokite priests, the high-priestly Zadokite line was thought to have continued uninterrupted until the Maccabees took over the high priesthood. It was this Maccabean break with tradition more than anything else—more even than the open commercialization of the high priesthood during the rule of Antiochus IV—that led to the formation of the Qumran sect. One of the self-designations of this sect is "sons of Zadok" (bĕnê ṣādôq), and its founder came to be known as "the legitimate teacher" (môreh haṣṣedeq, also formed with the stem ṣdq).

Prophetic texts from the Persian period often refer to priests, but never to Aaronite or Zadokite priests. The pseudonymous Malachi, perhaps a dissident member of the Jerusalem temple clergy, delivers a blistering attack on contemporary priests, accusing them, inter alia, of neglecting their educational role and offering defective sacrifices (Mal. 1:6–2:9). He sees the priesthood as constituted by a covenant made with Levi (2:4–9) and therefore refers to priests generically as "sons of Levi." The identity of this covenant has been much discussed. The main options have always been the "ordination" of the sons of Levi in the golden-calf episode (Ex. 32:28–29) and the covenant of peace and everlasting priesthood granted to Phineas,

grandson of Aaron, at Baal Peor (Num. 25:10–13), both following on enthusiastic participation of the clergy in bloody purges. But these may be specific instantiations of a more general idea of priestly legitimacy that, like so
much else in Malachi, can be traced to Deuteronomy. In Deuteronomy,
priests are referred to throughout as Levitical, and the oracle on Levi delivered by Moses on his deathbed speaks of the covenant fidelity of Levi's descendants (Deut. 33:8–11). Further confirmation is a passage of Deuteronomic origin in Jeremiah that refers explicitly to a covenant made with
Levitical priests (Jer. 33:20). Malachi therefore follows Deuteronomy in looking to Levi as founder and patron of the priesthood and, like Deuteronomy,
appeals to venerable antiquity to oppose the practice and pretensions of the
contemporary official clergy.

The data base on the priesthood provided by Ezra-Nehemiah, mostly in
the form of lists and genealogies, seems to exemplify Wellhausen's dismissal
of what he called "the statistical fantasy of the Jews" expressed in names
and numbers that "simply stand on parade and neither signify nor do anything."[35] A century after Wellhausen, we can probably move quite easily beyond such prejudicial judgments, but we still have the problem of deciding
how much useful information, on the priesthood or on anything else, can
be distilled from Chronicles-Ezra-Nehemiah. The ideology of the author/ed-
itor required that all priests and temple personnel connected with the rebuilt Temple originate in the Babylonian Diaspora. No other priests are
mentioned, the offer of the locals to participate in the rebuilding is rebuffed
(Ezra 4:1–3), and the worship in the newly constructed Temple is viewed
as an absolutely new beginning. It is hardly likely that this represents the
real situation. The Babylonians would not have deported all the priests in
the country, we have seen indications that some form of cult continued on
or near the site of the Temple, and Ezra-Nehemiah itself refutes the thesis
of total depopulation with its frequent allusions to the "people(s) of the
land," who certainly included the indigenous population of Judah (e.g., Ezra
4:4–5; 6:21).

Granted all this, we can still accept the historical reality of a resettlement
in the early Persian period, one that included descendants of Judeans deported by the Babylonians. Persian policy tended to support or, where necessary, put in place a favored elite in the provinces, one whose loyalty could
be counted on and that could help preserve the *pax Persica*. As noted earlier, it was also Persian policy to support local priesthoods and their cults
as part of the apparatus of imperial control. It is therefore by no means implausible that the rebuilding and endowment of the Jerusalem temple
should be financed, at least in part, out of the imperial treasury (Ezra 6:4,

8–10; 7:15, 20–23; 8:25, 33) and that prayers for the royal family be incorporated in the temple liturgy (Ezra 6:10).

The list reproduced in Ezra 2 and Nehemiah 7 purports to be a roster of the first '*ôlîm*, "those who went up at the beginning" (Neh. 7:5). But the numbers involved—42,360, according to the Ezra 2 version—would seem to be too large for any one return. Certain indications in the list—for example, the names of localities in which the immigrants eventually settled— also suggest a later date. One possibility is that the list represents a census of adult males, lay and clerical, in good (or in some few cases dubious) standing in the temple community, probably in the second half of the fifth century B.C.E. This community is constituted as an assembly or congregation (*qāhāl;* Ezra 2:64; Neh. 7:66), more specifically as the diaspora assembly (*qěhal haggôlâ;* Ezra 10:8) or simply the diaspora group, literally, "sons of the diaspora" (*běnê haggôlâ;* Ezra 4:1; 6:19–21; 8:35; 10:7, 16). These expressions refer to a distinctive social group with its own organization and leadership, a socially and economically dominant elite enjoying the support of the imperial government and centered in the Temple as its religious and temporal power base. To judge by the census list, temple personnel constituted about one tenth of the diaspora group as a whole.

According to these lists, the priests, 4,289 of them, belonged to four large ancestral houses of about the same size as the lay phratries (kinship groups) and, incidentally, as those of contemporary Iranian society, that is, numbering some 800 to 1,200 adult males (Ezra 2:36–39). Over the course of two centuries, the number and size of the groups could be expected to vary. New groupings might hive off from established ones (as, perhaps, Pashhur from Immer; cf. the Pashhur ben Immer of Jer. 20:1–6), and some others might simply disappear. If we put together the lists of priests in Chronicles-Ezra-Nehemiah, we have the following results: *five* priestly houses in the Chronicler's list of the first repatriates (1 Chron. 9:10–13), *six* in another list of priests living in Jerusalem (Neh. 11:10–14), and *twenty-one* in yet another list of first-generation priests (Neh. 12:1–7). The process of division and classification eventually terminated in the *twenty-four* priestly courses (*miš-mārôt*) in the late Persian or early Hellenistic period (1 Chron. 24:1–19), a system that remained in place until the end of the Second Temple. It will be recalled that a priest belonging to the eighth of the twenty-four courses is mentioned at the beginning of Luke's Gospel (1:5).

A notable feature of the lists in Ezra-Nehemiah is the absence of any reference to these priests as Zadokite or Aaronite. Ezra is supplied with a patently fictitious Aaronite pedigree (Ezra 7:1–5), which is borrowed from the genealogy in 1 Chron. 6:1–15 and was doubtless contributed to the Ezra narrative by the Chronicler as editor. Representatives of the priestly houses of Phineas and Ithamar are said to have accompanied Ezra on his mission to Judah (Ezra 8:2), and another priest, Eleazar ben Phineas by name, awaited them in Jerusalem (8:33). According to the P genealogies, Eleazar and Ithamar were the surviving sons of Aaron, whereas Phineas was the son of Eleazar. These three, and not Aaron, occur in the Ezra autobiography, which permits the suggestion that Phineas and Ithamar represent Judeo-Babylonian priestly houses, similar to the four in the Ezra 2 list (Jedaiah, Immer, Pashhur, Harim), and that their eminence secured for them a very prominent place in the "canonical" Aaronite genealogy. In its final form, attained at a later point in time, that genealogy would correspond to the final stage in the consolidation of the power of the Aaronite priesthood.

PRIESTS AND LEVITES

The priestly genealogies that Wellhausen found so exasperating could, if we knew how to decode them, reveal important aspects of the history of the priesthood, including internecine strife among different branches and the eventual ascendancy of one of these branches, the one claiming descent from Aaron. A key issue was control of the rebuilt Temple during the first century of Persian rule. Given the situation in the province, whoever controlled the operations of the Temple enjoyed not only spiritual hegemony but a large measure of political and economic power as well, including control of membership in the qāhāl (assembly), on which civic status and perhaps also title to property depended. It is not entirely surprising, then, that the priesthood took over some of the trappings of the monarchy, including items of the royal regalia and the rite of anointing.[36] An obscure passage in Zech. 6:9–14 even suggests the possibility that the contemporary high priest, Joshua ben Jehozadak, was secretly crowned after the hope of restoring the native dynasty in the person of Zerubbabel was dashed.[37]

The pretensions of the Jerusalem priesthood to wield power in both the spiritual and temporal realms did not go unnoticed and uncontested. Priests were often the target of prophetic diatribe at that time (see especially Isaiah 56—66 and Malachi), and one of the principal aims of Nehemiah, the lay governor of the province from about the middle of the fifth century, was to curb the power of the priesthood and secure some measure of control over the temple and its considerable economic assets (see Neh. 13:4–10, 13, 28–29).

The incident of the rebellion and execution of the Levite Korah, described in the Priestly history (P) as taking place in the wilderness, testifies to opposition to the priesthood emanating from both the lower ranks of the clergy and the laity, since the Levitical protest was supported by 250 leaders of the assembly (Num. 16:1–17:26 [16:1–17:11]). The demand was for decentralization of spiritual and temporal power on the grounds that holiness was not confined to the de facto leadership. In his reply, Moses rebuked the Levitical rebels for seeking to break the Aaronite monopoly of the priesthood and, in effect, usurp the priestly office. The historical situation reflected in this narrative was that Aaronites had succeeded by the time of writing in ousting other claimants to the priestly office, with the result that the latter either simply disappeared or were obliged to accept a role ancillary to the sacrificing priests. After Korah and his supporters were summarily executed—as examples—the bronze censers offered by the rebels were hammered out to make a covering for the altar and thus to remind all and sundry that "no outsider, who is not of the Aaronite line, shall approach to offer incense before Yahweh, lest he become like Korah and his faction" (Num. 17:5 [16:40]).

Mention of Korah the Levite raises an important point of nomenclature. We have seen that *Levite* came to serve as a primary and generic designation for priests in that, according to the prevailing view, all priests were ideally descended from Levi. We also saw that Deuteronomy speaks of "Levitical priests" with the intent of reaffirming the traditional priestly status over against more recent challenges. For the same reason Malachi calls contemporary priests "sons of Levi" and reminds them of the covenant of Levi (Mal. 2:4, 8). Yet in the course of time, *Levite* came to have a more restricted connotation, referring to a class of *clerus minor* (a lower priesthood) debarred from access to the priesthood in the strict sense, that is, from the ranks of the sacrificing altar priests descended from Aaron. How did this situation come about?

The first general observation to make is that the Aaronite claim, successfully pressed, to exclusive title to the priestly office displaced the traditional generic designation *Levite* so that it acquired the more restrictive connotation of minor clergy, in the sense of Levites *other than* Aaronite altar priests. The displacement is reflected in the genealogies in which Levi has to do double duty as ancestor to both priests and Levites so redefined, a requirement that called for some ingenious genealogical adjustments. We cannot say for sure when and under what circumstances these changes took place. Levites as *clerus minor* are not unambiguously attested before the Neo-Babylonian period. Allusions to Levites carrying the ark in the early period are among the clearest indications of Deuteronomic editing (Josh. 3:3; 1 Sam. 6:15; 2 Sam. 15:24; 1 Kings 8:4). In Deuteronomy, a distinction between priests and Levites occurs only in the latest strand of the Shechem covenant account in which the Levites pronounce the curses (Deut. 27:14), as they do later in covenant making at Qumran (1QS III). This suggests that the displacement occurred as a result of conflict within priestly circles in the Neo-Babylonian and early Persian periods, the context no doubt being control of worship in the Babylonian Diaspora and especially of the preparations for resuming worship after return to the homeland. Since Levites who chose to return would have to resign themselves to a subordinate role in temple affairs, it is understandable that few chose to do so—only seventy four as against 4,289 priests, according to the census in Ezra 2 = Nehemiah 7. The same situation explains why Ezra had to take special measures to recruit Levites for his own caravan (Ezra 8:15–20).

Chronicles-Ezra-Nehemiah, our principal source of information on Second Temple Levites, reveals a progressively broad range of functions and tasks that this order was called on to discharge. The age of admission to the Levitical ranks may also have been gradually lowered in response to this situation—from thirty (Numbers 4; 1 Chron. 23:3) to twenty-five (Num. 8:24–26) and, eventually, twenty (1 Chron. 23:24, 27; 2 Chron. 31:17; Ezra 3:8)—but since the texts in question cannot be dated with certainty, other explanations are possible. The retirement age, set at fifty, does not seem to have changed. It can be compared with a retirement age of sixty for priests and judges in the *Damascus Document,* the reason given being the eminently plausible one that "God has ordained that their understanding should depart even before their days are complete" (CD 10:8–10; 14:7).

A clearer indication of development in the office is the inclusion within it of temple musicians and gatekeepers. These are listed separately from Levites in the census list (Ezra 2:40–42 = Neh. 7:43–45) and elsewhere in the book (Ezra 7:7; Neh. 13:10), but in Chronicles, the composition and rendition of liturgical music and control of the entrances to the Temple precinct are routinely described as Levitical tasks. We conclude, then, that the scope of Levitical activity was broadened to include these functions not long before the composition of Chronicles, in the late Persian or early Hellenistic period.

While this progressively more inclusive definition of Levite does not necessarily entail a corresponding increase in power and influence, the Levitical phratries and guilds provided, often with lay support, a counter to the dominance of the priestly aristocracy. Levitical responsibility for the interpretation, administration, and teaching of the law also played an important part in the eventual emergence of Judaism as a lay religion, in contrast to

Christianity in which a priestly aristocracy or clerical hierarchy very quickly established control.

The author of Chronicles describes the Israel of David's day in glowing terms as a church or ideal theocracy. Prominent in this description is his account of David's establishment of the Levites to whom certain tasks are assigned (1 Chron. 23:1–6). In descending order of importance, they are to be caretakers of the Temple, administrators and magistrates, gatekeepers, liturgical musicians. The first category, involving about two-thirds of the (obviously fictitious) total of thirty-eight thousand, includes responsibility for the furnishings and appointments of the Temple, the sacred vessels, and the different commodities used in the sacrificial ritual. It is stated several times that Levites are to serve as sacristans for the priests, to which a veiled threat against any temptation to take over priestly functions is occasionally added.[38] Levites were also responsible for the storerooms and temple treasury and for the distribution of tithes and payments, always under priestly supervision.[39] How delicate and potentially problematic this task could be is seen in Nehemiah's measures to prevent abuses and ensure equitable distribution, as well as some measure of civic control (Neh. 13:13). As an extension of this function, Levites were also charged with collecting the Temple tax (2 Chron. 24:4–7; 34:9).

As part of their "outside work" (1 Chron. 26:29), Levites served as administrators and magistrates. Nehemiah may have been the first to co-opt Levites into the civil service; at any rate, they supported his program, especially where it conflicted with the interests of the priestly aristocracy. They also took part in the rebuilding of the city wall, and some seem to have served as district administrators (Neh. 3:17–21; see also 1 Chron. 26:29–32).

Of prime importance for the future was their role as teachers of the law, already implied in their having charge of the ark of the covenant, which contained the tablets of the law (2 Chron. 5:4–12; 7:6). Chronicles also has them playing a significant part in the religious reforms initiated by several Judean kings, always on the basis of a written law (2 Chron. 19:4–11; 31:4; 35:3). During the reign of Jehoshaphat, we hear of a panel of lay and clerical officials, including Levites, going in circuit around Judah instructing the people out of a law book that they took with them (2 Chron. 17:7–9). Like so much else in this author's history, the incident is probably a pious fiction, no doubt suggested by the name of the king in question (Jehoshaphat means "Yahweh judges" or "Yahweh has judged"), but could be an important witness to practice at the time of writing. Levites also played a part in the public reading and interpretation of the law, led by Ezra (Nehemiah 8).

Here, too, we suspect a borrowing from contemporary practice, perhaps a kind of protosynagogal service involving the reading and study of the law accompanied by prayer. The steadily increasing emphasis on the study of the law and on prayer, in both of which Levites played a prominent role, necessarily affected attitudes toward the sacrificial cult and tended to deemphasize it, thus enabling Judaism to survive the loss of the Temple and cessation of sacrifice.

Since instruction is generally taken to be one of the goals of preaching, we have to conclude that Levites, rather than priests, played the dominant role in the development of homiletics. Chronicles provides several samples of Levitical sermons, or, given their brevity, abstracts of sermons. Gerhard von Rad argued that these brief addresses punctuating the Chronicler's narrative, even when not attributed to Levites, derive from Levitical homiletic instruction.[40] According to von Rad, a Levitical homily would typically contain doctrine; application, including appeal to examples from past history; and final exhortation. Many homilies also incorporated reference to earlier authoritative writings, thus anticipating the typical congregational sermon of today.

The two smallest Levitical divisions established by David, numbering four thousand each, were gatekeepers and liturgical musicians (1 Chron. 23:5–6). The temple gatekeepers or porters (šō'ărîm) were organized in guilds, some of the names of which have been preserved (1 Chron. 9:17–27; Ezra 2:42; Neh. 12:25). As the successors to the threshold priests of the First Temple (2 Kings 12:10; 22:4; 23:4; 25:18), their main duty was to protect the ritual purity of the Temple compound. They also had responsibility for the storerooms located near the gates (1 Chron. 9:26–27; Neh. 12:25) and the collection boxes for the offerings of the faithful (2 Chron. 34:9). Like his Mesopotamian counterpart (the atūtu or naṣṣāru), the Jerusalem gatekeeper was not a prominent ceremonial role player; probably the highlight of his day would have been the solemn opening of the gates at dawn, perhaps comparable to the pīt bābi ceremony in Mesopotamian temples of the Neo-Babylonian and Achaemenid periods.

The co-option of the liturgical musicians into the Levitical ranks probably had something to do with the increasing emphasis on prayer, including prayer musically rendered, throughout the Second Temple period. In this process, the Book of Numbers, which has a great deal to say about Levites but nothing about liturgical musicians, represents an earlier stage than Chronicles, which gives prominence to liturgical music. The source material in Ezra-Nehemiah that lists musicians and gatekeepers separately from Levites would presumably represent an intermediate stage.

A peculiar feature of the Chronicler's account is his description of the composition and rendition of liturgical music as a prophetic activity (1 Chronicles 25), which has prompted the suggestion that these *měšōrěrîm* (liturgical poets) were the successors of the cult prophets on the staff of Solomon's temple. In his account of Josiah's religious reform, for example, the author of Chronicles speaks of the participation of priests, *Levites,* and the people, whereas his source has priests, *prophets,* and the people (2 Chron. 34:30; cf. 2 Kings 23:2). A connection between First Temple cult prophets and Second Temple liturgical musicians is plausible but would carry more weight if we knew that these cult prophets sang or chanted their oracles. In any case, the prophetic attribution can be explained in other ways—as one aspect of the author's understanding of the Levitical office in general, or in function of David as prophet and founder of the musical guilds.

We have seen that liturgical prayer comes increasingly into view in the later period. Originally ancillary to sacrifice, it expressed the sentiments considered appropriate to the particular kind of sacrificial offering being made. It is therefore not so surprising that neither the P ritual material nor the "law of the Temple" in Ezekiel ever mentions prayer as part of worship. Certain categories of prayer in hymnic form corresponded to categories of sacrifice—the thanksgiving psalm with the *tôdâ* and *minḥâ,* confession of sin with the *ḥaṭṭā't* and *'āšām.*[41] The author of Chronicles informs us that the morning and evening burnt offering (*tāmîd*) was accompanied by thanksgiving and praise rendered by Levitical singers (1 Chron. 23:30), and he summarizes their contribution as invoking, giving thanks, and praising (*lěhazkîr, lěhôdôt, lěhallēl;* 1 Chron. 16:4). The shift toward prayer as an independent rather than a satellite activity would have been furthered by erosion of confidence in the Jerusalem priesthood, apparent in much of the extant literature from the Persian period on, and especially after the commercialization of the high-priestly office under the Seleucids. Since the sacrificial system was itself open to exploitation as providing significant perquisites for those who controlled it, a crisis of confidence in the priesthood and its operations would give greater weight to those cultic acts for which the presence of a priest was not a requirement.

The composition and rendition of liturgical music required professional training, both theoretical (musical, literary) and practical (voice), no doubt provided in the Temple precincts. Some obscure vestiges can still be detected in the titles and rubrics attached to many of the Psalms. We hear of the teacher–pupil relationship (1 Chron. 25:8) but can only speculate on the curriculum. The names of one or two master musicians crop up in our sources—a certain Mattaniah at the time of Nehemiah (Neh. 11:17; 12:8–9) and Chenaniah, a precentor or musical director, allegedly during David's reign (1 Chron. 15:22, 27).[42] As in other temples in the Achaemenid Empire, the liturgical musicians were organized in guilds. Of most frequent occurrence are Kohath, Gershon (Gershom), and Merari, later displaced by Asaph, Heman, Ethan, Jeduthun, and others less prominent. Attempts have been made to trace their history, determine their relative size and importance, and even describe their religious views, but there is too little to go on to make it worthwhile.[43] Some of the productions of these guilds have come down to us in the Book of Psalms, which might be described as the "Hymns Ancient and Modern of the Second Temple": twelve from Asaph, eleven from Korah, one from Ethan. After temple worship came to an end in 70 C.E., the function of these musical guilds was continued, though obviously in much changed circumstances, by those Masoretes who prepared the biblical text for recitation or chanting in the synagogue.[44]

By way of rounding off this discussion of Levites, it should be added that they occupied an intermediate position in the Temple hierarchy. Below them were the *nĕtînîm* (literally, "the ones given"), who served the Levites (Ezra 2:43–54; 8:20) and occupied a position comparable to the *širkutu* in Mesopotamian temples of the same period. Ancient tradition links them with the Gibeonite "hewers of wood and drawers of water" who survived Joshua's war of annihilation by means of a ruse (Josh. 9:23, 27).[45] The Jerusalem temple also provided employment, but not of the equal-opportunity kind, to a wide range of professions organized, like those of Mesopotamia, in guilds. About fifteen hundred legal and economic texts from the Neo-Babylonian and Achaemenid periods and many more from the Hellenistic period provide a wealth of information on personnel attached to the great Eanna shrine of Uruk/Tell el-Warka in the flood plain of southern Mesopotamia, including scribes, exorcists, bakers, brewers, carpenters, and the like.[46] Sadly, nothing of the kind is available for the Jerusalem temple, but we do know that it employed slaves, no doubt predominantly of foreign descent (Ezek. 44:7, 9; Ezra 2:55–58).

In sum, the Second Temple was the focus of a more or less rigidly organized and self-enclosed hierarchical community, exclusively male, constituting perhaps as much as 10 percent of the population of the province. This was the immediate social context for the role playing of priest and Levite, though the impact on the province and beyond was profound and long-lasting. We will now try to determine more precisely what these roles were and in what sense, if at all, we can speak of the role players as the originators or bearers of an intellectual tradition.

PROFESSIONAL TRAINING FOR
THE PRIESTHOOD

In Max Weber's discussion of the contribution of intellectualism to the development of religions, he noted how in certain societies, including early Judaism, a priestly caste established exclusive control over theology, ethics, and the conferring or denying of benefits in the religious sphere. He went on to note the priestly tendency to codify doctrine, elaborate a rational system of religious concepts, and produce a systematic ethic, all of which translated into a considerable amount of social control. In societies with their own canonical writings, priests would also have the task of issuing authoritative and binding interpretations, especially where important questions of community life were involved.[47]

Weber's generalizations provide a useful point of departure for our inquiry, but we shall see that they call for some modification. The struggle to achieve dominance in the ranks of the priesthood had already schooled the Aaronites in the art of wielding coercive power, but they did not have it all their own way. Opposition came not only from the laity, including prophets, but also from the Levitical guilds within the Temple organization. While most of the literature extant from the Second Temple period is of clerical origin, other writings (discussed in the chapter on the sage) have survived from lay sources indifferent rather than hostile to the priestly and cultic establishment. The task now is to identify what is peculiar to or characteristic of the thought-world of the Jerusalem priesthood and to ask in what sense, if any, it qualifies as an intellectual tradition.

The first step is to get some idea of the kind of professional knowledge and skills required for the priest to fulfill his role. We saw earlier that in Israel divination never attained the level of organization and sophistication to which the Mesopotamian omen literature attests. The manipulation of Urim and Thummim by the priest presumably did not call for much training or skill (Lev. 8:8). The situation was different with the rudimentary but extensive medical knowledge required for the diagnosis of conditions, including pathological conditions, resulting in loss of body fluids of different kinds (Lev. 15:1–33). The priest also had to be able to diagnose various dermatological conditions, extended, by a rather odd analogy, to clothing and buildings (Leviticus 13—14). Maintenance of the distinction between clean and unclean also involved a considerable knowledge of flora and fauna, categorized according to complex ritual criteria (Lev. 11:1–47). The fixing of the liturgical calendar, a matter of the greatest importance, would in addition have entailed a knowledge of astronomy on the part of at least a small cadre of priestly specialists (Lev. 23:1–44).

The list of forbidden sexual relations in Lev. 18:6–30 covers incest in its different forms as well as other kinds of deviant sexual behavior, including adultery, homosexuality, and bestiality. The list suggests that the Temple priesthood, like the rabbinate in Israel today, exercised or at least claimed considerable control over marriage. Genealogical matters, on which one's status in the congregation depended, also fell within the province of the priesthood. We have had occasion to note more than once that legal competence had always been expected of the priesthood. As a fifth-century B.C.E. seer put it, "The lips of a priest should guard knowledge, and men should be able to seek instruction from his mouth" (Mal. 2:7). By the Persian period, then, the office of priest called for a wide range of competence and knowledge of a kind bearing directly on many aspects of the day-to-day existence of the individual.

We have, unfortunately, practically no information on how priests were educated. Mastery of ritual and cultic matters could hardly have been attained without formal instruction of some kind, presumably carried out in the Temple precincts. Before setting out from the river Ahava, Ezra recruited temple personnel from "the place Casiphia" somewhere in southern Mesopotamia (Ezra 8:15–20). The unusual repetition of the designation "place" (*māqôm*), elsewhere a synonym for "temple" (Deut. 12:5; 1 Kings 8:29), led to the suggestion that Casiphia was the site of a Jewish temple that, like the one then standing on the island of Elephantine in Upper Egypt, served the local Jewish ethnic minority.[48] While this is obviously speculative, it is no more so than the alternative proposal that the reference is to a kind of clergy training center under the regency of a certain Iddo, presumably a priest.

Some idea of the kind of situation that may have obtained, *mutatis mutandis*, in Jerusalem may be gained from the operation of the "house of life" (*pr-'nk*) in contemporary Egypt. These houses of life were colleges for the training of priests and the study of priestly matters. They were attached to some of the major temples, for example, the Temple dedicated to the goddess Neith at Sais. The curriculum included medicine, the practice of which implied religious and magical aptitudes described as "secrets of the house of life." In addition, the entire range of ritual and cultic law was covered. The faculty was composed of scribes who had the status of priests, who could be called on to provide guidance for the conduct of festivals or the authentication of sacred animals, and who were also charged with writing annals, laws, and rituals.[49] While we have no comparable information for the (much smaller and poorer) Persian province of Yehud, something in some respects comparable, if on a much smaller scale, there must have been.

CREATION AND DISTINCTION: THE MAKING
OF A CONCEPTUAL SCHEME

We now go on to ask whether the knowledge that the priest had to acquire and pass on to others entailed the existence of an intellectual tradition specific to the priesthood. Our point of departure is the ostensibly rather unpromising one of the dietary laws concerning clean and unclean animals in Lev. 11:1–47 and Deut. 14:3–21. The search for the rationale behind the clean-unclean distinction has occupied and vexed generations of scholars since late antiquity and will no doubt continue to do so. Leaving aside the view that the distinction is simply there to be obeyed as a divine command, the more prominent solutions appeal to historical or cultural considerations (the unclean animals were used in pagan rituals), or invoke hygiene (the pig as a carrier of the trichinosis pathogen), or fall back on symbolism (ruminants are clean because they suggest rumination, that is, meditation). This is not the place to evaluate these options. More recently, attention has focused on the animal series as part of a taxonomic system reflecting societal values. This Durkheimian approach has entered the discussion primarily through the well-known essay of anthropologist Mary Douglas on "The Abominations of Leviticus," which, though wrong on several points of detail, provides valuable clues to the conceptual system of which the clean–unclean distinction is part.[50]

Douglas's essay makes the essential connection between the animals listed according to their habitats—water, air, land—and the creation account in Genesis 1. The point deserves further elaboration. That the connection is not coincidental can be seen in the tenfold repetition of the phrase "according to its [their] kind" in Genesis 1, with reference to the flora and fauna in the order in which they were created. A further link is the reference to creation as a work of division or separation. It should be noted that this process is limited to the first four days of creation: God divides light from darkness on the first day, the superior from the inferior waters on the second, water from dry land on the third, and day from night on the fourth. In each case, with the exception of the third day, the technical term *hibdîl* (separated) is used, as it is for the distinction between Israel and the nations and between clean and unclean. What this arrangement insinuates is that the work of separating clean from unclean creatures, the creation of which

occupies the fifth and sixth days, is being left to humanity and Israel in particular and is to be carried out as a continuation of the work of creation.
Creation at the beginning is therefore only the first stage of a process that
must be continued. In the conclusion to the relevant law in Leviticus 11, the
same categories and much the same language occur as in Genesis 1:

> These, then, are the instructions concerning land animals, winged crea-
> tures, and all living creatures swarming in the water, and all creatures
> creeping on the ground; to make a distinction [lĕhabdîl] between un-
> clean and clean, and between living things that may be eaten and those
> that may not be eaten.
>
> (Lev. 11:46–47)

Consistent with and analogous to the cosmic and zoological distinctions is
the separation of Israel from the nations, stated in the form of an elegant
ring composition (a–b–a):

> I am Yahweh your God, who have separated [hibdaltî] you from the
> peoples; so you must distinguish [hibdaltem] between clean and un-
> clean animals, between unclean and clean flying creatures. You must
> not render yourselves unclean by means of any animal, or flying crea-
> ture, or anything crawling on the ground that I have set aside [hibdaltî]
> for you to regard as unclean. You shall be holy to me, for I Yahweh am
> holy. I set you aside ['abdil] from the peoples that you may be mine.
>
> (Lev. 20:24–26)

The homology between the status of the individual and that of the land,
between the *physical body* and the *body politic,* is the subtext to much that
is said about both in the Priestly source, whether dealing with boundaries
(orifices) or marriage and proselytism (what the body may or may not ingest). The integrity of the borders of the land, and therefore of the body
politic, must be protected with the same sedulous care with which the dietary laws and the laws concerning clean and unclean safeguard the integrity of the physical body, whose borders are its orifices. The body
metaphor underlines much of what the Priestly source has to say about the
land. The land cannot ingest idolatry but must vomit out those who practice it (Lev. 18:25; 20:22). Uncleanness affects the land, whether rot or
mildew in buildings (Lev. 14:33–34), violation of the laws governing sexual
relations (Lev. 18:25–28), or, most of all, the shedding of blood (Num.
35:33–34). In a later section we will return to this theme of the priestly understanding of the land.

The structure of the creation week in Genesis 1 also sets in high relief the importance of habitat. The six days in which creation takes place are arranged in parallel triads, which may be set out as follows:

1	Light Separation of light and darkness	4	Sun, moon, stars Separation of day and night
2	Firmament Separation of superior and inferior waters	5	Water and air creatures
3A	Dry land Separation of water and dry land	6A	Land creatures, humans
3B	Vegetation	6B	Vegetation as food

Thus to the first day (light) corresponds the fourth (heavenly bodies); to the creation of the firmament and separation of the waters on the second day correspond the aquatic and air creatures on the fifth; and after the separation of the dry land from water on the third day, land creatures and human beings can finally appear on the sixth. The final item establishes a vegetarian diet for both humans and animals. The columns therefore distinguish between habitat and created entities, especially living creatures, and habitat is the chief criterion deciding the categorization of living creatures in Leviticus 11. Creatures manifesting (apparent) taxonomic irregularities are excluded as anomalous and therefore unclean. Thus the bat is unclean since, though equipped with wings, it has fur instead of feathers; the eel is excluded since it does not have scales and fins and its mode of locomotion is not deemed appropriate for its watery environment; the ostrich is disqualified because it has wings but is earthbound and therefore out of its right environment; and so on.

To the scientific mentality, this way of looking at nature admittedly makes little sense. But for those who accepted it, it contributed to social maintenance by keeping alive a reverent regard for the created order, for the place of living things in that order, and for care of the body as that part of the world for which one was especially responsible. The dietary laws therefore were part of a complex and internally consistent sociocultural code, by means of which the individual Israelite could locate himself or herself within an orderly society and cosmos.

We might add that the *ethical* aspect of diet comes more clearly into view with the correspondence between the creation of vegetation on the third day and the stipulation of a vegetarian diet for humans and animals on the sixth. The first creation is therefore a kingdom of peace without bloodshed. The permission to kill for food, given after the Deluge (Gen. 9:3–5), indicates a lower level of performance in a world in which peaceful coexistence is no more than an ideal. In this damaged world the prohibition of shedding blood, encumbent on humans and animals, and the command to drain the blood away before eating meat (Gen. 9:4–6), a command often repeated, serve to hold violence in check, to recall the original intention of creation, and to inculcate a discriminating ethical attitude toward the taking of life for food.

THE TEMPORAL AXIS: CHRONOLOGY
AND HISTORY IN P

The creation recital of Genesis 1 is the first chapter of a history that critical scholarship has assigned to the Priestly source (P), one of the main characteristics of which is a concern for precise chronology. No great critical acumen is needed to conclude that a chronological schema according to which, for example, Abraham is one hundred years old and his wife ninety when their child is born is probably fictive. Fictive is not, however, the same as arbitrary, for it can be shown that the P chronological data fit into a preconceived, internally consistent, and carefully worked-out schema. Many attempts have been made to decode the chronological system in the Hebrew Bible that are not our primary concern in this study. One clue may be noted, however, namely, the interval of 2,666 years between creation and the exodus from Egypt (Ex. 12:40–41), which is two-thirds of 4,000, understood to constitute a world epoch or "great year." If, to this span of 2,666 years, we add the 480 from exodus to the building of Solomon's temple (1 Kings 6:1); another 480, based on the biblical chronology itself, for the period of the kingdoms and the Babylonian exile; and the remaining 374, counting from the end of the exile in 538, the total of 4,000 is reached, in terms of absolute chronology, in 164 B.C.E., the year of the rededication of the Temple by the Maccabees. If this is not pure coincidence, it implies that the original chronology, focused on the sanctuary, was updated in the same spirit some time in the second century B.C.E.[51]

Within this chronological framework the Priestly author composed a narrative that is not so much a historical work as the working out of a conceptual schema along a temporal axis. It begins with the creation of the world as a cosmic sanctuary and ends, as argued earlier in this chapter, with the setting up of the sanctuary in the Promised Land (Joshua 18—19). The structurally cardinal points focus, therefore, on worship. P has no conquest and does not continue the story into the time of the "judges" and the monarchy. The reason is that everything necessary for the life of the community was laid down in the period before the rise of the state. In this respect, P is faithful to a dominant historiographical tradition in the Near East and the Levant that sought for identity, self-understanding, and legitimacy in the distant past.

Some of the main conceptual elements in the history are here briefly noted. The decisive structural feature in the history of early humanity (Genesis 1—11) is the great divide of the Deluge. To the consoling idea that judgment now lies in the past it adds dispositions for preserving a precarious hold on order in the present. It is arguable that the first creation already conveys the conviction that primordial chaos and anomie, though discomfited, persist as a threat around the insecure perimeter erected to keep them at bay.[52] We might say that P is involved in building dikes and ramparts to preserve a hard-won and insecure order within the perimeter. The P version of the Deluge omits the distinction between clean and unclean. The reason is not just to be sought in the tidy mind of the author, who knew that these institutions were promulgated only later at Sinai. The distinctions come later because they are dispositions for healing the damaged world that has survived the catastrophe.

As was noted earlier, permission to eat meat and therefore to kill for food (Gen. 9:4–6) is a concession to the different conditions of life for the survivors. The postdiluvian creation is inaugurated under the sign of an indefectible covenant with all living creatures, including humans (Gen. 9:8–17). This universalist perspective is in marked contrast to the more ethnocentric and even xenophobic *Weltanschauung* (view of life) of Deuteronomy. P assigns a religious qualification to all humanity, in that all are in the divine image and all survivors of the Deluge are the recipients of a covenant long before Israel appears on the stage of history (Gen. 1:26–28; 9:8–17).

The cultured despisers of the priesthood also tended to overlook evidence for the same liberal approach in the Priestly legislation, for example, in the frequently repeated insistence that the same law holds for the native-born and the resident alien (e.g., Ex. 12:49; Lev. 16:29; Num. 9:14). In the so-called Holiness Code (Leviticus 17—26), care for the resident alien is enjoined on the basis of a collective memory of having shared the same dubious status:

> When an alien dwells with you in your land you shall do him no wrong.
> The alien who dwells with you shall be to you like those among you

who are native-born; you shall love him as yourself, for you yourselves
were aliens in the land of Egypt.

(Lev. 19:33–34)

In the context of antiquity in general, it would be easy to miss the remarkable liberality of this injunction. As Elias Bickerman observed, commenting
on this verse, an Athenian contemporary of Ezra would have been aston-
ished to hear that he had to love the metics.[53]

If the P version of the early history of humanity reflects the experience
of living in the more open and diverse world of the Diaspora, the narrative
cycles about the ancestors in Genesis 12—36 encode themes and concerns
related to the establishment of a new commonwealth after the "return to
Zion." A major concern of the Babylonian-Jewish immigrants was the re-
covery of real estate confiscated after the Babylonian conquest (Jer. 52:16;
Ezek. 11:14–15). To this concern corresponds the promise of land (Gen.
17:8; 35:12) and the progressive elimination of rival claimants to the land,
beginning with Lot and continuing with Ishmael and Esau. One of the few
extended P narratives in this section is the account of Abraham's purchase
of a plot of land near Hebron after negotiations reminiscent of land con-
tracts from the Neo-Babylonian period.[54] An issue not unrelated to property
rights was intermarriage between immigrants and local women, amply documented in Ezra-Nehemiah. In the P version, Jacob's journey to Mesopotamia was undertaken to avoid the kind of problems created by Esau's marriage to foreign women (Gen. 26:34–35; 27:46–28:9). A close reading of the
ancestral histories brings to light other paradigmatic aspects that can be related to the newly founded commonwealth of the Persian period.

Passing to the sojourn in Egypt, exodus, and wanderings, we move from
prehistory to the actual founding of the commonwealth. We do not know
that the priest-author had a definite date in mind, similar to the founding of
the State of Israel on May 14, 1948, but we begin to hear for the first time
of Israel as an assembly or congregation (ʿēdâ) at the celebration of the first
Passover (Exodus 12). We are reminded that the diaspora group, the běnê
haggôlâ, inaugurated their temple community in the same way (Ezra 6:19–
22). Other indications that P's wilderness assembly prefigures the Judean
polity under Persian rule are the inclusion of resident aliens (gērîm) who
have accepted circumcision (Ex. 12:48–49; Ezra 6:21); organization of the
Israelites in the wilderness according to the ancestral house (bêt ʾābôt; Ex.
12:3), a social unit characteristic of the postexilic period;[55] and the formula
for excommunication ("that person shall be cut off from the congregation
of Israel"; Ex. 12:15, 19; cf. Ezra 10:8). The material assistance provided will-
ingly by the Egyptians to the departing Israelites—a development for which

the reader is completely unprepared—also brings to mind the largesse bestowed on the Babylonian immigrants as they prepared to depart for Judah (Ex. 11:3; 12:36; Ezra 1:6).

A crucial moment in the P history is the revelation of the divine name to Moses. In what was originally an alternative version, the incident of the burning thornbush, this event took place in the wilderness of Midian to which Moses had to flee because Yahweh could not appear in Egypt, a land polluted by idolatry (Ex. 3:13–15). But for P, as for Ezekiel, the experience of exile had raised in an acute form the issue of worship, and therefore of the divine presence, outside of Israel. Hence the appearance of the divine effulgence (*kābôd*) to Ezekiel in Mesopotamia, to which corresponds P's version of the revelation of the divine name in Egypt (Ezekiel 1; Ex. 6:2–3, 28). In general terms, P reconciles the present with the past by tracing the stages by which the revelation of the divine name (Elohim–Shaddai–Yahweh) and the realization of the divine presence in the institutions of worship came about. With the celebration of Passover and preparation for leaving exile in Egypt, we have reached the penultimate stage in that process.

The main lines of the P account of the Sinai event can easily be isolated. Israel arrived on the first day of the third month, counting from the exodus, and departed processionally on the twentieth of the second month in the following year (Ex. 19:1; Num. 10:11). The latter date was chosen to accommodate those who had incurred ritual contamination and who therefore had to celebrate the delayed Passover as prescribed in Num. 9:1–14. Moses went up the mountain and had a vision in which were revealed detailed specifications for the construction and furnishing of the sanctuary, the cult to be carried out in it, and the cultic personnel who were to staff it (Ex. 24:15b–18a; 25—31). Like Gudea of Lagash,[56] he was also shown a model or blueprint (*tabnît*) of the sanctuary. Construction was to conclude with the celebration of Sabbath, first announced by Moses, then officially promulgated (Ex. 31:12–17; 35:1–3), though anticipated earlier in the wilderness (Ex. 16:4–30). The detailed account of the implementation of these instructions is probably the work of a priestly scholar anxious to make the point that the instructions retained their validity in spite of Aaron having compromised himself in the matter of the golden calf.

All of the enactments in Leviticus and the first part of Numbers (to Num. 10:28) are issued at Sinai. This is no place for a detailed commentary, but some further indications of a striving for inner cohesion within the P work as a whole should be noted. Thus the vision on the mountain takes place on the seventh day (Ex. 24:16), work on the sanctuary is followed by a day of rest (Ex. 31:12–17; 35:1–3), and worship can actually commence after the seven-day priestly ordination ceremony (Lev. 8:33; 9:1). The sanctuary is erected on the first day of the month, that is, New Year's Day (Ex. 40:1, 17), following on the New Year's Day of the first creation and of the emergence of the new world after the Deluge (Gen. 8:13).

The most notable and controversial feature of P's version of the Sinai event is the absence of any account of covenant making.[57] The standard explanation is that P is meant to be read as an expansion of existing narrative in which the making, breaking, and remaking of the covenant are described. According to this view, in other words, P never existed as an independent narrative. However, a major problem with this view of P as purely redactional is the highly distinctive structure of the P narrative in Genesis through Joshua, alluded to earlier in this chapter. It also fails to explain why at all important junctures of the story except this one, P has either a separate account of its own (e.g., the Abrahamic covenant, the call of Moses) or a significant contribution to a conflated version (e.g., the Deluge, the plagues). The absence of either at this point seems, therefore, to call for an explanation.

An explanation is, I believe, forthcoming after surveying the Priestly view of covenant as a whole. The first covenant was with the human and animal survivors of the Great Deluge (Gen. 9:8–17), and the first and only covenant with Israel was at the time of the ancestors (Gen. 17:1–21). Both are perpetual (*bĕrît 'ôlām*), meaning a type of covenant that does not require periodic renewal, as was generally the case. For P, all that is required is that God remember, and the time for remembering is when his people are in exile (Ex. 2:24; 6:5; Lev. 26:42, 45). This type of covenant is also distinctive in that, unlike the standard Deuteronomic version, God's fidelity is not contingent on the fulfillment of obligations encumbent on the human partner. In other words, P has moved away from the idea of contractual arrangements entered into with the Deity in the direction of an antecedent disposition or dispensation. And since the one covenant with Israel is chronologically prior to the promulgation of the ritual law and the setting up of the instruments of worship, the latter are to be considered not a performance on which the validity of the covenant depends but rather Israel's way of appropriating the offer implicit in the promissory covenant with Abraham.[58] According to this view, therefore, the point of the covenant is not to provide a theological grounding for moral obligation so much as to create a community united in worship.

In the account of the wanderings, the intent is to create a paradigm or model of the ideal polity for Israel, viewed from within the conceptual world of the Aaronite priesthood. The actual political and social reality to which the paradigm was meant to apply was the new commonwealth in the process of formation during the first century of Persian rule (say, from the edict of Cyrus in 538 to the arrival of Nehemiah in 445 B.C.E.). The recurring theme of divine guidance on the journey to the land points fairly clearly in this direction (Ex. 13:21–22; 40:34–38; Num. 9:15–23). The frequent complaints about conditions in the land could be taken to reflect what Babylonian Jews were hearing about the bleak social conditions in Judah, and the insistence that only the second generation would enter the land (Num. 14:20–28; 26:63–65) would fit that situation also.

The most explicit clue to the narrative as paradigmatic is the designation of Israel in the wilderness as a congregation (*'ēdâ*) or assembly (*qāhāl*), terms that appear to be used interchangeably. The former is by far the more common in P, but the latter also occurs and is the preferred designation in Ezra-Nehemiah for the elite diaspora community in the province of Judah (*běnê haggôlâ*).[59] The role of lay leaders and elders (*něśî'îm, zěqēnîm*) is acknowledged (e.g., Num. 1:44; 2:3; 16:1–2, 22), and both classes played an important role in Jewish communities in the Achaemenid Empire.

However, what above all is emphasized in P is, not surprisingly, the spiritual hegemony and prestige of the sanctuary priesthood. Challenges to that hegemony, whether originating with Levites or laity, are firmly suppressed. Authoritative guidance is to be sought in the sanctuary where Moses received direct messages delivered from a space above the ark (Num. 7:89). The implementation of the priestly agenda is reinforced at critical junctures by the timely appearance of the *kābôd,* the divine effulgence, an interesting *theolological symbol* combining the ideas of divine presence and transcendence. Armed with divine authorization, community leaders could impose the strictest penalities, including the death penalty and the social death of exclusion from the assembly, for violation of the Sabbath command (Num. 15:32–36), blasphemy (Lev. 24:10–23), and mixed marriage (Lev. 24:10–23; Num. 25:6–15), this last of particular concern at the time of Ezra and Nehemiah.

We have seen that the P history ends with the setting up of the sanctuary at Shiloh, followed by the distribution of tribal territory (Joshua 18—19). In deference to political realities at the time of writing, the conquest history is omitted, though the Priestly hand is detectable at one or two points (Josh. 4:19; 5:10–12; 9:15–27). We are left with the overall impression of a well-thought-out conceptual system that required historiographical expression both to legitimate the system with its institutional embodiments and to display sequentially ideas about divine action on the world and, more specifically, on Israel.

THE SPATIAL AXIS: EARTH,
LAND, TEMPLE

The outline history of early humanity in Genesis 1—11 provides the clearest indication of the priest-author's participation in a learned mytho-graphical-historiographical tradition attested in the Near East and the Levant over many centuries. In its mature (or perhaps degenerate) form, this literary tradition is exemplified in the *Babyloniaka* of the Chaldean priest Berossus, commissioned by the Seleucid king Antiochus I around 280 B.C.E. As far as we can tell from the surviving fragments, a distinctive feature of this work is the linking of the history of Mesopotamian rulers with the archaic period, beginning with creation and the emergence of culture in the Euphrates Basin. Knowledge of the creation of the world was revealed by Oannes, first of the antediluvian seven sages (the *apkallu*) who emerged from the ocean. Ten kings ruled before and ten after the deluge, in which only Xisouthros (the Sumerian Ziusudra) survived with his kinsfolk and close friends. After the water had subsided, the writings that had been buried before the deluge in Sippar were recovered. By this means the knowledge and skills necessary for a new beginning were again made available.[60]

The *Babyloniaka* represents a fairly late version of a literary tradition very familiar to students of the ancient Near East. The pattern is reproduced in *Atraḫasis,* partially reconstructed from fragments dating from the seventeenth to the sixth century B.C.E.[61] As in the canonical creation poem *enuma elish,* it begins with a theogony and the rebellion of the lesser gods. The creation of humans, initially seven male and seven female, leads eventually to overpopulation and violence, which in turn induce the gods to take counteraction leading to a universal deluge lasting seven days and nights. Warned by his tutelary deity, Atraḫasis survives by building an ark, offers sacrifice on the purified earth, and leads humanity into a new phase of existence. As in the Sumerian king lists and the Gilgamesh epic, the great divide in early history is the deluge. Similar patterns and themes appear also in early Greek mythographic and logographic tradition, beginning with Hesiod in the eighth century B.C.E.[62]

There can be no doubt that the priest-author's history in Genesis 1—11 represents one version of that tradition, somewhere between *Atraḫasis* and the *Babyloniaka* but closer to the latter than to the former. Whatever cosmological learning is detectable in it derives, therefore, from access to that tradition. How extensive that learning was is very difficult to determine on the basis of such a succinct account as the P history in Genesis 1—11. The theosophical and cosmological speculations in the Enoch cycle, *The Book of Watchers* and the *Astronomical Book* in particular, are often read as wide-ranging exegetical developments of P's precise statement about the Enoch who walked with God and was not because God took him (Gen. 5:24). But this statement may just as plausibly be read as a succinct summary of speculations about this ancient worthy in circulation at the time of writing, speculations against which, as we suggested earlier, Ben Sira may have been polemicizing. In general, the P narrative material in the Pentateuch reads like an abridged version or precipitate of a much more extensive body of clerical learning, which, to the extent that it may have survived, lies buried in such apocryphal and pseudepigraphal writings as the Enoch cycle.

By appropriating an international literary tradition of great antiquity, the priest-author provided an appropriate introduction for the history of Israel following. Transition from the world to the land of Israel, from macrocosm to microcosm, was facilitated by the accident that the same word, *'ereṣ*, served for both "earth" and "land." Thus the command to subdue the earth (Gen. 1:28) links with the allusions to the land being subdued, which use the same substantive and the same verbal stem (*kbš*; Num. 32:22, 29; Josh. 18:1, both P). The work of separation or division carried out by God in creation is continued in the division of the land among the tribes (Lev. 20:24, 26; Num. 34:17, using the same verb). God has his Sabbath after the six days of creation, the land has its rest in the seventh year (Lev. 25:1–7), as also during the exile (Lev. 26:34–35, 43). In numerous ways, therefore, the creation prologue serves as a point of both departure and convergence for the various strands of the Priestly ideology.

In the thinking of the priest-author, the land of Israel embodies in a more intense and concentrated form the hallowing bestowed on the earth in the act of creation, and the sanctity of the land is concentrated in the highest degree in the sanctuary. This idea of gradated holiness, an essential feature of the priestly worldview, is expressed in spatial terms in the form of concentric circles or, alternatively, boxed squares, areas of diminishing sanctity as one moves away from the center. As a later midrash puts it:

> As the navel is situated at the center of the human being, so the land of Israel is the navel of the world, as it is written, "those who dwell at the navel of the earth" (Ezek. 38:12); the land of Israel is situated at the center of the world, Jerusalem at the center of the land of Israel, the sanctuary at the center of Jerusalem, the holy of holies at the center of the sanctuary, the ark at the center of the holy of holies, and the foundation stone, which marks the foundation of the world, is in front of the holy of holies.[63]

Laying claim to the center, the hub of the inhabited circle, is not, of course, peculiar to Israel. For the ancient Greeks, Delphi was the *omphalos,* the navel of the earth, and an early cuneiform map places Babylon at the center.[64]

These gradations of holiness along the spatial axis are set out schematically and in quadratic form in P's description of the wilderness camp (Num. 2:1–34; 10:13–28) and in Ezekiel's description of the visionary temple (Ezekiel 40—48). According to the latter, the Temple is five hundred cubits square and is situated at the center of the priests' domain, measuring twenty-five thousand by ten thousand cubits but protected by an open space, a kind of holy no-man's-land, fifty cubits wide. This domain forms one-half of a sacred area reserved for the Temple clergy, the other half belonging to the Levites, with a further band twenty-five thousand by five thousand cubits to the south for the city. This entire area formed a sacred *temenos* or precinct, a perfect square twenty-five thousand by twenty-five thousand cubits, at the center of the land. At this point, finally, the spatial dimension correlates with the temporal, since the vision occurs in the twenty-fifth year of the exile, halfway to the jubilee year of redemption (Ezek. 40:1).

The Mishnah has a rather different cartography, listing ten degrees of holiness in an ascending scale from the land of Israel to the Temple courts, the building itself, and, finally, the Holy of Holies (Mishnah *Kelim* 1:6–9).

It was part of the common theology of the ancient Near East that land was the property of the local deity—the Sumerian city of Lagash belonged to Ningirsu, Moab belonged to the national deity Kemosh, and so on. The land of Israel was therefore the property of Yahweh (Lev. 25:23; 27:30) and was ceded to Israel as a fief (Lev. 14:33–34; 20:24). The theoretical inalienability of patrimonial domain was a derivate of this theological feudalism (Lev. 25:23). The integrity of the borders of the land and therefore of the body politic must be protected in the same way that the laws of ritual cleanness and the dietary laws safeguarded the integrity of the physical body, whose borders are its various orifices. As we noted earlier, the body metaphor underlies much of what P has to say about the land. The land cannot ingest idolatry but must vomit out those who practice it (Lev. 18:25; 20:22). Uncleanness affects the land, whether rot or mold in buildings (Lev. 14:33–34), violation of the laws governing sexual relations (Lev. 18:25–28) or, most of all, the shedding of blood (Num. 35:33–34). The emphasis therefore is not on the independent possession of the land as an object of political aspirations, though that is not entirely foreign to the outlook of the Priestly narrative, but on the land as the proper and most congenial environment for the holy life.

The sanctuary was, in every respect, the central reality within the conceptual world of the priesthood during the biblical period and beyond. As noted earlier, the axial points of the history are the creation of the world, the construction of the wilderness sanctuary, and its erection at Shiloh after settlement in the land. Further along the same line, the seven years Solomon took to build the Temple (1 Kings 6:37–38) correspond to the seven days of creation. At this point, the temporal and spatial axes converge. Recent studies have drawn our attention to the topos of the Jerusalem temple as cosmic mountain, a familiar representation in many cultures and particularly in evidence in the Ugaritic texts.[65] The symbolic equivalence of cosmos and temple, creation and Temple building, are expressed in the questions God addressed to Job:

> Where were you when I established the earth?
> Tell me, if you are so clever!
> Who fixed its measurements—surely you know!
> Or who stretched the measuring line upon it?
> On what were its bases sunk?
> Or who laid the cornerstone
> when the morning stars sang together,
> and all the sons of God exulted for joy?
>
> (Job 38:4–7)

The cosmic symbolism of temple architecture, furnishings, and decoration is also well attested. In describing the wilderness sanctuary and the Jerusalem temple, both Josephus and Philo note a range of symbolic correspondences: the menorah represents the heavenly bodies, the twelve oxen supporting the laver stand for the signs of the zodiac, the laver itself is the cosmic ocean, the two columns Jachin and Boaz are the sun and moon, the colors of the high priest's vestments represent the four elements, and so on. The tripartite architectural plan, apparently based on a Phoenician blueprint, also lent itself to cosmic symbolizing, according to which the inner sanctum, or Holy of Holies, corresponded to the heavens; the main hall to the earth; and the entrance porch to the circumfluent ocean.[66] To enter the Temple and take part in the Temple cult is therefore to participate in some degree in the unceasing worship going on in heaven (e.g., Isa. 6:1–5).

One can think of several reasons why this kind of symbolic construct would not be found congenial today. It has little in common with what is generally considered to be the mainstream intellectual tradition, the agenda of which was set by the ancient Greeks. Its emphasis on the spatial and temporal, on the concrete (bodily states, food, corpse contamination, etc.), contrasts too starkly with the typical Christian concern for internal, spiritual states and makes it easy to dismiss it as unscientific, magical, and materialistic. The Priestly synthesis certainly embodies a different idea of rationality, in part because of the social situation in which it originated, that is, a temple state ruled by a hegemonic priestly class, which situation was totally different from the social world of the polis in which Greek philosophy flourished. The Judean temple state eventually passed away, but not without bequeathing important elements of the synthesis to the future.

SOME PROVISIONAL CONCLUSIONS

After the destruction of the Temple by the Romans in 70 C.E., there was no longer any scope for the exercise of the priestly role, though no doubt a good number of priests of different kinds survived the civil war, the revolt, and the prolonged siege of the city. But by that time the majority of Jews lived in the Diaspora and had no contact with the Temple and its priesthood except payment of dues for the support of the now-unemployed clergy (Mishnah *Shekalim* 8:8). And even Palestinian Jews had been prepared for the abolition of the sacrificial system by the institution of the synagogue or "house of prayer" (*proseuchē*), established wherever Jewish communities were to be found. Long before the disaster of the civil war and the revolt, instruction in the law and prayer had assumed a greater role in the religious life of the Jew than sacrifice, and the tradition of actual opposition to the sacrificial system dated back further still.[67] Once it became possible to articulate and carry out the essential elements of belief and practice without reference to the priesthood, Judaism was well on its way to becoming a lay religion.

Ironically, Christianity, which began as a lay movement within Palestinian Judaism—a movement that had its prophets but no priests—evolved quite rapidly in the direction of a hierarchical and clerical structure, though not without protest and opposition. Tension between the clerical and lay elements has been a feature of the history of Christianity to the present.

By the time of the fall of Jerusalem, in any case, the priesthood had made its contribution. The role of the priest could, with that of the sage, merge into the rabbinic leadership of the Tannaitic period, while the intellectual legacy of the priesthood, an impressive achievement, as we have seen, became part of the mainstream of Jewish culture.

Chapter 3

The Prophet

THE DEFINITIONAL PROBLEM

When readers of the Bible use the term *prophecy,* they probably have in mind the fifteen books attributed to prophetic authorship known as the Latter Prophets. But many other prophetic figures are named throughout the Hebrew Bible—fifty-five, including seven female prophets, according to a baraita (saying) in the Talmudic tractate *Megilla* (*b. Megilla* 14a). Moreover, the earliest of the Latter Prophets, Amos and Hosea, are dated by most scholars to the eighth century B.C.E., and both refer to prophetic predecessors who can be traced back some three centuries. During the entire course of the history, a great number of different types of individuals and roles have been subsumed under the rubric of prophecy, which greatly complicates the task of coming up with an adequate definition of the phenomenon. The problem will be more severe still if we take a comparativist approach to prophecy, if only because we must first decide on criteria that will guide our selection of comparable phenomena and types from other cultures; and on what basis do we elaborate our criteria in the first place? The value of comparative data is also greatly reduced when, as often happens, no serious attempt is made to understand the phenomenon in question as a precipitate of the society in which it functions, a fortiori when the differences between that society and ancient Israel are overlooked.[1]

In this chapter we nevertheless make use of comparative data where available to illustrate, sometimes by contrast, one or another aspect of prophecy in Israel. To reduce the possibility of distortion, we limit our choice to ancient examples from the same general culture area as Israel, namely, the Near Eastern–Levantine region.

One of the best-known definitions of prophecy is that of Max Weber, occurring in the chapter on "Religious Groups" in his masterwork *Wirtschaft und Gesellschaft.*[2] In spite of his brilliance, Weber had the same problem as any other student of prophecy, namely, where to start. To explain his strategy, we must return to the concept of the *ideal type,* discussed earlier in our study.[3] It will be recalled that, for Weber, an ideal type is a construct based on abstraction and conceptualization that has the purpose of guiding inquiry back into the mass of available data. Weber's ideal types were not intended to be normative. They served as a means of provisional classification, allowing for some preliminary understanding of the phenomenon, creating and testing hypotheses, distinguishing between constants and variables, and identifying deviations.

On this basis, then, Weber defined the prophet as "a purely individual bearer of charisma, who by virtue of his mission proclaims a religious doctrine or divine commandment."[4] The elements considered essential, the constants, are therefore the possession of charisma, a distinctive mission, and a specifically religious message. Weber borrowed the term *charisma* from early Christian literature as a way of encapsulating the irreducibly personal and nonascriptive element (i.e., an element not assigned by society) in social interaction, especially in the exercise of leadership roles. It is defined as "a certain quality of an individual personality by virtue of which he is set apart from ordinary men and treated as endowed with supernatural, superhuman, or at least specifically exceptional powers or qualities."[5] The possession of this elusive quality and its acknowledgment by the prophet's public—an essential concomitant—serve to legitimate the status, claims, and mission of the prophet. It will generally be manifested in miraculous or at least remarkable demonstrations of power that, again, must be interpreted in a positive sense by the society, or a segment of the society, in which the prophet functions.

The prophet is distinguished from other religious specialists, the priest in particular, by being called to a mission rather than simply occupying an office. In prosecuting that mission, the prophet disdains remuneration, relying instead on voluntary gifts from devotees and the public in general. Another distinguishing mark, in contrast to the legislator, teacher of ethics, religious reformer, or mystic leader, is the element of vital emotional preaching. In this respect, Weber even speaks of Israel's prophets as demagogues and pamphleteers. At this point of his exposition, however, he seems to have narrowed the focus to the emissary type, which he considered to be characteristic of Israel, as opposed to the exemplary type in which the individual's way of life is the message. The latter type, exemplified in the Buddha, Weber took to be characteristic of India, though in fact both types are attested in the history of Israel, as we shall see.

Weber's third criterion, the proclamation of a religious doctrine or divine commandment, implies that prophecy is to be considered an essentially religious phenomenon, and in fact, Weber offers no examples of secular prophets. This is in keeping with his strong assessment of the social impact of religion in general. What is emphasized at this point is the consciousness of divine mandate together with innovation; hence the prophetic status of the founders of religion—Moses, Zoroaster, Jesus, Muhammad.

We need hardly add that Weber's writing on prophecy and charisma has been the object of a considerable body of criticism. Some have found his theory of charisma set too much in opposition to institutions and too closely tied to extraordinary individuals. For Dorothy Emmett, for example, it smacks too much of the cult of the "great man," what she calls the *Führerprinzip,*[6] though this is to overlook what Weber has to say about the routinization of charisma in institutions. Others have complained that Weber gives little attention to communal prophecy of the kind that flourished in the early period of Israel's history. This is not quite true either, since he does write about charismatic communities based on an emotional form of communal relationship, without hierarchy, promotion through the ranks, and administrative apparatus. And in his monograph on *Ancient Judaism,* he gave due consideration to communal prophetic phenomena in the chapter dealing with war prophecy, Nazirites, and those "plebeian technicians of orgiastics" referred to in biblical narrative as "sons of the prophets," that is, members of prophetic conventicles or communities.[7]

Weber also drew our attention to the important juncture at which authority passes from the charismatic leader to a successor, the point of departure for his concept of the routinization (*Veralltäglichung*) of charisma.[8] The classic instance is the transfer of prophetic authority from Elijah to his disciple Elisha (2 Kings 2:9–18). Elisha requests a double portion of Elijah's spirit, that is, the portion due literally to the firstborn or metaphorically to the principal disciple. The transfer, as Elijah points out, is fraught with difficulty and can be accomplished only if the disciple gives proof of extraordinary gifts, such as the gift of second sight. In other words, Elisha must see him as he is taken up. He does so, and later he uses the master's cloak to divide the River Jordan; in other words, he proves that the transfer of charisma has really taken place by working miracles. His new status must also be verified and accepted by a public, in this instance the representatives of the ecstatic cenobia (members of religious communities) who acknowledge that "the spirit of Elijah rests on Elisha" (2 Kings 2:15).

Charisma is therefore not merely an individual and certainly not an incommunicable phenomenon, and its transfer involves more than an individual originator and recipient. Elijah, for example, is addressed as "father" (2 Kings 2:12); he is the acknowledged charismatic leader or abbot of the "sons of the prophets," and the same title will be given to Elisha as he presides over their assemblies, rather like the sheik who presides over the dervish *takiyyah* (2 Kings 13:14). The difficulty of sustaining charismatic leadership once the originator passes from the scene is particularly clear in the different versions of the commissioning of Joshua as successor to Moses. According to the Priestly version this took place during the trek through the wilderness, and the event was at one time followed by the original account of the death of Moses (Num. 27:12–23). While in this passage Joshua possesses the spirit (*rûaḥ*) before the ritual laying on of hands (*sĕmîkâ*) by Moses, in a revised version from a later member of the same Priestly school, Joshua is filled with the spirit of wisdom *as a result of* the ritual act by which he was installed in office (Deut. 34:9). Charisma, therefore, has become a purely formal element in a theology of ecclesiastical office.

Whatever its problems and shortcomings may have been, the Weberian comparativist approach to prophecy at least opened up perspectives beyond the theological and confessional presuppositions that controlled the study of Israelite prophecy during the nineteenth and the early twentieth centuries. One of the major achievements of the historical-critical method in the nineteenth century was the rediscovery of prophecy as a distinct form of religious experience and expression. The method was used to sort out the utterances of the prophets from editorial accretions and thus identify their authentic message. As it emerged from the work of Heinrich Ewald, Bernhard Duhm, Julius Wellhausen, and a host of lesser luminaries, the result was a composite portrait of a religious individualist (the term *religious genius* occurs often in the literature of that time), a recipient of an unmediated or direct revelation from God, a preacher of a spiritual and ethical religion in opposition to contemporary religious institutions, especially the sacrificial system; in other words, the prototype of the liberal Protestant. This profile had a significant impact on theology and church life (e.g., in the social gospel movement), but it also entailed some severe limitations.

The development of sociological theory and the rise of the history of religions school opened up new perspectives for the study of Israelite prophecy. One of the first to bring comparative data to bear on the subject was Gustav Hölscher, whose pioneering study *Die Propheten* appeared in 1914.[9] Hölscher argued that ecstatic prophecy was characteristic of the agrarian societies of Asia Minor and the Levant and that therefore the early Israelite variety must have been taken over from the indigenous population of Canaan. In spite of the fact that the data supporting this conclusion were, and still are, extremely sparse (consisting of an incident in the Egyptian story of Wen-Amon, preserved on papyrus Golenisheff, and the account of the Baalist prophets on Mount Carmel in 1 Kings 18), his thesis opened a new line of inquiry that was followed up by a number of scholars, including Theodore Robinson, Alfred Jepsen, and Johannes Lindblom.[10] We conclude, then, that comparative data have a corroborative, corrective, or contextualizing role to play, but that the main weight must lie with a careful analysis of the different social forms and functions of prophecy in Israel and the different roles prophets were called upon to play.

SOURCES FOR THE STUDY OF
ISRAELITE PROPHECY

With the exception of an inscribed potsherd from Lachish, written shortly before the fall of Jerusalem in 587 B.C.E. (to be considered in due course), the Hebrew Bible is our sole *direct* source of information on Israelite prophecy. We assume that the Hebrew Bible is a product of the Second Temple period and that it inevitably reflects the concerns of that time and the ideology of the religious and intellectual elite responsible for its final redaction. We should therefore be prepared to find that the historical phenomenon of prophecy is presented in a way consistent with the perspective of that elite. We also note that the term *prophet* (Hebrew, *nābî'*) has undergone a semantic broadening and standardization, becoming progressively more inclusive to the point where it can apply, inter alia, to teacher of ethics, writer of apocalyptic material, historian, and composer of liturgical music. In fact, we arrive at the point where practically any significant figure cherished in the tradition can be designated a prophet.[11]

The most important biblical sources are: (1) Deuteronomy and the national history from the death of Moses to the Babylonian exile known as the Deuteronomic history (Dtr); (2) the collection of fifteen prophetic books, the nucleus of which may have been put together as a supplement to Dtr; (3) the history comprising 1–2 Chronicles, Ezra, and Nehemiah, from the late Persian or early Hellenistic period, of value chiefly for ideas about prophecy current at the time of writing; (4) narrative in the Pentateuch in which several figures from the remote past are either called prophets (*nĕbî'îm*) or described as acting prophetically—Abraham (Gen. 20:7), Moses (Deut. 18:15–18; 34:10), Miriam (Ex. 15:20), Balaam (Numbers 22–24). Postbiblical sources, including such paraphrases of biblical history as the *Jewish Antiquities* of Josephus, rarely add anything of historical value. None of the information supplied by any of these written sources can be taken at face value. Unlike the Lachish ostracon (an inscription in clay) mentioned earlier, which alludes to a prophet delivering a letter during the advance of the Babylonian army on Jerusalem, all are colored by either the presuppositions of the writer or ideas about prophecy current at the time of writing.

Preeminent among the biblical sources is Dtr. There is now broad agreement that a first draft of this historical work was composed a few decades before the fall of Jerusalem, perhaps during the reign of Josiah (640–609 B.C.E.), and the final edition around the middle of the sixth century, in response to the political disasters of the extinction of the Judean state and subsequent deportations. The Deuteronomic school also had a hand in editing prophetic books, conspicuous among these Jeremiah. Deuteronomy itself is regarded as a kind of theological preface to the history, and an increasing amount of narrative material in Genesis and Exodus is being attributed to the same source. It seems that these people had very definite ideas about prophecy. The program laid out in homiletic and legal form in Deuteronomy constitutes, in effect, the first attempt to impose an orthodoxy, and Dtr reconstructs the past in keeping with this orthodoxy. To understand anything at all about the historical phenomenon of prophecy, we have to get behind this ideological barrier, and therefore it would be helpful to understand it.

Deuteronomy contains the first attempt to reflect more or less systematically on prophecy. The first mention of prophets in the book brackets them with those who divine by means of dreams and stipulates that prophets who encourage the cult of deities other than Yahweh are subject to the death penalty, even if their predictions turn out to be correct (13:2–6 [13:1–5]). Later in the book, Israelite prophecy is contrasted with techniques of divination, including necromancy, common in surrounding lands. (They were also commonly practiced in Israel, but this is not mentioned.) The claim seems to be that prophecy is different from these other forms of mediation and, as defined by the author, is a uniquely Israelite phenomenon. Prophets continue the role and activity of Moses the protoprophet, and the origins of prophecy are to be sought in the people's request for a mediating agency at Sinai/Horeb (Deut. 18:15–19; cf. Ex. 20:18–21; Deut. 5:23–29). The chief function of the prophet is therefore to promulgate the law, preach its observance after the manner of Moses, and transmit it to posterity. A secondary function is the prediction of the future, which, when successful, can serve to validate the prophet's mission (Deut. 18:20–22).

Since Deuteronomy provides the ideological basis for and the theological key to the meaning of the history (Dtr), it is no surprise that the prophets mentioned throughout the history serve to illustrate the Deuteronomic "doctrine" on prophecy. The point may be illustrated by the historian's reflec-

tive comment on the conquest of Samaria by the Assyrians and the deportation of its inhabitants:

> Yahweh had warned Israel (and Judah) by means of every prophet and
> seer: turn from your evil ways and observe the commandments and
> statutes as found in all of the law which I prescribed for your forbears
> and which I also sent to you through my servants the prophets.
>
> (2 Kings 17:13)

A reading of the entire passage (2 Kings 17:7–20) suggests that the original
version of this comment on the fall of Samaria, belonging to the first, late-
preexilic edition of the history, was amplified some sixty or seventy years
later to take in the collapse of the Judean state. The prophetic task is therefore to proclaim the law and to predict the consequences of ignoring or con-
travening it and, by so doing, to exonerate the Deity of responsibility for
bringing about these disasters.

This view of prophecy is also retrospective; it implies that prophecy, or
at least this kind of prophecy, essentially belongs to the past. Hence the frequent occurrence in the Deuteronomic oeuvre of the expression "his servants the prophets" (*'ăbādāw hannĕbî'îm*), referring to the prophetic succession as a whole viewed as replicating the office of God's servant Moses.[12]

What we find, then, in Deuteronomy and Dtr is a retrospective view on
prophecy and a redefinition of the phenomenon by associating it directly
with the law and with Moses as lawgiver; a shift, therefore, from historical
involvement to law, from *Geschichtsprophetie* to *Rechtsprophetie*.[13] This is
the beginning of the semantic expansion referred to earlier, for the promise
of a Moses-like prophet in Deut. 18:15–18 must cover the entire historical
continuum from the death of Moses to the extinction of the kingdoms.
Joshua must therefore be presented as the first of these prophetic "servants"
(Josh. 24:28), his military activities must not interfere with his study and application of the law (Josh. 1:8; 23:6–8), and he will even successfully predict exile as punishment for nonobservance (23:15–16). After Joshua's
death, his place is taken by those charismatic leaders raised up by Yahweh
whose exploits are recorded in the Book of Judges; and it is consistent with
the thesis of an uninterrupted prophetic succession that during this entire
period there is no mention of prophets as a distinct category, with the single exception of Deborah, who is both "judge" and prophet (Judg. 4:4). The
career of Samuel marks the decisive transition from "judge" to prophet in
the stricter sense, and with the advent of the monarchy there begins the descending spiral of infidelity, prophetic denunciation, and the fulfillment of
the prophetic word of doom.

A peculiar feature of Dtr is that it mentions a great number of prophets and speaks at length about several of them (conspicuously Elijah and Elisha), yet has practically nothing to say about the canonical Latter Prophets, those to whom books are attributed. Second Kings 18:13–20:19 contains prophetic legends about Isaiah in his relations with Hezekiah that have been copied into the Book of Isaiah (chapters 36—39), perhaps because they end with the prediction of exile in Babylon and therefore prepare for the exilic section of the book. But the protagonist of these legends is a very different figure from the author of the condemnatory oracles in Isaiah 1—39. The only other allusion in the history is to the prophet Jonah ben Amittai, who gave aid and comfort to Jeroboam II in his reconquest of occupied Israelite territory (2 Kings 14:25). Curiously, the account of Jeroboam's reign makes no mention of Amos, presumed to be active at that time (Amos 1:1; 7:9–11), unless he is referred to cryptically, and disparagingly, in the historian's comment that "Yahweh had not said that he would blot out the name of Israel from under heaven" (2 Kings 14:27). Amos did say something of this kind (Amos 9:8), and the comment is clearly polemical.[14]

Since it seems unlikely that the historian was unfamiliar with prophets active up to the time of writing, it may be that the original nucleus of Latter Prophets was put together as a supplement to the history. If so, we can only speculate on the contents of this first prophetic "canon." Titles that date a prophet's activity to synchronized reigns (Hosea, Amos) or to a ruler of Judah after the fall of Samaria (Isaiah, Jeremiah, Micah, Zephaniah) are sometimes referred to a Deuteronomic editor. For the rest, we have to rely on the uncertain procedure of identifying Deuteronomic language and themes in prophetic books. It is also arguable that the Deuteronomists thought in terms of a prophetic succession from Moses, the protoprophet (Deut. 18:15–18; 34:10), to Jeremiah, last of "his servants the prophets." The commissioning of Moses has much in common with that of Jeremiah (Ex. 3:1–4:17; Jer. 1:4–19), and the forty years of activity assigned to Jeremiah by the (Deuteronomic) editor, corresponding to the period 627–587 B.C.E. (Jer. 1:2–3), brings to mind the forty years in the wilderness and the forty days and nights Moses spent on the mountain. In spite of Jeremiah's denunciation of "handlers of the law" (2:8) and those who claimed to be wise by virtue of possessing a written law (8:8–9), the Deuteronomic editors of the book succeeded in aligning him with their redefinition of prophecy.

The extensive refashioning of the Jeremiah material is only one example of the problems involved in reconstructing the social situations in which prophets and prophetic groups carried on their activities and the roles that they assumed. Prophetic books were not protected by copyright. Sayings and collections of sayings were recycled to meet the needs of later generations of hearers or readers. We have spent some time on the Deuteronomic theory of prophecy and redefinition of the prophetic role because, in this respect as in others, Deuteronomic orthodoxy constitutes the first systematic attempt to reconstruct the past in its own image. Deuteronomic ideology was not, of course, the only factor shaping the understanding and practice of prophecy. In other circles prophetic sayings were being reinterpreted according to an eschatological and transhistorical worldview, a process clearly detectable in Isaiah. It will therefore be no easy task to work upstream through these various redactions and transformations to get at original social situations, identities, and roles. But, unfortunately, there is no alternative, and we can only hope that the results, however modest, justify the effort.

We have seen that the only nonbiblical texts bearing directly on Israelite prophecy are the Lachish ostraca, which mention a prophet who served as an intermediary in delivering a letter (ostracon 3:20). Elsewhere in this batch of ostraca, a prophet (*nb'*) is mentioned whose name, like that of Jeremiah (Yirmeyahu), ends in *-yahu,* but nothing is said about him (ostracon 16:5). According to a widely accepted restoration of the defective text of ostracon 6:5, an unnamed prophet was undermining morale in the period shortly before the Babylonian conquest. The complaint is couched in terms similar to accusations directed at about the same time against Jeremiah (e.g., Jer. 38:4). If the textual restoration is correct, the reference could be to Jeremiah, or at least to a prophet who belonged to the same party of appeasement as did Jeremiah.[15]

Texts dealing with prophets from other parts of the culture area to which Israel belonged, including the inscribed limestone plaster fragments from Deir 'Alla referring to Balaam the seer, will be discussed where relevant as our inquiry proceeds.

PROPHETIC ROLE LABELS

In common with other Near Eastern texts, the Hebrew Bible has an impressive number of designations for religious specialists. In the preceding chapter, we had occasion to discuss several involved at different levels in the operation of more or less permanent cultic enterprises, from priests to temple slaves. As far as we know, all of these specialist roles were occupied by males. The same is not the case with the quite different though overlapping set of role labels to which the prophet belongs. As we survey and briefly comment on this list of designations, it is important to bear in mind that they occur in sources which contrast them with prophecy and regard most of them as illegitimate even if efficacious. This is especially clear in Deut. 18:9–22. However, all the indications are that, in Israel as elsewhere, recourse to these practitioners and the associated techniques of mediation were a normal feature of the culture.

The terms most frequently occurring in association with the *nābî'* (prophet) are *rō'eh* (seer), *ḥōzeh* (visionary), and *'îš 'ĕlōhîm* (man of God). In addition, the Deuteronomic scribe gives us a list of eight types, which he presents as characteristically foreign and contrasts with native prophecy but which, in reality, belong to the same set and were a familiar part of popular religion (Deut. 18:10–11). The list, with approximate translations appended, is as follows:

> *qōsēm qĕsāmîm*—practitioner of divination
> *mĕʻônēn*—soothsayer
> *mĕnaḥēš*—augur
> *mĕkaššēp*—sorcerer
> *ḥōbēr ḥeber*—caster of spells, wizard
> *šōʼēl ʼôb*—one who consults ghosts
> *yiddĕʻōnî*—medium
> *dōrēš ʼel-hammētîm*—one who consults the dead, necromancer

These labels call for a brief comment.

rō'eh (seer) At the urging of a servant, Saul conferred with a *rō'eh*, also referred to as a *'îš 'ĕlōhîm* (man of God), about his wayward donkeys. The seer in question is not at first named but turns out to be none other than Samuel (1 Sam. 9:1–10:16). The seer is therefore one gifted with second sight or extrasensory perception. We learn that, like the Arabic *kahin,* the *rō'eh* expected to receive a fee for his services (1 Sam. 9:7–8; see also Num. 22:7; 1 Kings 14:3). He also carried out rituals at the numerous *bāmôt* (high places) around the country and appears to have had permanent residence in a town or village, in contrast to the itinerant *'îš 'ĕlōhîm*. The story about Saul, the donkeys, and the kingship is the only account we have of an Israelite seer, though a different regional type is represented by Balaam, whose activities and oracles are recorded, with much editorial overlay, in Numbers 22—24.

A solicitous editor has added a note to the Saul story to the effect that the one now (at the time of writing) called a prophet (*nābî'*) was then known as a seer (*rō'eh*). The note is added to 1 Sam. 9:9 but would more naturally follow 9:11, where *rō'eh* first occurs. This bit of information confirms a point made earlier, that *nābî'* became a catch-all term applied to a wide range of persons and roles.

ḥōzeh (visionary) A distinction between *rō'eh* and *ḥōzeh,* the latter of more frequent occurrence, is not easy to detect, and it is not always possible to distinguish clearly between the *ḥōzeh* and the *nābî'* either. Visionaries are often bracketed with seers (e.g., Isa. 30:10) and with prophets (2 Kings 17:13; Isa. 29:10; Micah 3:7), without any attempt being made to distinguish between them. In the account of Amos's run-in with the priest in charge at Bethel, the latter addresses him as *ḥōzeh,* but Amos replies by denying that he is a *nābî';* and the passage in question assumes that both *ḥōzeh* and *nābî'* engage in the same activity, namely, "prophesying" (Amos 7:12–15). At David's court, Gad is described as a *ḥōzeh* (1 Sam. 22:5; 2 Sam. 24:11) and his colleague Nathan as a *nābî'* (2 Sam. 7:2; 12:25; 1 Kings 1:8), from which, however, we may not deduce that they had distinct functions, much less that Nathan, *qua nābî',* must have been an Ephraimite.[16]

On the subject of distinct regional usage, we can at least conclude that *ḥōzeh* had wide currency in Jerusalemite Second Temple circles. The content of three prophetic books—Isaiah, Obadiah, Nahum—is described under the rubric of vision (*ḥāzôn*), and the activity of three other prophets—Amos, Micah, Habbakuk—is described, also in the titles, as being of the visionary kind. With few exceptions (1 Chron. 9:22; 2 Chron. 16:7–10), the author of Chronicles refers to inspired intermediaries as "visionaries" (*ḥōzîm*), appeals to (alleged) sources composed by authors belonging to the same category (2 Chron. 9:29; 12:15; 19:2), and puts the temple musician guilds founded by David into the same class (1 Chron. 25:5; 2 Chron. 29:30; 35:15). Choice of this title at that time and in those circles may be due to the low esteem into which the *něbî'îm* had fallen, to judge by their role during Nehemiah's administration (Neh. 6:7,10–14) and a denunciation of exceptional ferocity in a contemporary prophetic text (Zech. 13:2–6).[17]

'îš 'ĕlōhîm (man of God) This is another term that underwent a process of decontextualization, since, beginning with the Deuteronomists, it could describe great personalities of the past such as Moses (Deut. 33:1; Josh. 14:6; Ps. 90:1; etc.) and David (2 Chron. 8:14; Neh. 12:24, 36). In these cases the meaning is not significantly different from *nābî'.* In the early period *'îš 'ĕlōhîm* was in currency among ordinary people such as servants (1 Sam. 9:6, 8), soldiers (2 Kings 1:9–16), and pious women (1 Kings 17:18, 24; 2 Kings 4:9, 16). The general idea was of a person of preternatural and

potentially dangerous power; recall, for example, how Samson's mother, cowed by the awe-inspiring appearance of her heavenly visitor, took him to be a man of God (Judg. 13:6, 8). In this sense the term is used of Samuel (1 Samuel 9), Elijah (1 Kings 17:18, 24; 2 Kings 1:9–16), Elisha (2 Kings 4:1–37), and several other named and unnamed prophetic figures who make a brief appearance in the history. While most of these were active in the central highlands of Canaan, usage may not have been limited to this region, and there is no indication of a cultic connection.[18] All of these individuals were male, and therefore no "woman of God" (*'ēšet 'ĕlōhîm*) is attested, a circumstance probably due to the social conditions, especially itinerancy, in which these people operated.[19]

The deeds, especially the miraculous ones, of this kind of extraordinary individual are at home in the genre of *legenda sanctorum,* (stories of sacred persons), a comparative study of which will reveal many structural and thematic similarities. One thinks of the *Life of Anthony* by Athanasius, accounts of the "divine man" (*theios anēr*) in Late Antiquity, or tales of Hasidic masters.[20]

qōsēm qĕsāmîm (practitioner of divination) This first of the roles condemned in Deuteronomy appears to be the most inclusive and occurs in tandem with several others in the list (2 Kings 17:17; Jer. 27:9) as well as with priest, prophet, and oneiromantic (1 Sam. 6:2; Jer. 29:7; Ezek. 13:6; Micah 3:7; Zech. 10:2). The diviner, who expected to be paid for services rendered (Num. 22:7), could be male or female (Ezek. 13:23). We do not know much about techniques of divination in Israel, but whatever actions were performed eventuated in a message to the client, in which respect the *qōsēm* resembled the Babylonian *āpilu* (answerer). The Balaam narrative (Numbers 22—24) makes it clear that the *qōsēm* was also thought capable of inflicting psychic and physical harm, and no doubt often did.

mĕ'ônēn (soothsayer) None of the occurrences of this term provides much guidance as to its precise import (see Lev. 19:26; Deut. 18:10, 14; 2 Kings 21:6; Isa. 2:6; 57:3; Micah 5:11). The related activity is proscribed but was certainly familiar in Israel; witness the place name Elon Meonenim, "Diviners' Oak," in Judg. 9:37. A late passage in Isaiah (57:3–10) describes a female soothsayer or sorceress (*'ōnĕnâ*) who engages in sexual rites in the open, sacrifices children, and has commerce with the underworld.

mĕnaḥēš (augur) A kind of magic involving the manipulation of snakes (*nāḥaš*) is often suggested for this category, but without any basis in the few texts that mention it. From these (Gen. 30:27; 44:5, 15; 1 Kings 20:33) we can deduce only that it was a way of discovering secrets. Joseph was an adept, as also pharaoh who used a cup, perhaps in a way similar to reading tea leaves (Gen. 44:5, 15).

mĕkaššēp (sorcerer) While this term, like all of the others in the list, is masculine, most of the allusions to sorcery are to female practitioners (cf. the Akkadian *kaššaptu*), real or symbolic (Babylon, Isa. 47:9,12; Nineveh, Nah. 3:4, both represented as women). The loose association between sorcery and the transgressive woman (Jezebel, 2 Kings 9:22) comes to a head in the death penalty on the female but not the male practitioner, the *mĕkaššēpâ* (Ex. 22:17 [22:18]). At this stage we will not be surprised to discover that female sorcery posed a greater threat than the male variety.

ḥōbēr ḥeber (caster of spells, wizard) A *ḥōbēr* can be a snake charmer (Ps. 58:6) and, by analogy, one who uses sorcery to cast a spell or hex on people (cf. Isa. 47:9, 12). This seems to be the kind of activity attributed to the Judean "prophetesses" by Ezek. 13:17–23, though the stem *ḥbr* does not occur. One of the standard connotations of the stem (joining, binding) also suggests a connection with binding and loosing by magical means.

šō'ēl 'ôb (one who consults ghosts) The term *'ôb* is used both for the ghost or spirit, often of an ancestor, and for the medium who conjures it up for a client. The witch of Endor is a *ba'ălat 'ôb* (1 Sam. 28:7), literally, a "mistress of the ghost," one who commands the spirits, a role that seems to have been predominantly female (Lev. 19:31; 20:6; 2 Kings 21:6; 23:24; Isa. 8:19; 19:3, in which *'ōbôt* and *yiddĕ'ōnîm,* presumably female mediums and male wizards, occur). After muttering incantations and conjurations (Isa. 8:19) and perhaps digging a pit, the medium relays the whisperings of the ghost, perhaps by ventriloquistic means (Isa. 29:4), to the client. Saul asked the witch of Endor to divine (*qsm*) for him by means of a ghost (*'ôb*) and conjure up the shade of Samuel. She did so, but it appears she was the only one who saw "*'ĕlōhîm* coming out of the underworld" (1 Sam. 28:13). This circumstance would naturally arouse suspicion of chicanery, but there is no indication that the efficacy of such actions was doubted at that time.[21]

yiddĕ'ōnî (medium) This term invariably occurs in tandem with *'ôb* and is usually associated with the verbal stem *yd',* "to know," but whether the "knowing one" is the spirit or the one who commands the spirit, that is, the medium or wizard, is disputed. Since, however, it makes sense to impose the death penalty on the latter but not on the former (Lev. 20:27), *yiddĕ'ōnî* must refer to a living practitioner of the necromantic arts.

dōrēš 'el-hammētîm (one who consults the dead, necromancer) The list ends as it begins, with a generic term that is self-explanatory.

It has become customary to classify these roles and activities under the rubric of mediation, and of a type somewhat different from that of the priest. The difference is not, however, one between magic and religion, since the element of coercion can be present in different degrees in the activities characteristic of either necromancer or priest. It is more a matter that the priest is engaged in the operation of a fixed and permanent cultic enterprise, while appeal to soothsayers and the like is sporadic, at least at the level of social development attained in Israel under the monarchy.

Whatever the original derivation and meaning of the term *nābî'*,[22] it did not designate a role and corresponding activity entirely distinct from the series we have been considering. Why the Deuteronomic authors took it out of the series in order to emphasize its uniquely Israelite status can be understood in the context of the work as a whole. One of the basic aims of Deuteronomy *qua* state document was to undermine the established lineage system and the popular religious practices that undergirded it. Many of these revolved around the cult of the ancestors and communication with the world of the spirits that the ancestors, still integrated into the clan structure, inhabited. The Deuteronomic emphasis on the distinctiveness of Israel's religious life and the uniqueness of her institutions—for example, the intellectual tradition (Deut. 4:5–8) and the monarchy (17:14–20)—would also explain the proscription of aspects of religious life (e.g., divination, necromancy) popular throughout the entire culture area. According to the Deuteronomists, therefore, the prophet is elevated from a rather peripheral location in society to the status of spokesman (less commonly, spokeswoman) for a central morality religion.

The broadening of the semantic range of the term *nābî'* raises serious questions about the identity and role of the fifteen to whom prophetic books are attributed. None of these fifteen ever refers to himself as a *nābî'*, and only three—Habakkuk, Haggai, and Zechariah—are so designated in the superscriptions to their books. Isaiah is called a *nābî'* exclusively in the prophetic legends taken from Dtr (Isa. 37:2; 38:1; 39:3), which feature a very different type from the Isaianic version of the sayings. Jeremiah bears the title only in narrative passages, including the narration of his commissioning (Jer. 1:5), one of many passages betraying Deuteronomic style and ideology. The prophetic status of Ezekiel is referred to only obliquely (Ezek. 2:5). Amos appears to disavow the title (Amos 7:14), while Micah sets his own endowment with power and the spirit in deliberate contrast to contemporary prophets and seers (Micah 3:5–8). A further complication is introduced with the generally violent attack directed against the *nĕbî'îm* by several of the persons to whom books are attributed (Isaiah, Jeremiah, Ezekiel, Micah, Zephaniah), which leaves us wondering whether they would have been happy to be themselves identified by the same designation.

PROPHECY IN ITS SOCIAL SETTING:
THE EARLIEST STAGE

Before drawing any conclusions of a general nature about social roles, we need to take account of developments and discontinuities in the social and political milieu in which prophets of different kinds operated. Classical prophecy is generally, though not universally, taken to begin with Amos around the middle of the eighth century B.C.E., a view that is often accompanied by categorizing earlier prophetic figures as primitives. However, as we go on to survey prophetic phenomena during this early period of about three centuries, it is best to eschew the language of primitive and classical. It is also necessary to reckon with the limitations of our sources, with respect to both what they do not tell us and the way in which what they do tell us has been shaped by the presuppositions and beliefs of a much later time.

We commented earlier on how the biblical history of prophecy is conformed to and structured by the ideology of the Deuteronomic school. After the death of Moses, Joshua is the first of the "servants" committed to carrying on the work and mission of Moses (Josh. 1:1; 24:29). The conquest of Canaan is launched after an exhortation to observe the law of Moses (Josh. 1:7–8), the native population is annihilated following prescriptions laid down in Deut. 7:1–6, and the fate of the Gibeonites is decided according to guidelines for conducting warfare in the same source (Joshua 9; Deut. 20:10–15). Consistently, therefore, as long as Joshua is alive there is no need for prophetic agents in the strict sense, and none is mentioned.

After the conquest, Joshua's place in the Mosaic succession is taken by a series of "judges" (*šōpĕṭîm*), who are "raised up" to ensure Israel's survival during the time of the settlement in the land. Some of these (Judg. 10:1–5; 12:8–15) are tribal leaders who carry out purely or primarily judicial functions, but the majority are warlords or the like, impelled to decisive action in response to external danger. Here, too, prophecy in the stricter sense is almost entirely absent, and for the same reason. Apart from Deborah, the sole exception is an unnamed prophet who delivers a short homily in the Deuteronomic manner, laying out the divine benefits bestowed on Israel and Israel's sadly inadequate response (Judg. 6:7–10). The last of these "judges" is Samuel, as he himself avers, incongruously in the context, in a valedictory speech to the people (1 Sam. 12:11). His career marks the transition from the judgeship to prophecy in the stricter sense of the term (1 Sam. 3:1, 19–21). The precise point of the transition occurs when his sons prove unworthy to follow in their father's footsteps by violating the Deuteronomic laws governing judicial activity (1 Sam. 8:1–3; cf. Deut. 16:18–20). A new dispensation is therefore called for, and from that point on, attention is focused on the relations between prophet and ruler, adumbrated in Samuel's designation and eventual rejection of Saul as king.

Though Weber did not engage in a thorough discussion of the function of *sōpēṭ* in his study of ancient Israelite society, the activities of these individuals fit his description of the ideal type of charismatic rule.[23] The authority wielded by them was strictly ad hoc, local, and sporadic. It is significant that when offered the kingship after a spectacular military success, Gideon/Jerubbaal appeared to accept the offer, to judge by his subsequent behavior, but declined *hereditary* rule for himself and his descendants (Judg. 8:22–28). By its very nature, the dynastic, hereditary principle would appear to rule out the charismatic; and the persistence of the idea of charismatic rule in the Northern Kingdom explains in good part the kingdom's political instability during the two centuries of its existence.

The Deuteronomic historian goes out of his way to emphasize the socially marginal origin of most of these "judges." The names of some of them (Shamgar ben Anath, Jerubbaal) suggest Canaanite stock; Jephthah was an outlaw and the son of a prostitute; Abimelech's mother was one of Jerubbaal's concubines. That the only one who qualifies as a prophet (*nĕbî'â*) is a woman, Deborah, may be because, being a woman, she had no standing in the agnatic-patriarchal order of the kinship network and so qualified for this socially exceptional function.[24] But the role of Deborah deserves a more careful scrutiny, and we shall come back to her in due course.

INDIVIDUAL FIGURES

Attaching the prophetic label to some figures in the tradition (e.g., Abraham, Moses) is clearly the outcome of the process of generalizing the use of the term, which was discussed earlier in this chapter. From other cases, however, some useful information may be retrieved. One of these is *Miriam,* sister of Moses and Aaron according to a late and probably fictitious genealogical consolidation. Like so many incidents recorded as happening on the trek through the wilderness, the protest of Miriam and Aaron against the exclusive religious authority of Moses is paradigmatic, reflecting conflict at some point of the history between prophets, female and male, and an elite claiming to stand in the line of direct descent from Moses (Numbers 12).

More to our immediate purpose is the account of Miriam the prophet (*nĕbî'â*), accompanied by a retinue of women, celebrating the victory at the Red or Reed Sea with song and dance (Ex. 15:20–21). The description seems to assume familiarity with inspired female dervishes who, like the Arabic *kahina,* accompany the troops into battle, provide enthusiastic moral support, and take the lead in celebrating the victory. In both Arabia and Israel, music, percussion (involving a *tôp* or small drum), and dancing were the means to achieve a state of mental dissociation. The capacity of certain types of music, especially percussion, to destabilize psychologically, to induce altered states of consciousness, is well attested in both ancient and modern cultures.[25] Music served at one time to dispel Saul's "evil spirit from Yahweh," perhaps a profound depression (1 Sam. 16:14–23), though it could also result in a "bad trip," as in the spear-throwing incidents (1 Sam. 18:10–11; 19:9–10). The ecstatic prophets encountered by Saul at Gibeah disposed of a small orchestra including, inevitably, drums (1 Sam. 10:5), and it is worth noting that when David pretended, for his own good reasons, to be out of his mind, he drummed on the city gates (1 Sam. 21:12–15). Elisha also made use of music as the occasion warranted (2 Kings 3:15). At a much later time, the activity of the liturgical guilds of musicians, and that of David as their founder, would be described as a form of prophesying (1 Chronicles 25).

The song of *Deborah,* judge and prophet, is generally considered one of the oldest poetic compositions in the Hebrew Bible (Judges 5). It may therefore be used, with caution, to illustrate the kind of situation liable to precipitate certain types of prophetic activity: sporadic warfare, social upheaval, brigandage, in short, a general state of anomie. These are precisely the conditions that favor the emergence of ad hoc warrior-chieftains, charismatic figures like the old Nordic berserks mentioned in this context by Weber.[26] Samson seems to fit this pattern, and perhaps also Barak, to judge by his name or nickname (= lightning). The tradition of war ecstasy, if that is what it is, was carried on by Saul and, in more spectacular fashion, by the usurper Jehu who put an end to the Omri dynasty in a bloodbath without parallel in Israelite history. Jehu was anointed king by an acolyte of Elisha, a member of an ecstatic conventicle who was taken to be a madman (*mĕšuggā'*; 2 Kings 9:11), and we recall that Jehu himself, a religious fanatic if ever there was one, was notorious for intemperate behavior, including dangerous chariot driving (9:20). His close association with the Rechabites (2 Kings 10:15–16) parallels Saul's connections with both the Nazirites (*nĕzîrîm*) and dervishes (*nĕbî'îm*), both passionately involved in the attempt to block the Philistine advance into the hill country.

Deborah is described as carrying out judicial activities at a well-known site in the central highlands. The very little we are told about her suggests that she fits the profile of a seer who mediates divine oracles, including, in this instance, a call to arms. Another seer caught up in warfare is *Balaam*, whose activities are reported, with much editorial overlay, in Numbers 22—24. We are told that he was from Pethor (Pitru), a locality on the upper Euphrates a few miles south of Carchemish. He may therefore have been of Mesopotamian origin, and in fact, he resembles in some respects the Mesopotamian *bārū* ("seer," from the verb *baru,* "see"), a religious specialist in such things as omens and curses. The Balaam of the plaster texts discovered at Deir 'Alla in Transjordanian Gilead in 1967, from the eighth century B.C.E., is a seer of the gods (*ḥzh 'lhn*) who receives a night vision of doomful import and communicates it to community representatives. Put together out of over a hundred fragments, this Aramaic text combines narrative and prophetic first-person speech, not unlike prophetic texts in the Hebrew Bible. What we learn of the Deir 'Alla Balaam is consistent with the biblical description of one "falling down and with [the inner] eyes uncovered" (Num. 24:4), the typical trance state of the mantic seer.[27]

The traditions about *Samuel* in 1 Samuel 1—19, rounded out with a posthumous appearance in 1 Samuel 28, have created severe and very probably insoluble problems for historical-literary criticism. The point was made earlier that, for the historian of the monarchy, Samuel's career marks the transition from judgeship to prophecy in the more specific sense, that is, from *šōpēṭ* to *nābî'*. The Samuel story begins with his conception, birth, and dedication as a kind of oblate or attendant (*mĕšārēt, na'ar*) at the temple at Shiloh, an important Ephraimite religious center between Bethel and Shechem. During an incubation ritual in the temple, he received a communication from Yahweh condemning the priesthood of the sanctuary, and we are told that this marked the beginning not only of his prophetic career but also of a new phase of prophetic activity (1 Sam. 1:1–4:1; especially 3:1; 3:21–4:1). It is worth noting that the summons in the dream or vision had to be repeated three times, reminiscent of the authentication of dreams of prophetic figures by threefold repetition in texts from the kingdom of Mari (eighteenth century B.C.E.).[28] Whatever the historicity of the account, it may well correspond to one way in which certain individuals were launched on a prophetic career. But beneath the surface of this apparently straightforward story we can make out, like the original writing on a palimpsest, a tradition about the infancy of Saul rather than about Samuel. This is apparent in the first place in the explanation of the name, in which the verbal stem *š'l* (request, ask) occurs three times, including the passive participle, *šā 'ûl* (1 Sam. 1:20, 28; 2:20), which clearly point to Saul, not to Samuel. The requirement that the child's hair remain uncut indicates that he is to be a Nazirite (*nāzîr*), a point that is made explicitly in a Qumran fragment corresponding to 1 Sam. 1:22: "I will give him as a *nāzîr* all the days of his life" (4QSam[a]). In this respect, the annunciation type-scene recalls the story of the birth and conception of Samson, certainly a Nazirite (Judges 13).

Of all the roles assigned to Samuel, the one that appears to be historically the least suspect is that of "father," that is, abbot or sheik of a mantic group whose ecstatic behavior seems to have been contagious (1 Sam. 19:18–24). Samuel is presented as presiding over a prophetic conventicle (*lahăqat hannĕbî'îm*), rather like the Islamic dervish *takiyyah* presided over by its *muḥaddam*. The incident in question describes how, after David had taken refuge in Samuel's cenobium, Saul sent three lots of messengers to arrest him, all of whom, however, were caught up in the ecstatic exercises in progress and "prophesied," that is, raved out of control. Something similar happened to Saul when he arrived; he tore off his clothes and lay in a catatonic state on the ground for an entire day and night. The episode corresponds to the earlier prophetic seizure of Saul on encountering the prophetic band (*ḥebel nĕbî'îm*) on his way to his anointing (1 Sam. 10:5–7, 10–13); and the point may be that while Saul was enabled by ecstasy at the outset of his career, he was rendered impotent and shamed by it toward the end. This also explains why the proverb about Saul being among the prophets is quoted at both junctures (1 Sam. 10:11–12; 19:24).

While no "quest for the historical Samuel" is likely to be successful, his association with these bands of ecstatics has a higher percentage of probability than any other traditions about him. This is not to say that he was the originator of this type of communal prophecy or that he took it over from popular Canaanite religion, either of which is possible but unsupported by evidence.[29] Such bands of the economically and socially marginalized may have sprung up spontaneously as a result of external pressure from Philistine expansion into the hill country or internal pressures on a peasant subsistence economy brought about by limited resources, overpopulation, or a series of bad harvests. It is, at any rate, worthy of note that we hear of such groups only during the severe crises precipitated by the Philistines in the eleventh and the Syrians in the ninth century.

Indications are not lacking that several other prophetic figures who loom large in the tradition had some form of association with these marginal groups. The account of Elijah's going up in the whirlwind, one of the great masterpieces of classical Hebrew prose (2 Kings 2:1–12), occurs as he is making a final visitation to the ecstatic brotherhoods at Bethel, Jericho, and another settlement near the Jordan. We saw earlier that the passing on of the prophetic mantle to Elisha enabled the latter, by working a miracle, to be acknowledged by the representatives of the "sons of the prophets" as their leader in succession to Elijah (2 Kings 2:13–14), and in that capacity we find him presiding over their assemblies (2 Kings 4:38–41; 6:1–7). The title *father* (*'āb*) carried by Samuel, Elijah, and Elisha (1 Sam. 10:12; 2 Kings 2:12; 13:14), as also by Jonadab, founder of the Rechabites (Jer. 35:6), indicates a distinctive type of charismatic organization and corresponding leadership of a familial, emotional, and personal kind. In this respect these prophetic conventicles were analogues of the extended family structure. We must now take a closer look at the social status and function of these marginal groups.

COMMUNAL PROPHECY

We have seen reason to suspect that individual prophetic figures during the early period were associated in some way with the group phenomenon, at least in the northern and central parts of the country. We hear of the activities of these prophetic-ecstatic groups during the period of Philistine expansion in the eleventh century and under the Omri and Jehu dynasties two centuries later, but it would be rash to conclude that thereafter they simply disappeared from the scene. Though the meaning of Amos's assertion that he is neither a *nābî'* nor a *ben-nābî'* (Amos 7:14) has been endlessly discussed, it is possible to interpret it as a denial of membership in such a group, which would make sense only if such groups were still in existence.

The social world that precipitated these groups and in which they functioned was basically a peasant society with a mixed economy of agriculture and stockbreeding. Most of the place-names occurring in the relevant narratives—Shiloh, Bethel, Gilgal, Gibeah—are in the central hill country, occupied by the Joseph tribes and their southern, or Benjaminite, branch. There seems to have been little contact with those city-states that had survived from the Late Bronze Age. Within the tribal network, authority resided with the elders and, for some religious functions, the priesthoods of the local shrines. The prophetic-ecstatic groups had some connection with these holy places, but there is no evidence that they served as regular cultic functionaries, like the members of *bārū* and *maḫḫu* guilds in Mesopotamia.[30] They belonged, in short, to the ranks of the socially marginal and peripheral.[31]

As was noted earlier, the thesis of Hölscher (1914), developed and modified by Jepsen (1934), that early Israelite ecstatic prophecy was a heritage from Canaanite culture is postulated on an understanding of Israelite origins that we now know to be inadequate. It is also unsupported by evidence, apart from the biblical account of the behavior of the Baal prophets on Mount Carmel (2 Kings 18:26–29). Other parallels sometimes alleged, including the Wen-amun narrative, the Mari letters, the stelae of Zakir (Zakkur) and Mesha, are from states with official means of mediation and religious specialists; and in any case, none speaks of communal prophetic activity analogous to the "sons of the prophets." It therefore makes sense to conclude that this phenomenon was an indigenous product, precipitated by local conditions of a kind that have produced comparable phenomena in other societies and at other times.[32]

The existence of such ecstatic groups presupposes a society that recognizes the possibility of forces from beyond the human sphere—the world of the gods, the spirits, the dead—impinging on human affairs, as well as the possibility of directing these forces toward specific ends by certain techniques, including ecstatic exercises. The ethical component, at least in terms of our categories, is not prominent; witness the punitive miracles worked by Elijah and Elisha and the fanatical commitment to war *à l'outrance* of these prophetic bands. Comparable phenomena from other cultures help us understand what "ecstasy" does for its practitioners and how group performance provides powerful reciprocal reinforcement, which has its own rewards. The impact of these groups on the society at large is more observable in the later than in the earlier period. While many would have dismissed them as crazy and completely beyond the pale, or at least as a social nuisance, there is evidence that they also served to bolster the morale of a society faced with intense political and social pressure. This role becomes increasingly apparent with the encroachment of the state system on a traditional way of life based on kinship and patrimonial domain, a process that we have seen is well documented by the Samaria ostraca. Among the northern and central tribes, the traditional clan system ceded much more reluctantly to the state system than was the case in Judah, and we find that the prophetic conventicles and their charismatic leaders played, at times, an important role as brokers of political power.

Deborah's song (Judges 5) shows that intertribal solidarity, always partial and sporadic, was the result of direct, external military threat, especially from the Canaanite city-states as, later, from the Philistines. At such times the prophetic-ecstatic bands were particularly active, and some may have come into existence as a direct response to such threats. Our sources place them in the direct line of Philistine expansion into the hill country—at Shiloh, which housed the war palladium (the ark), and at Gibeah, site of a Philistine garrison (1 Sam. 10:5; 13:3–4, 23; 14:11–12). Equally fanatical in their devotion to the tribal war god were the Nazirites (*nĕzîrîm*), whose presence in the peasant army may be alluded to in Deborah's song.[33] The best known of the Nazirites is Samson, though hardly a shining example since he broke all three of the Nazirite vows (Judges 13—16). At a later time, the usurper Jehu was assisted in his purge of the Baalist faction by Jonadab ben Rechab, putative "father" of the Rechabite order that rejected the indigenous culture and, to judge by their title, owed allegiance to Yahweh as warrior-god.[34] That Elijah and Elisha were connected in some way with the Rechabites (the name means, roughly, "charioteers") is suggested by the visions of heavenly chariots referred to at several points in the stories about the two prophets (2 Kings 2:11–12; 6:17; 13:14).

The "sons of the prophets" were deeply involved in the Syrian campaigns under the Omri and Jehu dynasties, issuing instructions and predicting successful outcomes (1 Kings 20:13–15, 22, 28, 35–43). Elisha appears to have been the driving force behind political coups in both Samaria and Damascus and served as intelligence agent during the wars between the two states. The ecstatic performance of Israelite prophets under the leadership of a certain Zedekiah preceding one of these Syrian campaigns, whatever its historical value, probably gives a fair idea of "prophetic" behavior during this period:

> The king of Israel and Jehoshaphat king of Judah were seated on their thrones dressed in their robes on the threshing floor at the entrance to the gate of Samaria, and all the prophets were in delirium in their presence. Zedekiah ben Chenaanah had made for himself a pair of iron horns and pronounced, "Thus Yahweh has spoken: with these you will gore Aram and finish them off." All the prophets prophesied in the same way: "Go up to Ramoth Gilead and triumph; Yahweh has handed it over to the king."
>
> (1 Kings 22:10–12)

The pattern of prophetic delirium, often during a religious or (as in this case) quasi-religious ceremony, in which the mantic gives a favorable oracle, is well attested in Israel and elsewhere. The aforementioned Egyptian tale of Wen-amun, for example, relates how, during a sacrificial ceremony in the presence of the ruler of the Phoenician city of Byblos, "the god seized one of his youths and made him possessed"—in which state he conveyed a message from the god that prevented Wen-amon from being expelled from the city.[35]

Extraordinary performances of this kind could be, and often were, induced by external stimuli, including music, percussion, dancing, chemical agents of different kinds, and self-laceration (for this last, see 2 Kings 18:28 and Zech. 13:6). But it would be naive to conclude that extreme behavioral changes were invariably interpreted as a sign of possession by a god or a spirit; on the contrary, they were often seen as symptomatic of sickness or insanity (2 Kings 9:11; Jer. 29:26). People were also aware that such conditions could be simulated. Finding himself in a tight corner, David, for example, pretended to be mad when serving with the Philistine ruler Achish:

> He changed his behavior when he was with them and acted madly in
> their presence, drumming [or "scrabbling"] on the doors of the city gate
> and dribbling down his beard. So Achish said to his retainers, "What
> you see here is a madman ['îš mištaggēa']; why did you bring him to
> me? Do I lack madmen [mĕšuggā'îm] that you bring this fellow to rave
> in my presence? Is this fellow to come into my palace?"
>
> (1 Sam. 21:14–16)

At the same time, there must have been a lurking fear of the psychic harm such people were thought capable, and therefore were capable, of inflicting. We detect it in the incident in which a mantic revealed his identity to a king of Israel by removing a bandage from his head to display a wound (1 Kings 20:35–43), and it is prominent throughout the prophetic legends dealing with Elijah and Elisha. The foreigner Jezebel, clearly a quite remarkable woman, seems to have been the only one immune to it.

What were the social and economic status and way of life of these prophetic-ecstatic cenobia? We saw earlier that they belonged economically to the lowest strata of society and may have been recruited from the marginal, landless class, disinherited as a result of bad economic conditions. We hear of a wife of one of the "sons of the prophets" about to lose her child to a creditor (2 Kings 4:1–7), and during a famine, some of them were reduced to subsisting on wild herbs—a dangerous diet, as it turned out (2 Kings 4:38–41). Their organization would not have been highly developed. Analogy with the cultic guilds of Mesopotamia is misleading, though many parallel terms are attested (e.g., *rabu* or *abu,* "leader," "father"; *aplu,* "son"; *aḫu,* "brother"). The collectivity itself is referred to as *ḥebel,* "union" or "band" (1 Sam. 10:5), and *laḥăqâ,* "company" (1 Sam. 19:20), though the latter is textually dubious. It has been suggested that the equally dubious *nwyt* (*navah?*) is a technical term analogous to the dervish *takiyyah,* but this is speculative.[36] But it does seem that these settlements were located in the precincts of sanctuaries, or at least in their vicinity, and that the members took part in the sacrificial cults offered there.

The members, or "sons," with their wives and families (2 Kings 4:1–7) owed obedience to the leader, or "father"; a fictive familial setting, therefore, analogous to certain religious orders today. As disciples, they sat before the master (1 Kings 22:10; 2 Kings 4:38; 6:1) who presided over their meals when present and led them in their ecstatic exercises. Other terms used for the individual member are *na'ar,* usually translated "youth" (1 Sam. 1:22, 24–27; 2 Kings 8:4; 9:4), and *mĕšārēt,* "servant" (1 Sam. 2:11, 18; 3:1; 2 Kings 6:15), both used of the luckless Gehazi, acolyte of Elisha.[37] Since biblical figures are often unreliable, we have no secure information on the size of these settlements. One text mentions fifty (2 Kings 2:7), and the pious Obadiah, majordomo of Ahab's palace in Samaria, speaks of hiding a hundred prophets in two caves, fifty in each (1 Kings 18:13). In the same general narrative context Elijah refers to the 450 prophets of Baal and 400 prophets, perhaps female prophets, of Asherah (1 Kings 18:19); all of which suggests that fifty and multiples of fifty were used to express round numbers of a certain magnitude.

PROPHETS UNDER THE STATE SYSTEM: CONTINUITY AND DISCONTINUITY

The distinction between *primitive* and *classical* prophecy has become one of the basic consensuses in Old Testament scholarship, but like other widely accepted assumptions, it should not be allowed to pass without scrutiny. At the political level, at any rate, there is no discontinuity. Throughout the two centuries of the existence of the Ephraimite kingdom there is, according to Dtr, an unbroken sequence of prophetic figures active in both supporting and undermining successive rulers and dynasties. Their intervention in state affairs, unthinkable in the great riverine empires, was made possible by the peculiar character of political rule in the territory of the northern and central tribes. The extension of David's rule in that part of the country was not imposed by force but negotiated by tribal representatives (2 Sam. 5:3). Solomon's attempt to impose the apparatus of state control led to the undoing of that agreement. The implications of that attempt are set out precisely in Samuel's response to the popular request for a king: a regular army, with a corresponding "defense budget"; conscription for military service and for the corvée; sequestration of land to provide royal domain and fiefs for royal retainers; tribute in kind, consisting of 10 percent of the harvest; and the division of the kingdom into administrative regions, primarily for fiscal purposes (1 Sam. 8:10–18; 1 Kings 4:7–19). Opposition to these measures, led by the Ephraimite Jeroboam, resulted in what from the Judean point of view was a secession from the Davidic dynasty but in reality was a return to the traditional pattern, a reaffirmation of tribalism ("to your tents, O Israel!"; 1 Kings 12:16). But the process of state control inevitably took its course in Jeroboam's kingdom as well; and the resulting tension between tribal ethos and state system, evident in the incident of Naboth's vineyard (1 Kings 20), created a situation of chronic political instability in the Northern Kingdom.

The outcome was a rapid turnover of rulers during the two centuries from the accession of Jeroboam I to the fall of Samaria to the Assyrians in 722 B.C.E. The nineteen who ruled during this time (twenty if we include Tibni, Omri's rival) belonged to nine dynasties, if we may call them that, the longest being that of Jehu, which lasted about a century, the shortest that of Zimri, who committed suicide after reigning for a week. Of these rulers, seven were assassinated and another, the last, died or was executed by the Assyrians during the siege of Samaria. A regular feature of political life, not unlike the situation in some Latin American countries in recent history, was the military coup carried out by disaffected or ambitious army commanders. One of these was Omri, who came to power in 883 B.C.E. and succeeded for the first time in creating a measure of stability. Not surprisingly, Israel now begins to appear for the first time in Assyrian records, being referred to as "the house of Omri" (*bīt ḫumria*).[38]

The greater resistance among the northern and central tribes to the apparatus of state control permitted a much larger role to prophetic collectivities and individuals than is attested in the relatively stable kingdom of Judah. The account of prophetic activity has no doubt been enhanced and expanded by the historian, but there is no particular reason to doubt that prophetic figures such as Ahijah of Shiloh and Jehu ben Hanani played a significant role as brokers of political power during the first century of Jeroboam's kingdom.[39] The Phoenician connections of the Omrids; the marriage of Omri's son Ahab to the Tyrian princess Jezebel, a dedicated devotee of the Tyrian Baal; and the founding of Samaria as the personal domain of the ruler explain the dominant role played by prophets in the resulting

Kulturkampf. Their struggle against the Canaanizing tendencies of the dynasty was crowned with success when a disciple of Elisha anointed the army commander Jehu as ruler designate (2 Kings 9:1–13).

At this point we encounter a certain ambiguity in our sources with respect to the Jehu dynasty. The historian (Dtr) is generally favorable to the dynasty, though of course he could not condone the dissident cult set up by Jeroboam I. The dynasty had prophetic support—Elisha and his disciples—at its inception, and Jehu was even given the extraordinary prophetic assurance that his descendants would reign to the fourth generation (2 Kings 10:30; 15:12). The historian is therefore careful to note how the three rulers after Jehu enjoyed divine favor, manifested in military success or deliverance from danger (2 Kings 13:4–5; 13:12; 14:8–15, 25–27). Jeroboam II, the third of these, enjoyed prophetic support in the person of Jonah ben Amittai (14:25), in which connection the historian goes on to make the obviously polemical statement that "Yahweh had not said he would blot out the name of Israel from under heaven" (14:25), a remark that we have seen to be almost certainly directed at Amos, who said just that (Amos 9:8; cf. 8:2). The reason for the historian's rejection of Amos, who is also recorded as having predicted—incorrectly, as it happened—the violent death of Jeroboam (7:11), may be that Amos contradicted the earlier prediction concerning the duration of the dynasty. Since an earlier oracle has precedence over a later one,[40] Amos's opposition to the dynasty could be safely ignored, which may also help to explain why both he and Hosea, who also spoke against the Jehu dynasty, are absent from the history.[41]

There is therefore no essential discontinuity between the "school" of Elisha that supported the Jehu dynasty and Amos and Hosea who opposed it, between the representatives of "primitive" and "classical" prophecy. The impression of discontinuity, of distinct and discrete phases in the history of prophecy, can be explained by the inevitable but misleading tendency to periodize and also by the nature of the source material at our disposal. The most obvious point is that beginning, as most would agree, with Amos, we have collections of prophetic sayings rather than prophetic legends. As to why this is so, why we have a Book of Amos and not a Book of Elijah, we can only speculate. If the sayings of Amos were collected by either the prophet himself or a disciple, the impulse may have been provided by the threat posed by the Assyrian *Drang nach Westen* (push to the West) after the accession of Tiglath-pileser III in 745 B.C.E. In any event, the dissolution of the kingdom of Samaria, already well underway by 734 B.C.E., would have provided strong motivation for the preservation in the surviving kingdom of Judah of the sayings of those who had predicted it.

A NEW KIND OF
INTELLECTUAL LEADERSHIP?

socially speaking,

The careers of Amos and other prophetic figures from the eighth century
B.C.E. do not, therefore, mark an absolutely new phase in the history of Israelite prophecy. We cannot, for example, exclude the possibility that communal prophecy continued beyond this point just because our sources no
longer mention it. Amos denies being a *ben-nābî'*, but other prophetic figures at that time or later may have emerged from the anonymity of the group
phenomenon. Yet, making all due allowance for lines of continuity and the
changed perspective involved in putting together collections of sayings, it
is possible to detect an element of newness when we examine closely the
sayings of Amos, Hosea, Isaiah, and Micah, all dated either shortly before
or shortly after the extinction of the kingdom of Samaria. The first task,
clearly, is that of sifting out the original content of these books from editorial accretions, the results of which rarely exceed probability or approxi-
mation. I believe, notwithstanding, that enough progress can be made to
enable us to identify some novel features on the basis of which certain conclusions about a new type of intellectual leadership can be drawn.

The first step is to note the relatively high level of literary skill in discourse
that can reasonably be assigned to the original nucleus. Literary analysis of
the four books in question is the subject of an extensive literature to which
I do not propose to add, but one or two examples may be helpful. The fre-
quency in Amos of rhetorical questions, numerical sayings, riddle-like poems, and similar rhetorical devices has persuaded most commentators that
the author must have belonged in some way to the very restricted circle of
the literati, in either Judah or Israel.[42] These features even led Hans Walter
Wolff to speculate that Amos belonged to what he called a "clan wisdom
school" at Tekoa in the Judean wilderness from which the "wise woman" of
Tekoa, mentioned in 2 Samuel 14, had graduated two centuries earlier.[43]
Wolff unfortunately failed to tell us what such a school would look like, what
its curriculum would be, or what it was doing in such an unpromising location. It will suffice, at any rate, to assume that Amos belonged to a socially
and economically superior, *literate* stratum of the population, in which of
the two kingdoms we do not know, and that the impressive literary features
alluded to derive from his participation in the intellectual activity of his day.

Similar conclusions have been drawn with respect to the other three
books. To take one more example, Hosea's ability to compose sustained
and well-structured discourses points to a different kind of prophetic opposition to the ruling elite in the kingdom of Samaria.

All four also exhibit a much broader historical perspective than their predecessors, including interest in and acquaintance with current international affairs. Both Amos and Hosea seem to be well informed on Assyrian campaigns of the previous century, including the campaign of Shalmaneser III in 841 B.C.E. during which the Assyrians first entered Israelite territory, typically leaving desolation in their wake. (Their destruction of Beth-arbel [Irbid in Jordan] is referred to in Hos. 10:14 and Amos 6:2.) All four are also well informed on the foreign policy being pursued by contemporary rulers, frequently denounce foreign alliances,[44] and are in touch with current events (e.g., Amos 6:13; Hos. 5:8–14). Isaiah was even involved in shaping policy, not always successfully, due to his close contacts with the Judean court.

These considerations based on the surviving writings of the four public figures in question lead to the conclusion that they belonged to a socially much more elevated stratum than did the nĕbî'îm who preceded them, with the exception of such court prophets as Gad and Nathan. The question then arises: In what sense did they belong to the ranks of the nĕbî'îm at all? To repeat a point made earlier, none of the four identifies himself as a prophet or is identified as such by others. The only exception is the Isaiah of the legends in chapters 36—39, who is closer to the early nĕbî'îm than he is to the Isaiah of the sayings. The frequent dismissal of contemporary prophets as fraudulent (e.g., Hos. 4:4–6; Micah 2:6–11; 3:5–7, 11; Isa. 3:2; 28:7) makes it very unlikely that any of the four would have presented himself as a nābî'. We have seen that Amos unequivocally dissociated himself from the prophetic office while defending his credentials as divinely authorized critic of contemporary mores.[45] Micah also appears to have been forbidden to speak in public (Micah 2:6; cf. Amos 2:12; 7:12–13). More to the point, he defines his status as spokesman for Yahweh in contrast to that of contemporary prophets (3:5–8). It is therefore understandable that he has left no account of a prophetic calling, hardly ever uses the standard prophetic incipit "thus says Yahweh," and almost always speaks in his own name rather than quoting the deity's words as is customary with prophets—and this even when referring to "my people."[46]

From all this we conclude that these four public figures from the eighth century B.C.E. saw themselves, in a limited respect, as heirs to the old nĕbî'îm but shied away from using the same designation to describe their own public personas and functions.[47] A partial explanation is that the increasing consolidation of the state system had created openings for prophets as stipendiary functionaries attached to court and temple, thus obliging them to represent official policies and, in general, play a corroborative rather than a critically independent role in society. Hence the frequent pairing of priests and prophets in the diatribe of these four directed against political and social abuses (Hos. 4:4–5; Micah 3:11; Isa. 28:7).

We now pass to an important feature of this new phase of social protest, namely, that it cohered into a tradition which lasted for the two remaining centuries of the history of the kingdoms. This point might easily be missed since these individuals do not follow our convention of acknowledging literary dependence and referring to sources by name. It is nevertheless clear that they are aware where they stand in relation to their predecessors and contemporaries and freely borrow and adapt the message of these others as circumstances dictate. So, for example, it can be shown that Isaiah is applying the message of Amos, and to a lesser extent, of Hosea, to the situation of the Judean state a few decades later. In the Isaian poem on the divine anger (Isa. 5:24–25; 9:8–10:4), there may even be a covert allusion to Amos in the reference to a word sent by Yahweh against Jacob (9:7). But in any case, Isaiah's debt to Amos is apparent in his criticism of the cult (1:12–17; cf. Amos 5:21–24), the women of the royal court (3:16–17, 24–26 cf. Amos 4:1–3), and those who oppress the poor (3:15; cf. Amos 2:6–8; 8:4). In general, Isaiah's denunciations follow along the same lines as Amos's (e.g., Isa. 10:1–2; 17:1–6; 28:1–4) and are often couched in the same form, for example, in the woe saying (5:8–23; cf. Amos 5:7, 18; 6:1, 4).

Isaiah's debt to Hosea is less clearly in evidence, but it has been detected in allusions to unfaithful sons (1:2–3), the harlot city (1:21–26), and Israel as a vineyard (5:1–7; cf. Hos. 10:1) and in the frequent use of the title "the Holy One of Israel" (e.g., 1:4; 5:19–24; cf. Hos. 11:9; 12:1).

It also seems likely that Hosea was familiar with the public pronouncements of his near contemporary Amos. Both announce the end of the special relationship between Yahweh and his people—a momentous and unprecedented message—and it may not be coincidental that in Amos the terminal point is reached in the third of five visions, in which intercession is no longer possible (7:7–9), while in Hosea it is announced in the symbolic name of the third child, Lo-ammi (1:6: "You are not my people and I am not your I AM"; with which compare Amos 8:2: "The end has come upon my people Israel").

Similar borrowings and adaptations from Amos have also been detected in Micah,[48] and the close association between Micah and Isaiah has long been acknowledged. Micah 4:1–5 and Isa. 2:2–5 are variants of the same saying, Micah's attitude to the sacrificial cult is similar to that of Isaiah, and the reference to going stripped and naked in Micah 1:8 recalls Isa. 20:1–6. This is as far as we need go, but similar connections and concatenations could be demonstrated for the next two centuries: for example, in Jeremiah's use of Hosean imagery (Jer. 1:1–8:3) and in Ezek. 7:1–27, which reads like a sermon on the text of Amos's fourth vision (Amos 8:1–3).

These indications of the existence of a prophetic literary tradition inscribing a tradition of social and political protest could be developed further, but they suffice to make the point. We could sum up by saying that the four public figures on whom our inquiry is focusing saw themselves as engaged in a common *activity* rather than as belonging to a specific *profession*. We are not well informed on what any of them did for a living before engaging in this activity or, for that matter, since prophesying was not necessarily a full-time occupation, while they were so engaged. We have a few bits of biographical information about Amos (1:1; 7:10–17) on which there has been interminable and inconclusive discussion. We cannot be sure that the matrimonial vicissitudes described in Hosea 1—3 have any biographical reference, and the prophetic legends about Isaiah are of uncertain historical value and, in any case, cover only the later part of his career. We are also ignorant as to how these four would, if asked, have characterized their societal role as public speakers. Perhaps the closest we can come, making all due allowance for the perils of importing modern categories into ancient contexts, is to describe them as dissident intellectuals. What this is meant to say is that they collaborated at some level of conscious intent in the emergence of a coherent vision of a moral universe over against current assumptions cherished and propagated by the contemporary state apparatus, including its priestly and prophetic representatives.

Some help in unpacking the implications of this way of thinking about these prophetic figures may be found in modern discussions of the role of the intellectual in the formation, maintenance, transformation, and disintegration of traditions. Intellectuals (not necessarily the same as academics) can function as creators of symbols and models by which the society understands itself and sustains its sense of identity and morale. They can also serve in an official, representative function by elaborating an intellectual account of the world supportive of the dominant ideology in a particular society. In contrast, the intellectual often plays a socially destabilizing role in taking an independent, critical, or innovative line over against commonly accepted assumptions or a dominant ideology. In fact, radical change rarely, if ever, comes about without the cooperation or intervention of an intellectual elite.[49]

The description of the eighth-century prophets as dissident intellectuals and agents of change also makes a fit with the concept of an "axial age" first elaborated by Karl Jaspers.[50] As generally understood, the concept states that there occurred in the course of the first millennium B.C.E. in various parts of the world, including Greece and Israel, a breakthrough to a coherent vision of a transcendental reality and a construction of the world in keeping with it. Essential to the form it took in Israel was the conviction of a personal, ethical deity whose demands, arising out of his very nature, led to a voluntary, contractual relationship between deity and people, the creation of an autonomous sphere of law, and an emphasis on human accountability. Tension between the transcendental and mundane spheres led to the elaboration of a doctrine of salvation in which ethical performance played an indispensable role.[51]

The thesis can be clarified somewhat by contrasting Israel with ancient Mesopotamia, which never developed the idea of a legal sphere independent of the will of the ruler and never progressed significantly toward the point of rationalization of the world represented by monotheism. Babylonian and Assyrian writing reveals significant achievements in abstract and analytic thinking, for example, in mathematics and astronomy, but is remarkably deficient in self-consciousness and interiority. It is at least possible that this condition has something to do with the failure of an intellectual tradition to develop independently of the state and, correlatively, with the absence of prophecy of the kind that emerged in eighth-century Israel.

In spite of some fairly obvious problems, not least the extremely broad and ill-defined chronological parameters of the "axial age," the thesis at least draws attention to the new aspects of prophecy that emerged in the eighth century. In some important respects Jaspers's idea was anticipated by Max Weber's concept of *rationality* as applied to Israelite prophecy. Toward the end of his study of prophecy (section 3 of chapter 6, "Religious Groups," in *Economy and Society*), Weber concluded:

> Regardless of whether a particular religious prophet is predominently of the ethical or predominantly of the exemplary type, prophetic revelation involves for both the prophet himself and for his followers . . . a unified view of the world derived from a consciously integrated, meaningful attitude towards life. To the prophet, both the life of man and the world, both social and cosmic events, have a certain systematic and coherent meaning, to which man's conduct must be oriented if it is to bring salvation.

And he continues a little later:

> The conflict between empirical reality and this conception of the world as a meaningful totality, which is based on the religious postulate, produces the strongest tensions in man's inner life as well as in his external relationship to the world. To be sure, this problem is by no means

> dealt with by prophecy alone. Both priestly wisdom and secular phi-
> losophy, the intellectualist as well as the popular varieties, are some-
> how concerned with it. The ultimate question of all metaphysics has al-
> ways been something like this: if the world as a whole and life in
> particular were to have a meaning, what might it be, and how would
> the world have to look in order to correspond to it?[52]

It seems to me that Weber has described very well the tacit assumptions behind the public discourse of Amos, Hosea, Micah, and Isaiah. It remains to
ask what the social and cultural determinants of this kind of language were,
a language that at least insofar as it cohered into a powerful tradition of dissent, was genuinely new.

A major factor, alluded to earlier, was the consolidation of the state system with its political and religious bureaucracies and the consequent re-
morseless grinding down of older patterns based primarily on real or fictive
kinship relations. This was the idea behind the comprehensive centralization policy inscribed in the Deuteronomic program. The requirement that
all adult males present themselves three times a year at the state sanctuary
(Deut. 16:16) was transparently aimed at undermining the annual clan sacrifice and common meal (e.g., 1 Sam. 20:6, 28), a principal focus of lineage
solidarity and often of political disaffection. Another, no less important factor was the decisive phase of Assyrian expansion set in motion after the accession of the usurper Tiglath-pileser III in 745 B.C.E. From that point on, to
the end of the biblical period and beyond, every aspect of life in Israel and
early Judaism was determined almost without interruption by the policies
of Near Eastern and Levantine empires and, following them, the Roman Empire. The impact on local cults and deities is well attested; it is an integral
part of imperial propaganda, as in the boastful claim of the Assyrian official
during the siege of Jerusalem in 701 B.C.E.:

> Has any of the gods of the nations rescued his land from the power of
> the Assyrian king? Where now are the gods of Hamath and Arpad?
> Where are the gods of Sepharvaim, Hena, and Ivvah? Did they rescue
> Samaria from my hand? Who of all the gods of the countries ever res-
> cued their land from my power that Yahweh should deliver Jerusalem
> from my hand?
>
> (2 Kings 18:33–35)

Imperial theology of this kind, expressed in equally crude terms in Assyrian royal inscriptions, gave rise to a crisis of theodicy among the devotees
of local cults and a situation in which such cults could survive, if at all, only
at the cost of a drastic rethinking of the effective power and jurisdiction of
the resident deity.

This leads to the observation that one of the most impressive aspects of "classical" prophecy, first clearly enunciated in Isaiah (e.g., 10:5–19), is its critique of imperial ideology and its refusal to take it with absolute seriousness. That ideology is turned back on itself by the statement that the Assyrians and, after them, the Babylonians and the rest are instruments in the hands of the God of Israel. A corollary of this counterclaim was the abandonment of the idea of Yahweh as a locative deity, one whose writ ran only within the borders of Israel. We can therefore appreciate a point made by Weber, namely, that the primary concern of Israelite prophecy was with international politics, since this was the arena of their God's activity. Their preoccupation with issues of social justice, he continued, was related to that primary concern as a means of explaining the course of events in the political sphere as they impinged, eventually with fatal consequences, on the Israelite kingdoms.[53] The shift from the tribal and territorial to the international scene was therefore an important aspect of the axial breakthrough to a new construction of reality in the eighth century.

We might mention, as a corollary, the observation of Moshe Weinfeld that one result of the prophetic critique of imperialism was the transfer of the language and ideology of imperium, as a kind of mirror image, into the metaphor of a spiritual kingdom, the kingdom of God.[54] It will not escape notice that so much of our metaphorical and analogical language about God, including the language of prayer, is rooted in the different expressions of the imperial idea in the ancient Near East.

THE SOCIAL SITUATION THAT GENERATED PROTEST AND DISSENT

The eighth-century dissenters sometimes expressed themselves in generalizing terms, but for the most part, their critique was itemized and their targets specific, namely, the ruling elite and its dependents. They spoke or wrote on behalf of the socially and economically disadvantaged, the victims of the gradual and inexorable undermining by the state of the cohesion and ethos of a more or less egalitarian system based on the kinship network.

Little need be added to what was said in chapter 1 on the subject of early Israelite society. The individual was located at the center of concentric circles of real or fictive kinship, or to use a different spatial metaphor, at the point of intersection of a horizontal line representing the living and a vertical line representing the past and future members of the kinship group. Hence the expression "to be gathered to one's fathers," or to paraphrase, to be aggregated, at death, to the totality of the group. Within these social units there was little differentiation of function, since practically all able-bodied members, male and female, would be engaged in raising crops, tending livestock, or doing the usual household chores. We saw also that the normal exercise of judicial authority would be in the hands of the *zāqēn* or paterfamilias and that some issues of a specifically cultic nature would have been the responsibility of the priest of a local sanctuary. Larger issues—external threats to the group, a protracted internal crisis, a serious intertribal dispute—would have required the convening of an assembly of elders or, in extraordinary circumstances, the ad hoc appointment of an individual leader to whom authority would be delegated for the duration of the crisis.

In this kind of subsistence agrarian economy, ownership of a parcel of land and access to common grazing rights were essential for the survival of the individual social units. Patrimonial domain was passed on from one generation to the next and was, in theory, inalienable; hence Naboth's refusal to accept Ahab's offer to purchase his vineyard: "Yahweh forbid that I hand over to you the patrimony [*naḥălâ*] of my ancestors" (1 Kings 21:3). Inalienable right to land was also undergirded by the theological premise that the entire land belonged to the national deity, who granted it in fief to those who shared in his cult (Lev. 25:23). Hence the legal requirement, a requirement as easy to circumvent as it must have been difficult to enforce, that expropriated land be returned to its original owner in the fiftieth or jubilee year (Lev. 25:8–17). Hence also the legal right to repurchase land, when the opportunity presented itself, after a forced sale or expropriation for insolvency (Lev. 25:25–28).[55]

In the earlier stages, to the time of Solomon, the transition to a state system would not have had a substantial impact on this traditional way of life. Gradually, however, and more gradually in the north than in the south, the demands of centralized government destabilized and eroded the old tribal structure and ethos. The high price to be paid for centralization is set out in Samuel's reply to the popular demand for a king. The incident may well be fictitious, but the situation as described is well attested:

> This will be the customary procedure of the king who will rule over you: he will take your sons and draft hem for his chariotry and cavalry, and they will run ahead in front of his chariots; he will appoint for himself commanders of thousands and of fifty, and others to plough his land, take in his harvests, and manufacture weapons and chariot equipment; he will take your daughters as perfumers, cooks, and bakers; he will requisition the best of your fields, vineyards, and olive orchards and give them to his underlings; he will take a tenth of your grain and the produce of your vineyards and give it to his officers and underlings; he

will requisition your male and female slaves, the best of your cattle, and your donkeys and put them to work; he will, finally, take a tenth of your flocks, and you shall be his slaves.

(1 Sam. 8:10–18)

This list of impositions reflects the harsh reality of life under the monarchy and errs, if at all, on the side of understatement. The monarchy brought with it the whole apparatus of a central government run by an army of bureaucrats. The historian has preserved lists of royal officials from the time of the United Monarchy (2 Sam. 8:15–18; 20:23–26; 1 Kings 4:1–6) that can be augmented with later allusions in Dtr and in various inscriptions including seals and bullae. Titles appearing on the latter include *na'ar* and *'ebed* (royal pages and servants), *'al habbayit* (majordomo of the palace), *śar hā'îr* (governor of the city), and *ben hammelek* (member of the royal family).[56] Solomon, moreover, is said to have divided his kingdom into twelve districts, primarily for fiscal purposes, and these too had their administrative staffs, which were, of course, at the public expense. The historian informs us that these provincial governors were jointly responsible for provisioning the royal court and supplying fodder for horses (1 Kings 4:7, 27–28).

The phasing out of the tribal levy in favor of a standing army, supported by its own "military-industrial complex," was an additional heavy drain on the country's economic resources, especially when mercenaries were employed (2 Sam. 15:18; 20:23). To take one example: during Solomon's reign a chariot and horse, both imported from abroad, cost 750 shekels, that is, roughly twenty pounds of silver bullion (1 Kings 10:29), and to this must be added the cost of equipment and provisions for both horse and man, more likely for two horses and three men, not to mention stables and barracks in several cities (1 Kings 9:19).[57] As is still the case today, the burden of the defense budget was borne by the ordinary citizen.

Changes in land tenure introduced by the monarchy posed the most serious threat to the survival of a free peasantry. Rulers needed land as a source of revenue. The need could be met by direct purchase (2 Sam. 24:24; 1 Kings 16:24); by confiscation, as when David took over the real estate belonging to Saul's family (2 Sam. 9:7; 16:4); or by vacant possession, as happened after the judicial murder of Naboth (1 Kings 21:1–16). By a process of gradual accumulation, the monarchy in both kingdoms came to possess extensive estates worked by slaves or day laborers, each with its own administrative staff. Land acquired by the ruler was also granted in fief to royal retainers as a means of ensuring their loyalty, and it is probable that laws were enacted to facilitiate acquisition, laws that inevitably posed a threat to the landowning peasant. (Isaiah refers to the publication of iniquitous decrees resulting in the oppression of the poor; Isa. 10:1–4). The shift from patrimonial toward prebendal domain was encouraged by the foreclosure on land following on the insolvency of the owner. In these cases, the traditional requirement of inalienability could be circumvented by the fiction that the creditor enjoyed the usufruct of the property without holding title to it. That this process was well advanced by the eighth century is apparent not only from the volume of protest directed against it but also from the scant archaeological evidence available—the Samaria ostraca referred to earlier and the *lmlk* ("belonging to the king") stamps from different sites in Judah.[58]

By the eighth century B.C.E., the two kingdoms were moving inexorably toward a situation in which the coercive power of the state, supported by a class of nouveaux riches parasitical on the monarchy and court, legitimated by state cults exercising their own forms of hierocratic coercion, and resting on a broad basis of peasant serfdom and slavery, was reaching out into every sphere of social life. That this process did not work its way to its anticipated term was due in the first place to Assyrian intervention, which terminated the existence of one kingdom and reduced the other to vassalage. But it was also the result of sustained protest coming not from the peasant class, which lacked the resources and leadership to generate it, but from the educated and literate stratum, in some instances within the "system" itself. It remains to outline briefly the forms that this protest took.

THE SUBSTANCE OF DISSENT

If we survey the sayings attributed to Amos, Hosea, Micah, and Isaiah against the background of the situation as described, we observe that their animus is directed primarily against the ruling elite in the two kingdoms. All of them, in one way or another, denounce the capital cities where these elites reside.[59] In reading them we also detect a more diffuse animus against urban living in general; Amos, for example, condemns leisure activities such as singing and listening to music, in themselves perfectly unexceptionable but characteristic of contemporary urban living (Amos 6:4–7). Attitudes toward the monarchy itself vary. Amos predicted the violent death of the contemporary ruler and the extinction of the dynasty that ruler represented (Amos 7:9–11). Hosea, the most utopian of the four, rejected the institution as such and regarded the passage to monarchy as the "original sin" of Israel

(Hos. 5:8; 9:9; 10:9). Isaiah, by contrast, limited his condemnation to specific policies pursued by Ahaz of Judah (Isa. 7:1–17). Their indictment also takes aim at officialdom in the service of the monarchy. Those condemned include *rā'šîm*, a vague term referring to leading officials (Micah 3:1–4), *qĕṣînîm*, "prefects" or "royal appointees" (Micah 3:9–12; Isa. 1:10; 3:7); and *śārîm*, "princes" or provincial "governors," military or civil, who also exercised a judicial function (e.g., Amos 2:3; Hos. 7:3, 5; Isa. 1:21–23).

An interesting confirmation of the role of the provincial *śar* came to light with the discovery of an ostracon at Yavneh-Yam (Mesad Hashavyahu on the Mediterranean coast, about nine miles south of Yafo) from a century after Amos. In this inscription, a farm laborer petitions the local *śar* for the return of a confiscated garment:

> The attention of my lord the commandant [*haśśar*] is drawn to the complaint of his servant. As for your servant—your servant was harvesting at [*ḥṣar 'asām*]; and your servant had reaped and measured and stored (grain) for the days agreed before stopping. After your servant had measured his (quota of) grain and put it in store for the days agreed, along came Hashabiah son of Shobai, and appropriated your servant's garment. . . . But all my comrades can testify on my behalf . . . that it was as I say—I am not guilty of any (crime. So please return) my garment, that I may be given satisfaction.[60]

The situation is reminiscent of Amos 2:8,

> On garments seized in pledge they stretch out
> beside every altar,

which itself recalls the law in Ex. 22:25–26:

> Whenever you distrain your neighbor's garment you must return it to him before sunset, for it is his only covering, it is his cloak [to cover] his body; what else does he have to sleep in? If he makes complaint to me I will hear him, for I am compassionate

(though neither the Yavneh-Yam plaintiff nor Amos appeal to the law in question).

A feature peculiar to Isaiah is the condemnation of royal counselors, perhaps, as has been suggested, because he belonged to their ranks (Isa. 3:2–3; 5:18–23; 29:14). Particularly intense criticism is concentrated on the corruption of the judicial system by favoritism and bribery, since it removed the last resort for the struggling poor to maintain their property and family or even just to ensure survival (e.g., Amos 2:7; 5:10; Micah 3:9–12; Isa. 3:1–3; 5:18–23). Control of the judicial system by state functionaries also permitted the enactment of "iniquitous decrees" (Isa. 10:1), probably so characterized because they subverted individual rights sanctioned by tradition but inconvenient in the new situation of state control.

Especially disconcerting for many modern readers is the rejection by all four, if with varying degrees of intensity, of contemporary forms of worship and the cult personnel, including prophets, who staffed the national sanctuaries.[61] This antireligious polemic had little to do with the idea of a spiritual as opposed to a materialistic concept of worship or of sacrifice as a kind of magical coercion of the Deity. It had a great deal to do with state-sponsored cults as part of an oppressive apparatus of control and their personnel as the exponents of the official state ideology. State cults also called for a large corps of employees over and above the sacrificing priesthood. Temples in antiquity were not just places of sacrifice and prayer but institutions, often very wealthy, with their own capital and work force. Since the wealthier temples also owned arable and grazing land, estate managers and overseers would be necessary. In fact, one hypothesis about Amos's profession, based on an interpretation of *nōqĕdîm* in the opening verse of the book, assigns him the task of overseeing the temple herds in one or other of the kingdoms.[62]

Temples also employed slaves, and there is no reason to believe that the Jerusalem temple was an exception. Temple personnel were also exempt from taxation, which of course increased the burden on the rest of the population, already under obligation to contribute to the support and maintenance of the temple personnel and temple fabric (2 Kings 12:4–16). In addition, the sacrificial cult itself was a heavy drain on commodities and livestock and contributed significantly to the perquisites of the temple officialdom.

The point was made earlier that the practice of land grants posed a direct threat to the traditional system of land tenure. It is therefore not surprising that protest took aim at "those who join house to house, who add field to field" (Isa. 5:8), and "those who oppress a man and his house, a man and his inheritance" (Micah 2:2). Beginning, according to the historian, with the United Monarchy, the practice represented the first stage in the formation of latifundia and the emergence of a kind of rent capitalism. In spite of legal safeguards (Ex. 22:24–27; Deut. 23:19; Lev. 25:35–37), these holdings were enlarged by the enclosure of land forfeited as a result of insolvency, a situation that could come about as a result of a series of bad harvests exacerbated by various royal exactions (Amos 5:11; 7:1). The predictable result would be forfeiture of livestock, perhaps also land, and in severe cases the reduction of family members to indentured service.

What can happen in a time of prolonged famine is set out in narrative form in the Joseph story. The scene is set in Egypt, but the conditions and their consequences reflect a Palestinian milieu. The agricultural laborers lost first their cattle, then their land holdings, and finally their freedom. They continued to work the land, but 20 percent of the produce went to the crown (Gen. 47:13–26).[63] In one of the bitterest indictments surviving from the eighth century B.C.E., the exploitation of peasant misery along these lines is compared with cannibalism:

> You who tear the skin from off them,
> and their flesh from their bones;
> who eat the flesh of my people,
> flaying the skin from their bodies
> and grinding up their bones;
> chopping them up like flesh in a pot,
> like meat in a cauldron.
>   (Micah 3:2–3)

The cumulative effect of these developments was a drastic redistribution of resources to the advantage of a new, urban class of upwardly mobile state employees and dependents and to the disadvantage of a downwardly mobile peasantry. That the material remains tell us much more about the former than about the latter is in great part due to the predilection of archaeologists for monumental architecture and public buildings, illustrated by the two excavations of Samaria (1908–1910 and 1931–1935), which were restricted to the palace enclosure on the western brow of the hill. (We therefore know nothing about the living conditions of the 27,290 inhabitants of the city deported by Sargon II, as recorded on his Display Inscriptions.) The scanty evidence we can assemble points, nevertheless, to a widening gulf between rich and poor. The evidence would include imported luxury items, including ivory and lapis objects, discovered in the royal enclave in Samaria, and the arrangement and size of houses, indicative of social ranking, in Tirzah (Tell el-Far'ah north, stratum VIId), rebuilt in the eighth century B.C.E.[64] There are also indications of the expansion of trade in the same period, which would have benefited the urban, commercial class and those wealthy enough to buy from them.[65]

In this kind of situation, it is understandable that protest should take aim at the accumulation of wealth and the luxurious lifestyle enjoyed by the few at the expense of the many. Amos lashes out at those who store up (the fruits of) violence and robbery (3:10) and live at ease in houses, the walls and furniture of which are inlaid with ivory (3:15; 6:4). Both he and Isaiah have nothing but scorn for the idle rich and depict, no doubt with hyperbole, an endless round of drunken carousal (Amos 6:4–7; Isa. 5:11–12; 28:7–8) in which the women of the court also participate (Amos 4:1–3; Isa. 3:16–4:1; 32:9–13).

The concentration of power and resources in the hands of the few, in this instance the political and hierocratic establishment and its clientele, is always liable to generate protest, especially if it is accompanied by the impoverishment of the many. A few decades after Amos, Hesiod claimed divine inspiration in denouncing unjust rulers and predicting their destruction by Zeus, protector of justice (*dikē*), and he did so in response to a situation similar to the one we have been describing. We have practically no biographical information on either Hesiod or the eighth-century Israelite prophets. Hosea's background is unknown; Micah was a provincial from Moresheth near Lachish, perhaps a provincial elder; Isaiah belonged in some capacity to the Jerusalemite court circles; and Amos may at one time have served on the staff of temple or palace, in which kingdom is not clear. What is clear is that all four belonged to the very small minority of the population that was literate and educated, and it was from that socially privileged position that their protest was launched.

It is remarkable that no other ancient Near Eastern society that we know of developed a comparable tradition of dissident intellectualism and social criticism. Prophets and intermediaries of different kinds are attested practically everywhere in the region. A Syrian ruler contemporary with Amos consulted visionaries (*ḥzyn*), who assured him of military success; a king of Moab a century earlier received messages from the national deity, presumably by the same means, commanding the capture of this or that city; Mesopotamian ecstatics, diviners, "answerers," and "proclaimers" conveyed guidance and words of assurance from different deities. There is the occasional inoffensive chiding of the ruler—perhaps he had neglected a ritual or overlooked an earlier oracle—but the role of these intermediaries is almost exclusively supportive, and there is no breath of challenge to the political or social status quo.[66] Only in Israel and, to a lesser extent, Greece did a tradition of dissent and social protest develop.

What impact the criticism of Amos and the others had at the time is unclear. Attempts were made, understandably, to silence both Amos and Micah (Amos 7:10–17; Micah 2:6). Hosea seems to have been dismissed as a fool (Hos. 9:7–8), and Isaiah went into retirement after his unsuccessful intervention in the foreign policy of Ahaz (Isa. 8:16–22). But whatever reception they were accorded, their message not only survived but attained a degree of official if unacknowledged recognition in the Deuteronomic program. We must now go on to see how this transformation took place.

FROM DISSIDENCE
TO OFFICIAL RECOGNITION

A theme recurring often in prophetic discourse is that social injustice and political disaster are related as cause and effect. The question we now ask is: Who listened to this message and what impact did it have? It is assumed, with reason, that the prophet cannot function without a support group of some kind, and the further assumption is generally made that these people gathered around themselves a group of disciples who preserved and transmitted their messages. This is reasonable enough, especially if we assume some connection with the group phenomenon of which discipleship was an integral element. But the evidence for prophetic disciples beginning in the eighth century is not exactly overwhelming. Of the four dissenters under consideration, only one actually refers to disciples, and on one occasion only, where Isaiah speaks of instruction committed to disciples (*limmudîm;* Isa. 8:16). Perhaps, then, Israelite society at that time had its own informal means of disseminating information of public interest, including the pronouncements of prophetic demagogues, to use Max Weber's term, especially if the extant texts represent a deposit of several performances delivered, with local adaptations, in different places throughout the kingdoms. If we can believe Dtr, Micah's prediction of the destruction of Jerusalem was remembered and quoted verbatim at Jeremiah's trial a century after it had been uttered; and the fact that it was quoted by certain "elders of the land" may provide a clue to the transmission of prophetic sayings, to which we shall return (Micah 3:12; Jer. 26:18). The priest Amaziah's report to Jeroboam of a similarly dire prediction of Amos, with the added comment that the land could not put up with his sayings (Amos 7:10–11), is another indication that knowledge of at least the more spectacular pronouncements of these people was not confined to a small circle of disciples. Isaiah, finally, was well known in court and temple circles, and his activity and sayings were no doubt a matter of public record.

In whatever manner and to whatever extent these sayings were originally transmitted, the decisive factor in their survival was that the course of events proved them to be correct and vindicated the truth and coherence of their authors' visions. After the fall of Samaria in 722 B.C.E. they had to be taken seriously, and we have seen that the message of Amos and Hosea was reapplied to Judah after that event. Witness to this recycling of the prophetic message are the comminations of Amos against Judah and Jerusalem (Amos 2:4–5; 6:1). Hosea seems to have addressed both Samarians and Judeans, but there are also indications of later application to Judah (Hos. 1:7; 2:1–3;

3:4–5). Isaiah, who replicated the dire warnings of Amos for the benefit of his Judean audience, linked both kingdoms in his diatribe against social abuses. His contemporary Micah warned that, in imitating the "statutes of Omri and Ahab." Judah was heading in the same direction as Samaria (Micah 1:13; 6:16).

The first clear indication that dissent was accorded a degree of official recognition is the reform carried out, according to the historian, by Hezekiah, the first Judean king to come to the throne after the fall of Samaria. (The historian may have altered his accession year from seven years after to six years before that event, in order to bring the reform into more direct contact with the fate of the Northern Kingdom; see 2 Kings 17:1 and 18:1, 13.) In general, religious reform went in tandem with movements of political emancipation, in this instance an attempt to throw off the Assyrian yoke. Hezekiah's predecessor Ahaz had appealed to Tiglath-pileser III for assistance against a hostile coalition of Damascus and Samaria; the Assyrian king was happy to oblige, but the price was vassal status for Judah (2 Kings 16:7–9). Some time later, Hezekiah rebelled; the Assyrians attacked and invested Jerusalem, but both the city and the king somehow survived. The circumstances under which this happened (documented in both biblical and Assyrian annals) are obscure and need not concern us here.

As described in 2 Kings 18, supplemented here and there by 2 Chronicles 29—31, the reform consisted in the abolition of the "high places," thus providing the Assyrian commander with a convenient theological argument justifying aggression (2 Kings 18:4; 2 Chron. 31:1; the address of the Rabshakeh before the walls of Jerusalem is a free composition of the historian). Confirmation of the disestablishment of the *bāmôt,* initially under Hezekiah, definitively under Josiah, is claimed on the basis of a cult installation discovered during excavation at Arad in the Negev—though the experience of numerous disconfirmations of such archaeological claims suggests caution. At any rate, the sacrificial altar seems to have gone out of use in the late eighth century (stratum VIII), and the temple was no longer in use by the late seventh to early sixth centuries (stratum VI).[67]

Another measure was the removal of objectionable cult objects, including representations of male and female deities, from the temple precincts and, according to the author of Chronicles, restoration of the temple fabric. But what is remarkable about these accounts is not what they say but what they omit. There is not the slightest allusion to the removal of social abuses, and this in spite of the fact that, according to the record, Hezekiah was influenced by the Judean prophets Micah and Isaiah and therefore presumably by the tradition of dissent which they represented. Here, too, we have to begin with the ideology and *Tendenz* of our principal source. We have to ask why Dtr shows so little interest in matters of social justice in general, never alludes to the removal of social abuses, and never identifies such abuses as factors contributing to the eventual disaster. The author was certainly familiar with the standard topos that the ruler was responsible for the maintenance of justice and righteousness, and he even alludes to it in passing (2 Sam. 8:15; 1 Kings 10:9), but it is still odd that he makes so little use of it. We would be justified in suspecting that the omission is deliberate and perhaps not unconnected with the omission from the history of any reference to Amos and his colleagues. The omission may, in other words, be explained by the historian's ambivalent attitude toward prophecy, discussed earlier, combined with a very definite thesis in explanation of the fall of Samaria and Jerusalem. In any case, it is unlikely that Hezekiah and those who backed his reform were unaware of the need to remove the social, economic, and judicial abuses that had contributed to the disaster of 722 B.C.E., even if their concern did not, in the event, translate into a successful campaign of social and administrative reform.

Here, as elsewhere, we are at the mercy of our sources—what they choose to tell us and what they overlook or suppress. Several pieces of the interlocking puzzle are missing, obliging us to fall back on more or less educated guesswork. But there is one clue to the process by which dissent won a degree of official recognition that I believe is worth following up. Beginning in the latter part of the ninth century, we begin to hear of the political activity of a social entity that the historian refers to as "the people of the land" (*'am hā'āreṣ*). The contexts in which the designation occurs strongly suggest a specific social class rather than a generic term for a large segment of the population. Its influence appears to have been on the increase from that time to the end of the kingdom of Judah. We first hear of them collaborating in the coup against the Baalist queen Athaliah, engineered by the priest Jehoiada and resulting in the restoration of the Davidic dynasty in the person of Joash (ca. 837 B.C.E.). In the process, the Baal temple built by Athaliah in Jerusalem was destroyed and its cult officials executed (2 Kings 11:14, 18–20). Both Joash and his son Amaziah were victims of palace coups (2 Kings 14:5, 19–21), suggesting perhaps that the Baalist faction was still active. Much later, the "people of the land" dispatched the assassins of Amon and put his eight-year-old son Josiah on the throne (2 Kings 21:24), an intervention that must have put them in a strong position during the king's minority. It is reasonable to conclude that they played an important role in the cult reform and bid for independence from Assyria that followed. After Josiah's death at Megiddo, they made sure of the succession by their support of his son Jehoahaz (2 Kings 23:30).

The alignment of the "people of the land" with the nationalistic faction at the court and their allegiance to the Davidic dynasty are confirmed by the fact that they were among the first to be executed by the Babylonians after their conquest of Judah (2 Kings 25:18–21). The same conclusion is suggested by their opposition to Jeremiah, one of the chief proponents of appeasement, who lists them routinely among his enemies and accuses them of a whole range of improprieties (Jer. 1:18; 34:19; 37:2; 44:21). In the circumstances, it would be imprudent to take his allegations at face value.

To recapitulate: the expression ʿam hāʾāreṣ refers to the representatives of the Judean landed class outside the capital, which saw itself threatened by the encroaching state bureaucracy while supporting a limited but crucial role for the native dynasty. Their opposition to foreign rule, economically as well as politically onerous, went hand in hand with social and religious traditionalism and regret for the passing of the old order.[68] I suggest that it was this class which found a voice in the preaching of Micah and to which he refers as "my people." That Micah denounces the state bureaucracy yet, exceptionally, never condemns the monarchy is consistent with what we know about the "people of the land," and it will be recalled that it was certain "elders of the land" who quoted Micah's prediction of the destruction of Jerusalem at Jeremiah's trial. (If these "elders of the land" were representatives of "the people of the land," Jeremiah's opposition to the latter may have developed later, in connection with the bid for independence from the Babylonians.) It is, at any rate, arguable that the "people of the land" provided the channel through which the tradition of dissent represented by Micah found its way into the mainstream of the national life.

THE DEUTERONOMIC PROGRAM

None of the sporadic reforms carried out under the monarchy seems to have had much success. After Hezekiah's death (ca. 687 B.C.E.), his religious reform was quickly undone, and it remained undone during the long reign of Manasseh and the much shorter reign of Amon following. While the historian's portrait of Manasseh as the most villainous of Judah's kings, and one whose villainies helped bring about the extinction of the kingdom, is no doubt exaggerated and overlooks the not unimportant achievement of keeping the Assyrians at bay, we can at least accept his allusion to internal opposition with which Manasseh had to contend (2 Kings 21:16). I take this to imply that the reform party remained in existence and was still to some extent active. Its opportunity came with the assassination of Amon and the accession of the boy king Josiah, engineered, as we have seen, by the "people of the land."

The reform set in motion during Josiah's reign replicated Hezekiah's, but on a more impressive scale due to the declining power of Assyria. The Deuteronomic historian dates the reform to the eighteenth year of the reign, therefore 622, but the Chronicler places it six years earlier, which, if correct, has the advantage of moving it closer to the abdication of Ashurbanipal, last significant Assyrian king, which took place in 631 followed by his death in 627. We have seen that reforming activity and political emancipation generally go together. One of the most notable differences between the two reforms is the extension of Josiah's into the territory of the former kingdom of Samaria (now the Assyrian province Samerina), evidently with a view to eventual reunification. Like Hezekiah's reform, however, Josiah's was exclusively cultic. We are told that it came about as a result of concerted action by all segments of the population, lay and clerical (2 Kings 23:1–3), but the impetus, as far as social issues were concerned, must have come from the reform party, including the "people of the land."

We are also told that Josiah's reform was set in motion by the discovery of a law book during repair of the temple fabric (2 Kings 22:8–10). The identification of this book with Deuteronomy, perhaps an earlier version of the book as we have it, is one of the "assured results of modern scholarship," but whether it was a genuine product of Mosaic antiquity or a much more recent composition planted by the Jerusalemite priesthood or some other party interested in reform continues to be debated. Another possibility is that the story about the discovery of the book is a pious fiction of the historian. The idea would have been to explain how the law could have been neglected for so long and how, notwithstanding Josiah's piety, this neglect brought about the disasters that followed after a few decades. The same point is made in the historian's expanded version of Huldah's oracle (2 Kings 23:15–20; cf. 23:26–27). Consistent with this hypothesis is the absence of any reference to the law book in the account of the reform itself (23: 4–20).[69] It seems, then, that the Deuteronomic law represents a later attempt to give official sanction to the program of the reform party. In much the same way, the Athenian laws attributed to Solon aimed to perpetuate the reforms instituted by him during his tenure of office, a few years after the death of Josiah.

While a good part of the Deuteronomic law (chapters 12—26) is essentially an updated version of laws in the so-called Covenant Code (compare, for example, Deut. 15:12–18 with the law concerning slaves in Ex. 21:1–11), and additions continued to be made down into the Second Temple period (e.g., the law of membership in the assembly, Deut. 23:2–9), the nucleus can be dated to the reign of Josiah when the reform party, and the 'am hā'āreṣ in particular, came into their own. It represents, therefore, the agenda of the party set out in programmatic form. The cultic laws, most of which occur in the first half of the document (chapters 12—18), recall Hosea's vivid denunciation of alien cults and cult objects, the frequenting of high places, ritual prostitution, and other interesting but deviant practices. This, however, is the extent of Deuteronomy's debt to Hosea, for the latter did not take up the cause of agrarian reform and has little to say about such matters as the conduct of war and offices of state, with both of which Deuteronomy deals at length. It may be that Hosea represents a distinct constituency, in which case a likely candidate would be the Levitical clergy excluded from the state cult by Jeroboam (1 Kings 12:31).[70]

The Deuteronomic program gives clearest expression to protest against economic oppression and the widening gap between rich and poor in its agrarian measures. The basic issue was insolvency and its effect on the free, landowning peasant. In a subsistence economy, back-to-back crop failures would be enough to oblige the peasant to borrow seed for sowing at a high rate of interest and with the land, its produce, or the indentured service of members of his household as collateral; a situation exacerbated by the onerous exactions levied by the state.[71] We have no information on rates of interest during the monarchy, but in the Jewish military settlement on the island of Elephantine in Upper Egypt, the rate could go as high as 75 percent. For the same period, Nehemiah 5 provides a glimpse of the consequences of insolvency resulting from a combination of famine and imperial taxation.[72] In the Deuteronomic document, this contingency was countered by updating an old measure prohibiting interest on loans made to fellow Israelites while permitting it in dealings with foreigners, no doubt to encourage trade (Deut. 23:19–20; cf. Ex. 22:25). There were also laws forbidding distraint of anything necessary for the survival, livelihood, and basic comfort of the peasant (Deut. 24:6, 12–13, 17) and forbidding forcible entry to seize effects as pledge for unpaid debts (24:10–11). The old customary law about the seventh fallow year (Ex. 23:10–11) was enlarged to include the remission of debts in the seventh year, a law, however, that must have been practically unenforceable (15:1–3, 7–11). Along the same lines, the maximum stint of indentured service was set at six years, which no doubt represented a step forward in Israel but was twice the length permitted by the code of Hammurabi (#117).

Together with these remedial measures designed to alleviate some of the worst side effects of state control, those who drafted the program introduced a genuine innovation in the form of the triennial tithe, destined for the most disadvantaged members of society (14:28–29). This and similar measures, including gleaning rights (23:24–25; 24:19–22), amounted to a kind of rudimentary social-security system. Regulation of weights and measures (25:13–16) and the prompt payment of day laborers (24:14–16) corresponded to major concerns of the reform party (Amos 8:5; Hos. 12:7; Micah 6:10–11) and, indeed, of legislators in the Near East from the earliest times.

The main threat to social stability and the traditional way of life of the peasantry was undoubtedly the alienation and foreclosure under mortgage of land held in the family units for generations. Hence the violence of prophetic diatribe against those who covet fields and who join house to house, field to field (Micah 2:2; Isa. 5:8). Of some importance, therefore, was the prohibition of removing landmarks set up by the ancestors (Deut. 19:14; 27:17). These landmarks (*gĕbûlîm*) were stones set in the property that defined its limits. Like the *horoi* in ancient Greece, they may have been inscribed. In one of his poems, Solon claims to have removed the *horoi*, thus freeing the land, which suggests that the stones in this case may have recorded the insolvency of the owner and consequent foreclosure under mortgage.[73] Clearly, this was not the case with the Deuteronomic law, which took aim at the practice of cheating a neighbor out of land by repositioning the boundary marker.

Those who drafted the program were aware that any prospect of success depended on access by all to fair judicial process. The corruption of judges, who were recruited exclusively from the wealthy classes, was one of the principal targets of protest in the eighth century (Amos 5:10, 12; Micah 3:9, 11; Isa. 1:23; etc.). The Deuteronomic program addresses this issue by setting up local panels of judges in the towns and a central judiciary in the capital that served as a court of appeal (Deut. 16:18–20; 17:8–13). Precise guidelines for giving testimony were also established (19:15–20), and restrictions were placed on corporal punishment (25:1–3). Into all of this the program injects a note of urgency quite foreign to law codes ancient or modern:

> You shall not pervert justice; you shall not show partiality; you shall not take a bribe, for a bribe blinds the eyes of the wise and subverts the cause of the innocent. Justice, only justice you shall pursue, that you may live and inherit the land which Yahweh your God gives you.
>
> (16:19–20)

In Greece, shortly after the promulgation of the Deuteronomic program, Solon was putting into effect reforms of a similar nature during his tenure of office as archon in Athens (ca. 595–590 B.C.E.). His laws, written on tablets and set up in public places (cf. Deut. 27:2–3; 31:26), were intended to perpetuate the reforms and prevent the recurrence of abuses represented in the surviving fragments of his poetry as offensive to Zeus, guardian of justice. The social situation in Attica that provoked his denunciations was much the same as that of contemporary Judah. A rural, agrarian society, based on a clan system with hereditary landholdings, producing the same commodities (primarily grain, wine, olive oil), was being undermined by peasant insolvency, leading to the distraining of property, indentured service, enclosure, foreclosure, and a widening gap between the *aristoi* and the *demos,* the haves and the have-nots. To remedy this situation, in which social revolution seemed a distinct possibility, Solon took the radical step during his archonship of canceling all debts and prohibiting loans *epi tois sōmasin,* "with the debtor's own person," or the persons of his family members, as security. Other measures included the manumission of indentured laborers; the regulation of weights, measures, and coinage; and control of prices by prohibiting the export of essential commodities. In keeping with Hesiod's injunction to judges to hand down fair verdicts and put aside crooked judgments (*Works and Days* 263), Solon also reformed the judicial system and permitted appeal to the *dikasterion,* the popular court, in disputed cases.

Solon's reforms have been compared with those of Nehemiah during his governorship of Judah,[74] but they also correspond fairly closely to measures detailed in the Deuteronomic law. The connection between the preaching of the eighth-century prophets and the Deuteronomic program is also recalled by Solon's prediction of political disaster consequent on social injustice. The following passages, originally in verse, are taken from Demosthenes, *De Falsa Legatione* 254–55, and Diodorus Siculus, *Bibliotheke* 9.20:

> The ruin of our state will never come about by the doom of Zeus or through the will of the blessed and immortal gods; for Pallas Athena, valiant daughter of a valiant sire, is our stout-hearted guardian, and she holds over us her protecting arms. It is the townsfolk themselves and their false-hearted leaders who would fain destroy our great city through wantonness and love of money. But they are destined to suffer sorely for their outrageous behavior. They know not how to hold in check their full-fed lust, or, content with the merriment the banquet affords, to take their pleasure soberly and in order. . . . They are rich because they yield to the temptation of dishonest courses. . . . They spare neither the treasures of the gods nor the property of the state, and steal like brigands one from another. They pay no heed to the unshaken rock of holy Justice, who, though she be silent, is aware of all that happens now or has happened in the past, and in course of time, surely comes

to demand retribution. Lo, even now there comes upon the whole city a plague which none may escape. The people have come quickly into degrading bondage; bondage rouses from their sleep war and civil strife; and war destroys many in the beauty of their youth.

Out of the cloud come snow and hail in their fury, and the thunderbolt springs from the lightning's flash; so from great men ruin issues upon the state, and the people through their own folly sink into slavery under a single lord.[75]

Unlike the authors of prophetic dissent in Israel, Solon was able to bring about change by direct political action. Under the quite different political conditions in Judah, the proposal for reform had to come from outside the political mainstream, create its own constituency, and await the right set of circumstances to influence those with the power to effect change within the mainstream. We have proposed one way in which this may have come about, the end result being the official promulgation of a kind of social charter in Deuteronomy 12—26.

As a postscript, I note a certain ambiguity at the heart of the Deuteronomic program. In whatever form it was officially promulgated, if indeed it was, it is presented as an official state document, prescribes a constitution or polity, and concentrates authority in the organs of a centralized theocratic state. To the extent that such a political and religious program was successfully implemented, it would tend necessarily to undermine and replace the lineage network according to which Israelite society was structured from the beginning. However, the program incorporated, according to the hypothesis advanced above, important features of social reform sponsored by the "people of the land," who were committed to maintaining a traditional agrarian way of life. Perhaps that is why, when the "official" history came to be written, it passed over in silence both dissident prophecy of the type we have been considering and the social abuses against which it protested.

DEUTERONOMY AND BEYOND

Deuteronomy, therefore, marks the point at which dissent finally achieved a degree of official, if qualified and unacknowledged, recognition. Ironically, however, the promulgation of the Deuteronomic law was the first and decisive step toward the neutralization of prophetic dissent. The passage in the law dealing with prophecy (Deut. 18:15–18), perhaps not by accident located at its center, redefines the prophet as the continuator of the work of Moses the lawgiver and prophecy as essentially in function of the law. By placing the doctrine on prophecy in the chapter dealing with the official

organs of the state, alongside the judiciary, monarchy, and priesthood
(16:18–18:22), the drafters of the document indicated their intent to bring it
within the grid of their ideal commonwealth, thereby depriving it of its potentially disruptive and innovative character. Since it is generally agreed that
"the prophet like Moses" of this passage stands for the prophetic succession
as a whole, the reader is encouraged to view prophecy retrospectively, as
essentially belonging to the past. As was noted earlier, the same impression
is conveyed by the global allusion in Dtr to "his servants the prophets." The
idea seems to be that the promulgation of a written law renders appeal to
prophetic inspiration both unnecessary and undesirable, and the same message is conveyed in a number of rabbinic *baraitôt* that speak of prophecy
(*nĕbû'â*) as a thing of the past.[76]

The point emerges more clearly on the probable supposition that the
Deuteronomist school in the postdisaster period was responsible for putting
together the first collection of prophetic sayings, ending with those of Jeremiah.[77] A more or less official corpus of prophetic writings would not in itself rule out continued prophetic activity, but it would tend to shift the
weight from the present to the past, from the spoken to the written word,
and from direct prophetic utterance to the interpretation of written
prophecy. Here too, then, we see how the Deuteronomic redefinition of
prophecy marks the beginning of the process by which the prophetic role
was absorbed into those of sage (*ḥākām*), exegete, and eventually, rabbi.

Intellectuals have often been viewed as, typically, taking up a critical position vis-à-vis the status quo and functioning as the society's conscience, a
role requiring them generally, if not necessarily, to stand outside of the "establishment." So understood, the intellectual is expected to assume a critical posture also with respect to official or widely accepted understandings
of the dominant tradition, understood as "the reservoir of the most central
social and cultural experiences prevalent in a society, as the most enduring
element in the collective social and cultural construction of reality."[78] This
would correspond roughly to the role of the four eighth-century figures discussed in this chapter. Their language, needless to say, exceeded the
bounds of what would be considered tolerable for the social critic today;
take, for example, the systematic subversion of his public's expectations by
Amos: election does not lead to salvation (3:2), Israel's exodus is no different from those of other peoples (9:7), the expected "day of Yahweh" will
be darkness and not light (5:18–20), the sacrificial system and other cultic
acts as currently practiced are hateful to God (5:21–24), and so on.

It is perhaps not so surprising if this kind of diatribe had little positive
impact at the time of delivery. It is not even clear that it fared much better

as mediated through officially sponsored reforms, the accounts of which, as we have seen, never refer to the removal of social abuses. But by virtue of its incorporation in an official document, in the somewhat chastened form of the Deuteronomic program and law, it could function as a counterbalance to bureaucratic indifference to social issues. In subsequent centuries, it became an important part of the social conscience of synagogue and church, and it has continued to function in that way to the present.

Conclusion

We have now come to the end of our study of the ways in which the occupants of different roles contributed to the formation and maintenance of a basic but pluriform tradition. Many of the specialized activities implied by these roles have been identified in other ancient societies (e.g., Greece, Mesopotamia) and in traditional societies that have survived into the modern era (e.g., the Nuer of the Sudan, the Plains Indians). But whatever may have been the case elsewhere, we do not encounter in Israel a stable situation in which differentiated roles continued unchanged indefinitely. Israel was not a steady state society, and not only because it existed by courtesy of the great empires surrounding it. The movement toward political and economic centralization and consolidation resulted in these major roles or characters—scribal, priestly, prophetic—collapsing in on one another. So, for example, the didactic, aphoristic tradition became subordinated to the national cult, prophecy was reabsorbed into the priesthood, and a moralizing pedagogue like Ben Sira could claim, even if somewhat implausibly, to be fulfilling a prophetic role.

At the literary level, this process of consolidation corresponds to the formation of a canonical collection of writings. We are aware, of course, that in this context the term *canonical* is anachronistic and heavy with ambiguity. It is possible nevertheless to discern a process by which an authoritative literary corpus was put together. We could, for example, start out from the report of the Maccabean project to preserve the national literary heritage (2 Macc. 2:14) and the library allegedly established by Nehemiah (2 Macc. 2:13). Neither of these initiatives is historically implausible, and both presumably had some connection with the formation of a Torah—Prophets collection. Going further back, most scholars would agree that the Pentateuch is a product of the Persian period (sixth to fourth centuries B.C.E.) and that Pentateuchal law represents the civil and religious constitution of the Judean temple-state at that time. Going even further back, Deuteronomy has all the marks of an official, authoritative, and (to speak anachronistically) canonical text. Note, for example, the injunction not to add to or subtract from it (Deut. 4:2; 12:32), characteristic of an officially promulgated and binding document.

This literary construct in its successive stages was the product of specific social situations favoring the emergence and dominance of certain classes. Its strongly religious and cultic character correlates with the establishment, successively under Persian, Ptolemaic, and Seleucid aegis, of a type of political and social organization based on the temple as a political and economic as well as religious center. The dominant influence on the formation of the tradition was therefore exercised by the agenda of the priesthood and, to a lesser extent, of the aristocratic lineages whose interests coincided with those of the ruling priestly class. The emergence of a dominant tradition, inscribed in texts for which absolute authority was claimed, did not, needless to say, stifle the impulse toward other options. One of these is represented by the "new prophecy" emanating from millenarian sects and the writers of apocalyptic tracts and treatises, with their own brand of intellectuality. Another and more radical departure was the adoption of new forms of intellectualism inspired by Greek culture and its social and political embodiments—the polis, the *ephebeion* (youth center), the theater, and others. Both of these departures call for special treatment that exceeds the limits of the present study.

We noted at an earlier point the remarkable contrast between intellectualism in Judah and in Greek-speaking lands during the two centuries of Persian dominance (sixth to fourth centuries B.C.E.). We know of nothing in Judah or in the Jewish Diaspora remotely resembling the cosmological speculations of the Miletus school (Thales, Anaximander, Anaximenes), the Eleatics (Xenophanes, Parmenides), or the Pythagoreans. Geographical location no doubt had something to do with the contrast. As the archaeological record for the period in question attests,[1] Judah was a backwater, isolated from the coastal region and the major trade routes, while the cities on the Ionian seaboard were open to contacts from all sides. Unlike the Greek polis, the Judean temple community favored the emergence of a priestly elite serving as an instrument of Persian imperial control in the province. This, in turn, determined the main features of the officially sanctioned literary corpus put together at that time. There were also, as we have seen, elements of cultural deterrence and ressentiment already embedded in the tradition.

We have to admit, as we conclude our brief investigation, that this literary construct that came to be known as the biblical canon permits only occasional and poorly focused glimpses into the successive social worlds in which sages, priests, and prophets went about their business. Without that literary construct, however, the study of those worlds and those roles would be of interest only to social historians. For example, one of the most significant intellectual and religious achievements of ancient Israel, in contrast to the great empires, was the establishment of an autonomous sphere of law, independent of the will of a ruler. The "canonization" of the law meant that, although its interpretation could become an instrument of social control and oppression, and although its administration could be corrupted and subverted, the law rather than the will of a ruler was always the ultimate court of appeal. Or again, prophetic protest was neutralized by bureaucratic control, as we have seen, but the words themselves were preserved and eventually reclaimed as an essential element in the social consciousness of church and synagogue. In a word, the sage, the priest, and the prophet came, in their different ways, to contribute to the construction of an intellectual and moral universe that is still, in its main lines, habitable.

Notes

Introduction

1. The following remarks have been guided by my selective reading in role theory, including Ervin Goffman, *The Presentation of Self in Everyday Life* (Garden City, N.Y.: Doubleday, 1959); M. Banton, *Roles: An Introduction to the Study of Social Relations* (New York: Basic Books, 1965); B. J. Biddle and E. J. Thomas, eds., *Role Theory: Concepts and Research* (New York: John Wiley & Sons, 1966); T. Sarbin and V. Allen, "Role Theory," in G. Lindzey and E. Aronson, eds., *The Handbook of Social Psychology*, (Reading, Mass.: Addison-Wesley, 1968), 1:488–567; J. A. Jackson, ed., *Role* (Cambridge: Cambridge University Press, 1972); B. J. Biddle, *Role Theory: Expectations, Identities and Behaviors* (New York: Academic Press, 1979); idem, "Recent Developments in Role Theory," *ARS* 12 (1986): 67–92. On the limitations of the theory, see Margaret A. Coulson, "Role: A Redundant Concept in Sociology? Some Educational Considerations," in Jackson, ed., *Role*, 107–28; and the discussion between Malcolm Bradbury, Bryan Heading, and Martin Hollis, "The Man and the Mask: A Discussion of Role Theory," in Jackson, ed., *Role*, 41–64. The theory has been applied to prophecy by David L. Petersen, *The Roles of Israel's Prophets* (Sheffield, England: JSOT Press, 1981).

2. The theatrical analogy is developed—perhaps overdeveloped—by Peter Berger, *Invitation to Sociology* (Baltimore: Penguin Books, 1966).

3. Alasdair MacIntyre, *After Virtue*, 2d ed. (Notre Dame, Ind., and London: University of Notre Dame Press, 1984), 27–31.

4. Max Weber, *Economy and Society* (Berkeley: University of California Press, 1978), 1:18–22 (based on the 4th ed. of *Wirtschaft und Gesellschaft*, published in 1956).

Chapter 1: The Sage

1. R. Norman Whybray, *The Intellectual Tradition in the Old Testament* (Berlin: Alfred Töpelmann, 1974).

2. On the *logoi sophōn* genre, see James M. Robinson and Helmut Koester, eds., *Trajectories through Early Christianity* (Philadelphia: Fortress Press, 1971), 71–113; James M. Robinson, "Jesus as Sophos and Sophia," in Robert L. Wilken, ed., *Aspects of Wisdom in Judaism and Early Christianity* (Notre Dame, Ind., and London: University of Notre Dame Press, 1975), 1–16.

3. On this idea, see B. A. Van Groningen, *In the Grip of the Past* (Leiden: E. J. Brill, 1953).

4. See Joseph Blenkinsopp, *The Pentateuch: An Introduction to the First Five Books of the Bible* (New York: Doubleday, 1992), 1–19.

5. The *Einleitung,* running to nearly a hundred pages, was translated under the (misleading) title *The Legends of Genesis: The Biblical Saga and History* (New York: Schocken Books, 1964).

6. Hermann Gunkel, *Genesis,* 6th ed. (Göttingen: Vandenhoeck & Ruprecht, 1964).

7. On Gunkel's contribution, and on tradition history in general, see Douglas A. Knight, *Rediscovering the Traditions of Israel* (Missoula, Mont.: Scholars Press, 1975); Herbert F. Hahn, *The Old Testament in Modern Research,* 2d ed. (Philadelphia: Fortress Press, 1966); Douglas A. Knight, ed., *Tradition and Theology in the Old Testament* (Philadelphia: Fortress Press, 1977).

8. Max Weber, *Economy and Society* (Berkeley: University of California Press, 1978), 1:226–41.

9. Edward Shils, *Tradition* (Chicago: University of Chicago Press, 1981), 13.

10. Alasdair MacIntyre, *After Virtue,* 2d ed. (Notre Dame, Ind., and London: University of Notre Dame Press, 1984), 222.

11. *ANET,* 432–34.

12. See Saul Lieberman, *Greek in Jewish Palestine* (New York: Jewish Theological Seminary, 1942), 15–28; idem, *Hellenism in Jewish Palestine,* 2d ed. (New York: Jewish Theological Seminary, 1962), 100–114.

13. See Martin Hengel, *Judaism and Hellenism* (Philadelphia: Fortress Press, 1974), 1:157–162. An aretalogy is an encomium uttered by a deity in praise of the deity's attributes and great deeds. A translation of the most complete of the aretalogies, originally from Memphis, is available in Frederick C. Grant, *Hellenistic Religions* (Indianapolis and New York: Bobbs-Merrill, 1953), 131–33.

14. Hengel, *Judaism and Hellenism,* 1:147–49.

15. *ANET,* 421–25.

16. Max Weber, *Ancient Judaism* (New York: Free Press, 1952), 285.

17. Ibid., 336–82; on which, see Samuel N. Eisenstadt, "The Format of Jewish History: Some Reflections on Weber's *Ancient Judaism,*" *Modern Judaism* 1 (1981): 57–58.

18. André Lemaire, *Les Écoles et la formation de la Bible dans l'ancien Israël* (Fribourg, Switzerland: Editions Universitaires; Göttingen: Vandenhoeck & Ruprecht, 1981); idem, "Sagesse et écoles," *VT* 34 (1984): 270–81. Lemaire's attempt at reconstruction is criticized by James L. Crenshaw, "Education in Ancient Israel," *JBL* 104 (1985): 601–15.

19. Zeev Meshel, *Kuntillet 'Ajrud: A Religious Center from the Time of the Judaean Monarchy on the Border of Sinai* (Jerusalem: Israel Museum, 1976). Unfortunately, but typically, at the time of writing only a provisional account of the excavation, carried out in 1976, has been published.

20. D. W. Jamieson-Drake, *Scribes and Schools in Monarchic Judah* (Sheffield, England: The Almond Press, 1991).

21. See Emile Durkheim, *De la division du travail social,* 6th ed. (Paris: Libraire Félix Alcan, 1932), 149–57. The somewhat similar manner in which Saul was elected takes in only the *šēbeṭ* and the *mišpāḥâ* (1 Sam. 10:20–21).

22. To be distinguished from the *bêt 'ābôt* (ancestral house), a unit characteris-

tic of social organization in the province of Yehud under Iranian rule; on which see Joel Weinberg, "Das BĒIT ĀḆŌT im 6–4. Jh. v. u. Z.," *VT* 23 (1973): 400–414.

23. On kinship terms, with reference to ancient Israel, see Francis I. Andersen, "Israelite Kinship Terminology and Social Structure," *Bible Translator* 20 (1969): 29–39; C.H.J. de Geus, *The Tribes of Israel* (Assen and Amsterdam: Van Gorcum, 1976), 133–64; Niels Peter Lemche, *Early Israel: Anthropological and Historical Studies on the Israelite Society before the Monarchy* (Leiden: E. J. Brill, 1985), 245–85.

24. Elders functioned in Judean settlements in the Persian period (Ezra 10:14), in the cult assembly (Lev. 4:15; Judg. 21:16), and in the Babylonian Diaspora (Jer. 29:1; Ezek. 20:1).

25. On the material evidence for writing and literacy, in addition to Lemaire and Jamieson-Drake, see Amihai Mazar, *Archaeology of the Land of the Bible 10,000–586 B.C.E.* (New York: Doubleday, 1990), 361–63, 514–20.

26. Gen. 34:7; Deut. 22:21; Judg. 19:22–26; 2 Sam. 13:12; Jer. 29:23.

27. Albrecht Alt, "The Origins of Israelite Law," in idem, *Kleine Schriften zur Geschichte des Volkes Israel* (Munich: C. H. Beck, 1959), 1:278–332.

28. I am assuming that '*ibrî* in Ex. 21:2 denotes a social category and is not a gentilic. On the slave law, see Niels P. Lemche, "The 'Hebrew Slave': Comments on the Slave Law Ex. xxi 2–11," *VT* 25 (1975): 129–44.

29. See Carole R. Fontaine, *Traditional Sayings in the Old Testament* (Sheffield, England: The Almond Press, 1982).

30. For the recently discovered ninth-century B.C.E. Aramaic inscription allegedly containing the first nonbiblical reference to the *bet david*, see Avraham Biran and Joseph Naveh, "An Aramaic Stele Fragment from Tel Dan," *IEJ* 43 (1993): 81–98.

31. Mazar, *Archaeology*, 368–402; Lemaire, *Les Écoles*, 7–33.

32. John C. L. Gibson, *Textbook of Syrian Semitic Inscriptions*, vol. 1: *Hebrew and Moabite Inscriptions* (Oxford: Clarendon Press, 1971), 5–15; André Lemaire, *Inscriptions hébraïques*, vol. 1: *Les Ostraca* (Paris: Editions du Cerf, 1977), 23–81, 245–50.

33. Cf. 2 Chron. 17:2. The discussion of the date of the list goes back to Albrecht Alt, "Judas Gaue unter Josia" and "Bemerkungen zu einigen Judäischen Ortslisten des Alten Testaments," in idem, *Kleine Schriften zur Geschichte des Volkes Israel* (Munich: C. H. Beck, 1964), 2:276–305. See also Yohanan Aharoni, *The Land of the Bible: A Historical Geography*, 2d ed. (Philadelphia: Westminster Press, 1979), 347–56.

34. The expression *šēbeṭ sōpēr* in Deborah's song (Judg. 5:14) may mean "commander's staff" (cf. Akkadian *šapāru*, "command") or "bronze staff" (cf. Akkadian *siparru*, "bronze") but in any case has nothing to do with scribes.

35. The epic thesis as proposed by W. F. Albright was adopted, with modifications, by Frank Moore Cross, Jr., who takes J and E to be "variant forms in prose of an older, largely poetic epic cycle of the era of the Judges" (*Canaanite Myth and Hebrew Epic* [Cambridge, Mass.: Harvard University Press, 1973], 293). It has since been reproduced often by Cross's students, most recently by Brian Peckham, *History and Prophecy: The Development of Late Judean Literary Traditions* (New York: Doubleday, 1993).

36. Gerhard von Rad, *Old Testament Theology* (New York: Harper & Row, 1962), 1:48–56; idem, *The Problem of the Hexateuch and Other Essays* (Edinburgh and London: Oliver & Boyd, 1966), 69.

37. Mazar, *Archaeology,* 416–62.

38. *he'tîqû* probably refers to copying, as in modern Hebrew, but this would include collecting and editing. According to *b. Baba Batra* 15a, Hezekiah and his colleagues (*si'átô*) wrote—i.e., copied—Proverbs, the Canticle, Qoheleth, and Isaiah.

39. Johannes Fichtner ("Jesaja unter den Weisen," *TLZ* 74 [1949]: 73–82) and R. J. Anderson ("Was Isaiah a Scribe?" *JBL* 79 [1960]: 57–58) argue, I believe inconclusively, that Isaiah was at one time a scribe or counselor.

40. 2 Kings 22:3–14; Jer. 26:24; 29:3; 36:10–12; 39:14; 40:5. On hereditary scribalism in Mesopotamia, see D. E. Weisberg, *Guild Structure and Political Allegiance in Early Achaemenid Mesopotamia* (Baltimore: Johns Hopkins University Press, 1967), 79–81.

41. Patrick Skehan, *Studies in Israelite Poetry and Wisdom* (Washington, D.C.: Catholic Biblical Association of America, 1971), 43–45.

42. *ANET,* 420, 422.

43. *Ibid.,* 422, 423.

44. Moshe Weinfeld, "The Origin of the Humanism in Deuteronomy," *JBL* 80 (1961): 241–47. See also William McKane, *Prophets and Wise Men* (London: SCM. Press, 1965), 107–8.

45. Barnabas Lindars, "Torah in Deuteronomy," in Peter Ackroyd and Barnabas Lindars, eds., *Words and Meanings* (Cambridge: Cambridge University Press, 1968), 128–29.

46. The quasi-canonical status of Deuteronomy is apparent in the stipulations that nothing be added to it or subtracted from it (4:2; 12:32), that it be read publicly on specific solemn occasions (31:9–13, 24–26), and that a copy of the official text be in the hands of the ruler (17:18).

47. The verb *tāpaś* can refer to handling harp (Gen. 4:21), shield (Jer. 46:9), sword (Ezek. 38:4), sickle (Jer. 50:16), and bow (Amos 2:15).

48. See Joseph Blenkinsopp, *Prophecy and Canon* (Notre Dame, Ind., and London: University of Notre Dame Press, 1977), 39–53.

49. Weber, *Ancient Judaism,* 395.

50. On Proverbs 1—9 and 31 forming an interpretative framework for the book, see Claudia V. Camp, *Wisdom and the Feminine in the Book of Proverbs* (Sheffield, England: The Almond Press, 1985), 186–208.

51. See William Foxwell Albright, "The Goddess of Life and Wisdom," *AJSL* 36 (1919–1920): 258–94; idem, "Some Canaanite-Phoenician Sources of Hebrew Wisdom," in Martin Noth and David Winton Thomas, eds., *Wisdom in Israel and the Ancient Near East* (Leiden: E. J. Brill, 1955), 1–45; idem, *From the Stone Age to Christianity,* 2d ed. (Garden City, N.Y.: Doubleday, 1957), 367–70. More recent guesses along the same lines are those of Richard J. Clifford, "Proverbs IX: A Suggested Ugaritic Parallel," *VT* 25 (1975): 298–306; Bernhard Lang, *Frau Weisheit* (Düsseldorf: Patmos, 1975).

52. The woman of Zech. 5:5–11 who must be removed from Judah and transported to Babylon is designated by the unusual feminine form *hāris'â* (wickedness), suggesting by assonance the name of the goddess Asherah. On these poetic texts in relation to Proverbs 1—9, see Joseph Blenkinsopp, "The Social Context of the 'Outsider Woman' in Proverbs 1—9," *Bib* 72 (1991): 457–73.

53. In the Gospel of Thomas, for example, Jesus says of Mary Magdalene, "I my-

self shall lead her in order to make her male; for every woman who will make her-self male will enter the kingdom of heaven" (quoted from the translation of Thomas O. Lambdin, in James M. Robinson, ed., *The Nag Hammadi Library*, rev. ed. [San Francisco: Harper & Row, 1988], 138).

54. On this point, see the perceptive remarks of Carol A. Newsom, "Woman and the Discourse of Patriarchal Wisdom: A Study of Proverbs 1—9," in Peggy L. Day, ed., *Gender and Difference in Ancient Israel* (Minneapolis: Fortress Press, 1989), 142–60.

55. Blenkinsopp, "Social Context," 465.

56. This summary of the Weberian concept of rationalization, expounded at numerous points in *Economy and Society,* is taken from Shils, *Tradition,* 291.

57. LXX has *harmozousa,* followed by Vulg. *cuncta componens;* cf. Wisd. Sol. 7:22 and 8:6. *Midrash Bereshit Rabbah* 1:1 starts out with Prov. 8:22 and concludes that God created the world using Torah as a blueprint.

58. Grant, *Hellenistic Religions,* 132.

59. *ANET,* 320–21.

60. On Gen. 18:22–33 and its midrashic commentary, see Joseph Blenkinsopp, "Abraham and the Righteous of Sodom," *JJS* 33 (1982): 119–32; and idem, "The Judge of All the Earth: Theodicy in the Midrash on Genesis 18:22–33," *JJS* 41 (1990): 1–12.

61. Once *qādôš,* "the Holy One" (6:10). Beginning with chapter 3, the singular form *'ĕlôha* is the most common.

62. It bears the title "Counsels of a Pessimist" in Wilfred G. Lambert, *Babylonian Wisdom Literature* (Oxford: Clarendon Press, 1960), 107–9.

63. In Lambert, *Babylonian Wisdom Literature,* 139–49; see also *ANET,* 437–38.

64. The next three lines, *nittĕnû mērō'eh 'ehād* (they are given by one shepherd) do not make sense and are probably corrupt. One emendation is *kĕmardēa' hād* (like a sharp goad), by Louis Ginsberg, *Qohelet* (Tel Aviv: Neuman Press, 1961), 134.

65. For an assessment of the different "voices" in the book, see Roland E. Murphy, "The Sage in Ecclesiastes and Qoheleth the Sage," in John G. Gammie and Leo G. Perdue, eds., *The Sage in Israel and the Ancient Near East* (Winona Lake, Ind.: Eisenbrauns, 1990), 263–65.

66. D. Tsekourakis, "Studies in the Terminology of Early Stoic Ethics" (Ph.D. diss., University of London, 1971), 91–92, as quoted by A. A. Long, *Hellenistic Philosophy: Stoics, Epicureans, Sceptics,* 2d ed. (Berkeley and Los Angeles: University of California Press, 1986), 206.

67. On Stoic ethics, see, in addition to Long, *Hellenistic Philosophy,* 179–209, J. M. Rist, *Stoic Philosophy* (Cambridge: Cambridge University Press, 1969), passim; I. G. Kidd, "Moral Action and Rules in Stoic Ethics," in J. M. Rist, ed., *The Stoics* (Berkeley and Los Angeles: University of California Press, 1978), 247–58.

68. On the Zeno(n) papyri, see the brief article by Michael Stone in *EJ* 16:991–92; also Hengel, *Judaism and Hellenism,* 1:35–55; Victor Tcherikover, *Hellenistic Civilization and the Jews* (New York: Atheneum Press, 1975), 60–73.

69. See Blenkinsopp, *The Pentateuch,* 19–28, 54–97. A more detailed defense of this thesis appears in Andrew H. Bartelt, Astrid B. Beck, Chris A. Franke, Paul R. Raabe, eds., *Fortunate the Eyes that See: Essays in Honor of David Noel Freeman* (Grand Rapids: Wm. B. Eerdmans Publishing Co., 1995).

Chapter 2: The Priest

1. Julius Wellhausen, *Prolegomena to the History of Israel* (Edinburgh: Adam & Charles Black, 1885; reprint, Atlanta: Scholars Press, 1994), 361 (first published in German 1878).

2. Ibid., 509. Note, however, that the quotation is from the article "Israel," which appeared in the 9th edition of the *Encyclopædia Britannica* (1881) and was reprinted with the English translation of the *Prolegomena.*

3. E.g., Walther Eichrodt, *Theology of the Old Testament,* vol. 1 (Philadelphia: Westminster Press, 1961), 405; vol. 2 (Philadelphia: Westminster Press, 1967), 315, 442; Gerhard von Rad, *Old Testament Theology* (New York: Harper & Row, 1962), 1:259–60.

4. Her *Purity and Danger* (London: Routledge & Kegan Paul, 1966), especially the chapter on "The Abominations of Leviticus," is often quoted; several of the chapters in her *Implicit Meanings: Essays in Anthropology* (London and New York: Routledge & Kegan Paul, 1975) are also relevant, as is, more recently, "The Forbidden Animals in Leviticus," *JSOT* 59 (1993): 3–23.

5. The importance of ritual and gesture in sustaining tradition and social memory is emphasized in Paul Connerton, *How Societies Remember* (Cambridge: Cambridge University Press, 1989).

6. Joseph Blenkinsopp, *The Pentateuch: An Introduction to the First Five Books of the Bible* (New York: Doubleday, 1992), 229–32.

7. Yehezkel Kaufmann, *The Religion of Israel: From Its Beginnings to the Babylonian Exile,* translated and abridged by Moshe Greenberg (New York: Schocken Books, 1960), 175–200; Avi Hurwitz, "The Evidence of Language in Dating the Priestly Code," *RB* 81 (1974): 24–56.

8. William G. Dever, "Material Remains and the Cult in Ancient Israel: An Essay in Archeological Systematics," in Carol L. Meyers and Michael O'Connor, eds., *The Word of the Lord Shall Go Forth: Essays in Honor of David Noel Freedman in Celebration of His Sixtieth Birthday* (Winona Lake, Ind.: Eisenbrauns, 1983), 578–79.

9. Consult John S. Holladay, Jr., "Religion in Israel and Judah: An Explicitly Archeological Approach," in Patrick D. Miller, Jr., Paul D. Hanson, and S. Dean McBride, eds., *Ancient Israelite Religion* (Philadelphia: Fortress Press, 1987), 249–99; Amihai Mazar, *Archaeology of the Land of the Bible 10,000–586 B.C.E.* (New York: Doubleday, 1990), passim.

10. On the priesthood and cult at Elephantine, see Bezalel Porten, *Archives from Elephantine* (Berkeley and Los Angeles: University of California Press, 1968), 105–50 and passim. Priests are referred to in two of the papyri (AP 30:1, 18; 38:1, 12).

11. See Max Weber's remarks on ancestor cults and the priesthood of the paterfamilias in *Economy and Society* (Berkeley: University of California Press, 1978), 1:411–12. Recommended also is Herbert Brichto, "Kin, Cult, Land and Afterlife—A Biblical Complex," *HUCA* 44 (1973): 1–54.

12. Jer. 14:14; 27:9; 29:8; Ezek. 13:6–9; 22:28; Micah 3:5–7, 11.

13. *měšārēt* is used of cultic personnel (Jer. 33:21; Isa. 61:6; 1 Chron. 16:4; 2 Chron. 23:6), and *na'ar* sometimes occurs in cultic contexts, e.g., in describing Micah's Levite (Judg. 17:7, 11–12; 18:3, 15). According to Franz Dummermuth ("Josua in Ex. xxxiii, 7–11," *TLZ* 19 [1963]: 161–68, *na'ar* can carry the meaning of cultic ecstatic.

14. Mazar, *Archaeology*, 319–23.

15. On the Gibeonite cities, their location, and their role in the early history of Israel, see Joseph Blenkinsopp, "Kiriath-jearim and the Ark," *JBL* 88 (1969): 143–56; idem, *Gibeon and Israel: The Role of Gibeon and the Gibeonites in the Political and Religious History of Early Israel* (Cambridge: Cambridge University Press, 1972), 65–83. A more recent treatment with bibliography is Patrick M. Arnold, "Gibeon," *ABD* 2:1010–13.

16. The principal proponent of the thesis that Exodus 32—34 is basically a Deuteronomic composition is Lothar Perlitt, *Bundestheologie im Alten Testament* (Neukirchen-Vluyn: Neukirchener Verlag, 1969), 203–16.

17. Frank Moore Cross, Jr., *Canaanite Myth and Hebrew Epic*, (Cambridge, Mass.: Harvard University Press, 1973), 197–198. Cross's use of the designation "Mushite" for the priestly houses of Shiloh and Dan is debatable, since in the genealogies Mushi belongs to the Merari line and Moses to the Kohathite line.

18. John R. Bartlett ("Zadok and His Successors at Jerusalem," *JTS*, n.s., 19 [1968]: 1–18) argued that the Jerusalemite chief priests were royal appointees rather than descendants of Zadok.

19. Frank Moore Cross, Jr., "The Priestly Houses of Early Israel," in idem, *Canaanite Myth and Hebrew Epic*, 195–215.

20. Harold H. Rowley, "Zadok and Nehushtan," *JBL* 58 (1939): 113–41; in his *Worship in Ancient Israel* (London: SPCK Press, 1967), 73n4, he lists and documents previous proponents of this thesis, including Mowinckel.

21. Argued in Blenkinsopp, "Kiriath-jearim and the Ark," 156.

22. In the Sumerian city-states, the *en* (one in charge of the temple) could be male or female, depending on the gender of the deity; see Samuel N. Kramer, *The Sumerians: Their History, Culture and Character* (Chicago: University of Chicago Press, 1963), 141–44.

23. On the gender issue in general, see Phyllis Bird, "The Place of Women in the Israelite Cultus," in Miller et al., eds., *Ancient Israelite Religion*, 397–419.

24. Weber, *Economy and Society*, 1:440.

25. Ibid., 1:426.

26. On divination in Mesopotamia by priests, and the *baru*-priest in particular, see A. Leo Oppenheim, *Ancient Mesopotamia: Portrait of a Dead Civilization* (Chicago: University of Chicago Press, 1964), 206–27; J. Renger, "Untersuchungen zum Priestertum in der altbabylonischen Zeit," *ZA* 24 (1967): 110–88.

27. Amos 7:16; Micah 2:6, 11; Ezek. 21:2, 7. At Amos 7:16, for *lōʾ taṭṭîp*, NEB has "I am not to . . . go drivelling on," which is wisely abandoned in the revised edition.

28. Robert P. Carroll, "The Myth of the Empty Land," in idem, *Ideological Criticism of Biblical Texts* (*Semeia* 59; 1992), 79–93.

29. E.g., by Hans-Joachim Kraus, *Worship in Israel* (Oxford: Basil Blackwell, 1966), 98–99; Aelred Cody, *A History of Old Testament Priesthood* (Rome: Pontifical Biblical Institute, 1969), 113–14; Leopold Sabourin, *Priesthood: A Comparative Study* (Leiden: E. J. Brill, 1973), 130–33; Menahem Haran, *Temples and Temple Service in Ancient Israel* (Winona Lake, Ind.: Eisenbrauns, 1985), 81.

30. More detailed presentation in Blenkinsopp, *The Pentateuch*, 47–50.

31. The connection is rejected by Roland de Vaux, *Ancient Israel: Its Life and Institutions* (London: Darton, Longman & Todd, 1961), 369–71.

32. *ANET,* 315–16.

33. He accuses the Temple priests of venality (6:13; 8:16), culpable ignorance (14:18), arbitrary rule (5:31), idolatry (8:1–3), and ungodliness in general (23:11), all of which help to explain his rough treatment at the hands of Pashhur, chief officer of the Temple (20:1–6).

34. On these Zadokite passages in Ezekiel and their place in the history of the priesthood, see Walther Zimmerli, *Ezekiel 2* (Philadelphia: Fortress Press, 1983), 456–59.

35. Wellhausen, *Prolegomena,* 179–81.

36. Some examples: the high priest's headdress consisted of the *miṣnepet* (tiara) and *nēzer* (diadem), both of which were worn by rulers (Lev. 8:9; cf. Ezek. 21:31 [21:26]; 2 Sam. 1:10; 2 Kings 11:12; Ps. 132:18); the *sānîp* (tiara, turban) placed on the high priest Joshua's head (Zech. 3:5) also occurs in a royal context (Isa. 62:3). Rulers were anointed during the time of the kingdoms, never priests.

37. Alternatively, the crowning may be symbolic and honorific, indicating the increased judicial and administrative functions of the high priest under Persian rule; see Carol L. Meyers and Eric M. Meyers, *Haggai, Zechariah 1—8* (Garden City, N.Y.: Doubleday, 1987), 369–70.

38. Num. 1:50–54; 3:5–10; 8:13, 19, 23–26; 18:1–7; 1 Chron. 9:28–29; 23:2–4, 24–32.

39. 1 Chron. 26:20–28; 2 Chron. 8:15; 31:11–16; Ezra 8:24–30; Neh. 10:37–39; 13:13.

40. Gerhard von Rad, "The Levitical Sermon in I and II Chronicles," in idem, *The Problem of the Hexateuch and Other Essays* (Edinburgh and London: Oliver & Boyd, 1966), 267–80.

41. The close association between sacrifice and prayer is apparent in many psalms, e.g., Ps. 5:3; 27:7; 54:8. It is discussed in Sigmund Mowinckel, *The Psalms in Israel's Worship* (New York and Nashville: Abingdon Press, 1967), 2:20–25.

42. The latter is described as *śar hammaśśā'* which Mowinckel (*Psalms in Israel's Worship,* 2:56) translates "master of the oracle," based on the meaning of *maśśā'* in prophetic texts; the more usual meaning, however, would be "precentor," "musical director," or something of the sort.

43. Nothing certain can be concluded from the order in which Kohath, Gershon, and Merari are listed in the relevant texts (Num. 3:14–39; 4:24–25; 10:17, 21; 1 Chron. 5:27 [6:1]; 15:5–7; 23:6; 2 Chron. 29:12). According to the Chronicler (1 Chron. 5:27–6:15 [6:1–30]), Asaph, Heman, and Ethan were descended, respectively, from Gershom, Kohath, and Merari, with Jeduthun replacing Ethan. See Hartmut Gese, "Zur Geschichte der Kultsänger am Zweiten Tempel," in Otto Betz, ed., *Abraham unser Vater. Festschrift Otto Michel* (Leiden: E. J. Brill, 1963), 222–34.

44. M. Gertner ("The Masorah and the Levites: An Essay in the History of a Concept," *VT* 10 [1960]: 241–84) proposed the thesis that Levitical scholars of the Second Temple were the ancestors of the Masoretes.

45. On the Temple *nětînîm,* see Menahem Haran, "The Gibeonites, the Nethinim and the Sons of Solomon's Servants," *VT* 11 (1961): 159–69; Baruch A. Levine, "The Netinim," *JBL* 82 (1963): 207–12; Ephraim A. Speiser, "Unrecognized Dedication," *IEJ* 13 (1963): 69–73.

46. See Joseph Blenkinsopp, "Temple and Society in Achaemenid Judah," in Philip R. Davies, ed., *Second Temple Studies,* vol. 1: *Persian Period* (Sheffield: Sheffield Academic Press, 1991), 30–33.

47. Weber, *Economy and Society,* 1:425–26, 500–502.

48. Adolph Lods, *The Prophets and the Rise of Judaism* (London: Routledge & Kegan Paul, 1955), 218.

49. Alan H. Gardiner, "The House of Life," *JEA* 24 (1938): 164–76.

50. See n. 4, above. Also David P. Wright, *The Disposal of Purity: Elimination Rites in the Bible and in Hittite and Mesopotamian Literatures* (Atlanta: Scholars Press, 1987), and his article on "Unclean and Clean (OT)," *ABD* 6:729–41.

51. Further detail in Blenkinsopp, *The Pentateuch,* 47–50.

52. A thesis developed in interesting ways by Jon D. Levenson, *Creation and the Persistence of Evil* (San Francisco: Harper & Row, 1988).

53. Elias Bickerman, *From Ezra to the Last of the Maccabees* (New York: Schocken Books, 1962), 19.

54. Robert P. Carroll (*Jeremiah: A Commentary* [Philadelphia: Westminster Press, 1986], 620–23) suggests that Jeremiah's purchase of a plot of land near Jerusalem may also reflect the crucial issue of land tenure in the early Persian period.

55. See above.

56. *ANET,* 268.

57. Joseph Blenkinsopp, "The Structure of P," *CBQ* 38 (1976): 275–92; idem, *The Pentateuch,* 185–86.

58. This point is developed by Eichrodt, *Theology of the Old Testament,* 1:56–61 (= *Theologie des Alten Testaments,* 5th ed. [Göttingen: Vandenhoeck & Ruprecht, 1957] 1: 23–24).

59. Ex. 16:3; Lev. 4:13–14, 21; 16:17, 33; Num. 10:7; 14:5; 15:15; 16:2–3, 33; 17:12 [16:47] 19:20; 20:4, 6, 10, 12; 22:4.

60. Text and brief commentary in Stanley M. Burstein, *The Babyloniaca of Berossus* (Malibu, Calif.: Undena Publications, 1978).

61. Wilfred G. Lambert and Alan R. Millard, *ATRA-ḪASĪS: The Babylonian Story of the Flood* (Oxford: Oxford University Press, 1969).

62. John Van Seters, "The Primeval Histories of Greece and Israel Compared," *ZAW* 100 (1988): 1–22.

63. Solomon Buber, *Midrash Tanhuma': Qedoshim* 10 (Vilna: 1885).

64. Mircea Eliade dealt with the theme so repeatedly as to defy documentation, but see, e.g., his *Patterns in Comparative Religion* (New York and London: Sheed & Ward, 1958), 374–79; and *Images and Symbols* (New York and London: Sheed & Ward, 1969), 27–56. On the Babylonian *mappa mundī,* see James C. VanderKam, "I Enoch 77,3 and a Babylonian Map of the World," *RevQ* 42 (1983): 271–78.

65. Richard J. Clifford, *The Cosmic Mountain in Canaan and the Old Testament* (Cambridge, Mass.: Harvard University Press, 1972); Jon D. Levenson, *Sinai and Zion* (Minneapolis: Winston Press, 1985), 111–37.

66. The relevant texts are Josephus, *Ant.* 3.102–203; *War* 5.212–19; Philo, *Vita Mos.* 2.76–108.

67. E.g., Amos 5:21–27; Isa. 1:10–16; 66:1–4; cf. Ps. 51:16–17 and the corrective addition in v. 18–19.

Chapter 3: The Prophet

1. Two recent examples: Robert R. Wilson, *Prophecy and Society in Ancient Israel* (Philadelphia: Fortress Press, 1980), 21–88; Thomas W. Overholt, *Prophecy in Cross-Cultural Perspective* (Atlanta: Scholars Press, 1986).

2. Max Weber, *Economy and Society* (Berkeley: University of California Press, 1978), 1:439. A translation of chapter 6, "Religious Groups," was published separately as *The Sociology of Religion* (London: Methuen, 1965).

3. See above.

4. *Economy and Society,* 1:439.

5. Ibid. 1:241. See also Max Weber, *The Theory of Social and Economic Organization* (New York: The Free Press of Glencoe, 1964), 358; and the collection of Weber's writings on the subject in Samuel N. Eisenstadt, ed., *On Charisma and Institution Building* (Chicago and London: University of Chicago Press, 1968).

6. Dorothy Emmett, "Prophets and Their Societies," *JRAI* 86 (1956): 13–23. Other criticisms in David Little, "Max Weber and the Comparative Study of Religious Ethics," *JRE* 2 (1974): 5–40; David L. Petersen, "Max Weber and the Sociological Study of Ancient Israel," in H. M. Johnson, ed., *Religious Change and Continuity* (San Francisco: Jossey-Bass, 1979), 117–49.

7. Max Weber, *Ancient Judaism* (New York: Free Press, 1952), 90–117.

8. Weber, *Economy and Society,* 1:246–54.

9. Gustav Hölscher, *Die Propheten. Untersuchungen zur Religionsgeschichte Israels* (Leipzig: J. C. Hinrichs, 1914).

10. Theodore H. Robinson, *Prophecy and the Prophets in Ancient Israel* (1923; 2d ed., London: Gerald Duckworth, 1953); Alfred Jepsen, *NABI. Soziologische Studien zur alttestamentlichen Literatur und Religionsgeschichte* (Munich: C. H. Beck, 1934); Johannes Lindblom, "Zur Frage des kanaanäischen Ursprungs des altisraelitischen Prophetismus," in Johannes Hempel and Leonhard Rost, eds., *Von Ugarit nach Qumran* (Berlin: A. Töpelmann, 1958), 89–104. Peter Berger ("Charisma and Religious Innovation: The Social Location of Israelite Prophecy," *ASR* 28 [1963]: 940–50) criticizes the Duhm-Wellhausen approach as taken over by Weber but exaggerates the cultic connections of the prophets.

11. John Barton, *Oracles of God: Perceptions of Ancient Prophecy in Israel after the Exile* (Oxford: Oxford University Press, 1986).

12. 1 Kings 14:18; 15:29; 18:36; 2 Kings 9:7, 36; 10:10; 14:25; 17:13, 23; 21:10; 24:2; Jer. 7:25; 25:4; 26:5; 29:19; 35:14; 44:4. The same phrase occurs in Amos 3:7, a transparently Deuteronomic gloss.

13. The terms are taken from Hans-Joachim Kraus, *Die prophetische Verkündigung des Rechts in Israel* (Zurich: Zollikon, 1957), 15–16.

14. Practically the same statement is attributed to Yahweh in Amos 9:8a but modified by the almost certainly added v. 8b. On this question, see Frank Crüsemann, "Kritik an Amos im Deuteronomistischen Geschichtswerk," in Hans Walter Wolff, ed., *Probleme biblischer Theologie. Festschrift Gerhard von Rad* (Munich: Chr. Kaiser, 1971), 57–63. Peter R. Ackroyd ("A Judgment Narrative between Kings and Chronicles? An Approach to Amos 7:9–17," in George W. Coats and Burke O. Long, eds., *Canon and Authority* [Philadelphia: Fortress Press, 1977], 71–87) makes the interesting suggestion that the biographical passage in Amos 7:10–17 dealing with

the prophet's run-in with the priest Amaziah at Bethel may have originated as an alternative, and less favorable, account of Jeroboam's reign than the one in 2 Kings 14.

15. For the text of and brief commentary on the ostraca, see John C. L. Gibson, *Textbook of Syrian Semitic Inscriptions*, vol. 1: *Hebrew and Moabite Inscriptions* (Oxford: Clarendon Press, 1971), 32–49; Klaas A. D. Smelik, *Writings from Ancient Israel* (Edinburgh: T. & T. Clark, 1991), 116–31.

16. As proposed by Wilson, *Prophecy and Society*, 263–66.

17. On the role labels *rō'eh, ḥōzeh, nābî'* see David L. Petersen, *The Roles of Israel's Prophets* (Sheffield, England: JSOT Press, 1981), 35–88.

18. *Pace* Alfred O. Haldar, *Associations of Cult Prophets among the Ancient Semites* (Uppsala: Almqvist & Wiksell, 1945), 126–30.

19. On this label, see R. Hallevy, "Man of God," *JNES* 17 (1958): 237–44; N. P. Bratsiotis, " 'ish," in *TDOT* 1:232–35. The Mesopotamian equivalent *awil-ilum* or *amel-ili* is attached to different functions; see Haldar, *Associations of Cult Prophets*, 29–34, 126–30.

20. One of the best studies on the prophetic *legendum* is that of Alexander Rofé, *The Prophetical Stories* (Jerusalem: Magnes Press, 1988).

21. On the linguistic usage, see Harry A. Hoffner, " 'ob," in *TDOT* 1:130–34.

22. Not much is to be gained by speculation as to the etymology of *nābî'* and its possible connection with the Akkadian *nabû*, "to call" (the called one? the one who calls out?), though juxtaposition with comparable ancient Near Eastern designations (*āpilu, muḫḫû*, etc.) can be instructive; on which see Herbert B. Huffmon, "Prophecy (ANE)," in *ABD* 5:477–82.

23. See his remarks in *Ancient Judaism*, 82–87 and *Economy and Society*, 1:241–54.

24. On the judgeship from a Weberian perspective, see Abraham Malamat, "Charismatic Leadership in the Book of Judges," in Frank Moore Cross, Jr., Werner E. Lemke, and Patrick D. Miller, Jr., eds., *Magnalia Dei: The Mighty Acts of God. Essays on the Bible and Archaeology in Memory of G. Ernest Wright* (New York: Doubleday, 1976), 152–68.

25. Comparative material in Haldar, *Associations of Cult Prophets*, 118–20. A wealth of fascinating source material on these phenomena in general is to be had in I. M. Lewis, *Ecstatic Religion: A Study of Shamanism and Spirit Possession*, 2d ed. (London and New York: Routledge, 1989).

26. Weber, *Ancient Judaism*, 94–95.

27. J. Hoftijzer and G. Van der Kooij, *Aramaic Texts from Deir 'Alla* (Leiden: E. J. Brill, 1976); Jo Ann Hackett, *The Balaam Text from Deir 'Alla* (Chico, Calif.: Scholars Press, 1980); Michael S. Moore, *The Balaam Traditions: Their Character and Development* (Atlanta: Scholars Press, 1990).

28. *ANET*, 623–32 has a selection of the Mari material. A brief recent survey of the relevant Mari texts with bibliography is available in Huffmon, "Prophecy (ANE)," in *ABD* 5:478–80. The dream-incubation is dealt with extensively by Robert Gnuse, *The Dream Theophany of Samuel: Its Structure in Relation to Ancient Near Eastern Dreams and Its Theological Significance* (Lanham, Md.: University Press of America, 1984).

29. Argued by Jepsen, *NABI*, pp. 29–43.

30. On these cultic seers and ecstatics, see Haldar (note 18, above) and Huffmon (note 22, above).

31. For the central-peripheral distinction, see Lewis, *Ecstatic Religion* passim.

32. Examples in Lewis, *Ecstatic Religion;* and Johannes Lindblom, *Prophecy in Ancient Israel* (Oxford: Basil Blackwell, 1963), 6–46.

33. Assuming that *pĕrā'ōt* in Judg. 5:2 refers to long locks of hair; cf. Num. 6:5.

34. *rkb,* "chariot," has obvious warlike connotations and reminds us of the description of Yahweh in Ps. 68:5 as *rōkēb ba'ărāpôt,* "rider or [charioteer] on the clouds," emended following the Ugaritic description of Baal as *rkb 'rpt;* cf. Ps. 68:18. Cf. also the Syrian deity Rekub-el.

35. *ANET,* 26.

36. Lindblom, *Prophecy in Ancient Israel,* 102–3.

37. See chapter 2, note 13, above.

38. In the annals of Shalmaneser III; see *ANET,* 280–85. Omri is also named, and Ahab referred to but not named, in the Mesha stela; see *ANET,* 320–21.

39. 1 Kings 11:29–39; 14:1–18; 15:29; 16:1–4, 7, 12; cf. 2 Kings 15:12.

40. The point is made clearly in the story about the man of God from Judah and the old prophet of Bethel in 1 Kings 13.

41. Christopher Begg, "The Non-mention of Amos, Hosea and Micah in the Deuteronomistic History," *BN* 32 (1986): 41–53.

42. E.g., Amos 1:3; 3:3–8, 12; 6:12. The original home of Amos is an open question and will probably remain so. The superscription (1:1) places him among "the shepherds of Tekoa," a village about five miles south of Bethlehem in the Judean wilderness, but this superscription was added at a much later time, and the awkward subordinate clause '*ăšer hāyāh bannōqĕdîm mittĕqôa*' may have been added to that later still. This Tekoa would not be a likely spot for sycamore groves (Amos 7:14) either. Note, too, that Amaziah tells Amos to flee to Judah, not to return there (7:12). Proponents of a northern provenance include Victor Gold, "Tekoa," *IDB* 4:527–29; Stanley N. Rosenbaum, "A Northern Amos Revisited: Two Philological Suggestions," *HS* 15 (1977): 132–48; idem, *Amos of Israel: A New Interpretation* (Macon, Ga.: Mercer University Press, 1990), 31–33; Klaus Koch, *The Prophets: The Assyrian Period* (Philadelphia: Fortress Press, 1982), 70.

43. Hans Walter Wolff, *Amos the Prophet: The Man and His Background* (Philadelphia: Fortress Press, 1973) = *Amos' geistige Heimat* (Neukirchen-Vluyn: Neukirchener Verlag, 1964).

44. Hos. 6:13; 7:11; 8:9–10; 12:1; 14:3; Isa. 2:6–7; 7:1–17; 30:1–5; 31:1. See W. Dietrich, *Jesaja und die Politik* (Munich: Chr. Kaiser, 1976); J. Alberto Soggin, "Hosea und die Aussenpolitik Israels," in John A. Emerton, ed., *Prophecy: Essays Presented to Georg Fohrer on His Sixty-fifth Birthday* (Berlin: Walter de Gruyter, 1980), 131–36.

45. Amos 7:14 has been endlessly discussed, but the most obvious sense, i.e., a dissociation from the *nĕbî'îm,* still seems the most probable. The most recent commentaries available in English are J. Alberto Soggin, *The Prophet Amos* (London: SCM Press, 1987), 127–29; F. I. Andersen and D. N. Freedman, *Amos: A New Translation with Introduction and Commentary* (New York: Doubleday, 1989), 775–94; Shalom Paul, *Amos* (Hermeneia; Minneapolis: Fortress Press, 1991), 243–47.

46. Hans Walter Wolff, "Wie verstand Micha von Moreschet sein prophetisches Amt?" VTSup 29 (1978): 403–17.

47. The non-use of the *nābî'* label by the eighth-century prophets is discussed by A. Graeme Auld, "Prophets through the Looking Glass," *JSOT* 27 (1983), 3–21, and by Robert P. Carroll, "Poets not Prophets," *JSOT* 27 (1983), 25–31.

48. Compare Micah 1:2–4 with Amos 1:2; Micah 1:3 with Amos 4:13; Micah 2:3 with Amos 5:13; Micah 2:6–7 with Amos 7:15–16. In this last, note use of the verb *hēṭîp*, literally, "drip," for preaching.

49. The following are worth reading on the role of the intellectual: Max Weber, "Intellectualism, Intellectuals, and Salvation Religion," in idem, *Economy and Society* 1:500–518; Karl Mannheim, *Ideology and Utopia* (1929; New York: Harcourt Brace Jovanovich, 1985), 153–64; S. N. Eisenstadt and S. R. Graubard, eds., *Intellectuals and Tradition* (New York: Humanities Press, 1973).

50. Karl Jaspers, *Vom Ursprung und Ziel der Geschichte* (Munich: Piper Verlag, 1949); English translation, *The Origin and Goal of History* (London: Routledge & Kegan Paul, 1953).

51. See the essays in Samuel N. Eisenstadt, ed., *The Origins and Diversity of Axial Age Civilizations* (Albany, N.Y.: State University of New York Press, 1986).

52. Weber, *Economy and Society*, 1:450–51.

53. Ibid., 1:443.

54. Moshe Weinfeld, "The Protest against Imperialism in Ancient Israelite Prophecy," in Eisenstadt, ed., *Origins and Diversity*, 181–82.

55. Consult K. H. Henry, "Land Tenure in the Old Testament," *PEQ* 86 (1954): 5–15; Christopher J. H. Wright, *God's People in God's Land: Family, Land and Property in the Old Testament* (Grand Rapids: William B. Eerdmans, 1990), 119–28; Jeffrey A. Fager, *Land Tenure and the Biblical Jubilee* (Sheffield, England: Sheffield Academic Press, 1993).

56. L. H. Herr, *The Scripts of Ancient North-west Semitic Seals* (Missoula, Mont.: Scholars Press, 1978); Amihai Mazar, *Archaeology of the Land of the Bible 10,000–586 B.C.E.* (New York: Doubleday, 1990), 455–58, 518–20; Nahman Avigad, *Hebrew Bullae from the Time of Jeremiah: Remnants of a Burnt Archive* (Jerusalem: Israel Exploration Society, 1986).

57. The Monolith Inscription of Shalmaneser III (*ANET,* 279) records that Ahab put two thousand chariots into the field at the battle of Qarqar on the Orontes in 857 B.C.E. Even if we reduce this figure by a factor of ten, the cost of equipping such a force must have been very high.

58. For the texts see Gibson, *Textbook of Syrian Semitic Inscriptions,* 1:5–20, 71–83; André Lemaire, *Inscriptions hébraïques,* vol. 1: Les Ostraca (Paris: Editions du Cerf, 1977), 23–81, 245–50. They have been variously interpreted by Yigael Yadin, "Recipients or Owners: A Note on the Samaria Ostraca," *IEJ* 9 (1959): 184–87; Anson Rainey, "Administration in Ugarit and the Samaria Ostraca," *IEJ* 12 (1962): 62–63; idem, "The Samaria Ostraca in Light of Fresh Research," *PEQ* 99 (1967): 32–41; W. Shea, "The Date and Purpose of the Samaria Ostraca," *IEJ* 27 (1977): 21–22; Mazar, *Archaeology,* 409–10. On the *lmlk* jar handle stamps, see P. Welten, *Die Königs-Stempel* (Wiesbaden: Otto Harrassowitz, 1969); Mazar, *Archaeology,* 455–58.

59. Amos 3:9, 12; 6:1; Hos. 7:1; 8:5; 10:5, 7; 14:1; Micah 1:5–6; 3:10–12; 6:9–16; Isa. 1:21–23; 28:14–22.

60. The translation is from Gibson, *Textbook of Syrian Semitic Inscriptions,* 1:28–29.

61. Amos 5:21–24; Hos. 4:4–6, 9; 5:1; 6:9; 10:5 (note the use of the term *kōmĕrîm*, "pagan priests," galli, rather than the usual *kōhănîm*); Micah 3:5–12; Isa. 1:10–17; 3:2–3; 28:7; 29:10.

62. Arvid S. Kapelrud, *Central Ideas in Amos* (Oslo: Aschehoug, 1956), 5–7.

63. Bernhard Lang, *Monotheism and the Prophetic Minority* (Sheffield, England: The Almond Press, 1983), 117; G. A. Barrois, "Debt, Debtor," in *IDB* 1:809–10; J. van der Ploeg, "Slavery in the Old Testament," VTSup 22 (1972): 72–87.

64. On the Samaria ivories, first published in 1938 by J. W. Crowfoot and Grace M. Crowfoot, see Nahman Avigad, "Samaria (city): The Ivories," *NEAEHL* 4:1304–6; on Tirzah–Tell el-Far'ah, see Mazar, *Archaeology*, 414–15.

65. See Dan Barag, "Survey of Pottery from the Sea off the Coast of Israel," *IEJ* 13 (1963): 13–23.

66. For the text of the stela of Zakir (Zakkur?), ruler of Hamath and Lu'ath, see *ANET*, 501–2, 655–56; and Walter Beyerlin, ed., *Near Eastern Religious Texts Relating to the Old Testament* (Philadelphia: Westminster Press, 1978), 229–32; for the inscription of the Moabite king Mesha, see *ANET*, 320–21; on Mesopotamian prophecy, see note 25, above; also *ANET*, 449–52, 629–32; Beyerlin, *Near Eastern Religious Texts*, 118–28.

67. Yohanan Aharoni, "The Israelite Sanctuary at Arad," in David Noel Freedman and Jonas C. Greenfield, eds., *New Directions in Biblical Archaeology* (Garden City, N.Y.: Doubleday, 1969), 28–32; Mazar, *Archaeology*, 497–98.

68. Samuel Daiches, "The Meaning of 'Am-haaretz' in the Old Testament," *JTS* 30 (1929): 245–49; Marvin H. Pope, " 'Am Ha'arez' in the Old Testament," in *IDB* 1:106–7; J. Alberto Soggin, "Der jüdische 'am-ha'areṣ und das Königtum in Juda," *VT* 13 (1963): 187–95; Roland de Vaux, "Les Sens de l'expression 'peuple du pays' dans l'Ancien Testament et le rôle politique du peuple en Israel," *RA* 58 (1964): 167–72; Ernest W. Nicholson, "The Meaning of the Expression ' 'Am-ha'areṣ' in the Old Testament," *JSS* 10 (1965): 59–66; Shemaryahu Talmon, "The Judean 'am ha'areṣ in Historical Perspective," *Fourth World Congress of Jewish Studies* 1 (1967): 71–76.

69. I take 2 Kings 23:21–24 to be an appendix, added after the account of the reform had been rounded off with the celebration of Passover (vv. 21–23).

70. On Hosea's origins, see Hans Walter Wolff, "Hoseas geistige Heimat," *TLZ* 91 (1956): 83–94; and idem, Hosea (Hermeneia; Philadelphia: Fortress Press, 1974).

71. Referred to in Amos 5:11 and 7:1. See Barrois, "Debt, Debtor," in *IDB* 1: 809–10.

72. On the situation in Elephantine, see Porten, *Archives from Elephantine* (Berkeley and Los Angeles: University of California Press, 1968), 60–75; on Nehemiah 5, Joseph Blenkinsopp, *Ezra-Nehemiah: A Commentary* (Philadelphia: Westminster Press, 1988), 253–60; E. Neufeld, "The Rate of Interest and the Text of Nehemiah 5.11," *JQR* 44 (1953/54): 194–204; R. Maloney, "Usury and Restrictions on Interest-Taking in the Ancient Near East," *CBQ* 36 (1974): 1–20.

73. W. J. Woodhouse, *Solon the Liberator* (New York: Octagon Books, 1965), 98–116.

74. Edwin M. Yamauchi, "Two Reformers Compared: Solon of Athens and Nehemiah of Jerusalem," in Gary Rendsburg, Ruth Adler, Milton Arfa, and Nathan H. Winter, eds., *The Bible World: Essays in Honor of Cyrus H. Gordon* (New York: Ktav, 1980)

75. The translations are those of I. M. Linforth, *Solon the Athenian* (Berkeley: University of California Press, 1919), 141, 145.

76. *b. Yoma* 9b; *b. Yebamot* 121b; *b. Baba Batra 12a; b. Sanhedrin* 11a.

77. Proposed by David Noel Freedman, "The Law and the Prophets," VTSup 9 (1963): 250–65; idem, "The Earliest Bible," in Michael P. O'Connor and David N. Freedman, eds., *Backgrounds to the Bible* (Winona Lake, Ind.: Eisenbrauns, 1987), 29–37; see also Joseph Blenkinsopp, *Prophecy and Canon* (Notre Dame, Ind., and London: University of Notre Dame Press, 1977), 96–102.

78. Eisenstadt and Graubard, eds., *Intellectuals and Tradition*, 3.

Conclusion

1. Assembled by Ephraim Stern in his *Material Culture of the Land of the Bible in the Persian Period 538–332 B.C.* (Warminster: Aris & Phillips, 1982) (published in Hebrew 1973).

Suggestions for Further Reading

General

The reader is encouraged to check the suggestions made and conclusions reached against a close personal reading and study of the biblical texts. Further reading suggestions, restricted for the most part to recent English-language works, follow. The fullest selection of related texts from the Near East is still James B. Pritchard, ed., *Ancient Near Eastern Texts Relating to the Old Testament,* 3d ed. (Princeton: Princeton University Press, 1969), but a useful collection with notes and bibliography is available in Walter Beyerlin, *Near Eastern Religious Texts Relating to the Old Testament* (Philadelphia: Westminster Press, 1978). For Hebrew inscriptions, see John C. L. Gibson, *Textbook of Syrian Semitic Inscriptions, vol. 1: Hebrew and Moabite Inscriptions* (Oxford: Clarendon Press, 1971), or Klaas A. D. Smelik, *Writings from Ancient Israel* (Edinburgh: T. &. T. Clark, 1991). Several aspects of Israelite society are covered in R. E. Clements, ed., *The World of Ancient Israel: Sociological, Anthropological and Political Perspectives* (Cambridge: Cambridge University Press, 1989), and J. Andrew Dearman, *Religion and Culture in Ancient Israel* (Peabody, Mass.: Hendrickson, 1992). For the history of scholarship on the biblical literature, Douglas A. Knight and Gene M. Tucker, eds., *The Hebrew Bible and Its Modern Interpreters* (Chico, Calif.: Scholars Press, 1985), may be consulted. Patrick D. Miller, Paul D. Hanson and S. Dean McBride, eds., *Ancient Israelite Religion* (Philadelphia: Fortress Press, 1987), contains thirty-three essays on various aspects of cult. Rainer Albertz, *A History of Israelite Religion in the Old Testament Period,* vol. 1: *From the Beginnings to the End of the Monarchy* (Louisville: Westminster John Knox Press, 1994), is commendable for making the necessary distinctions between familial, tribal, and official state cults.

D. A. Knight, ed., *Tradition and Theology in the Old Testament* (Philadelphia: Fortress Press, 1977), is one of the few recent works in English dealing with the concept of tradition. Odil H. Steck, "Theological Streams of Tradition" (in Knight, ed., *Tradition and Theology* 183–214), and Morton Smith,

Palestinian Parties and Politics That Shaped the Old Testament (New York and London: Columbia University Press, 1971), identify specific traditions and related social entities in ways quite different from the present volume.

The Sage

Most of the relevant Near Eastern material can be found in the works listed above, to which add W. G. Lambert, *Babylonian Wisdom Literature* (Oxford: Clarendon Press, 1960). Standard treatments of the "wisdom literature" are James L. Crenshaw, *Old Testament Wisdom: An Introduction* (Atlanta: John Knox Press, 1981), and Roland E. Murphy, *The Tree of Life: An Exploration of the Biblical Wisdom Literature* (New York and London: Doubleday, 1990). The most comprehensive treatment of the sage in different lands and contexts is John G. Gammie and Leo G. Perdue, eds., *The Sage in Israel and the Ancient Near East* (Winona Lake, Ind.: Eisenbrauns, 1990), to which Leo G. Perdue, Bernard B. Scott, and William J. Wiseman, eds. *In Search of Wisdom* (Louisville: Westminster John Knox Press, 1993), serves as a companion volume. J. L. Crenshaw, "Education in Ancient Israel," *JBL* 104 (1985): 601–15, evinces a more cautious approach than André Lemaire, "Education (Israel)," in *ABD* 2:305–12 (with excellent bibliography). Joseph Blenkinsopp, *Wisdom and Law in the Old Testament* (Oxford: Oxford University Press, 1983), traces the confluence of the intellectual-sapiential and legal traditions, and Claudia V. Camp, *Wisdom and the Feminine in the Book of Proverbs* (Sheffield, England: The Almond Press, 1985), has an interesting treatment of issues dealt with in the present volume under the heading of "Feminine Wisdom: The Return of the Repressed". B. W. Kovacs, "Is There a Class-Ethic in Proverbs?" in J. L. Crenshaw and J. T. Willis, eds., *Essays in Old Testament Ethics* (New York: Ktav, 1974), 171–89, supplements the section on the same subject in the present volume.

Priest

The problems besetting the history of the priesthood in Israel explain why no one has attempted to write such a history since Aelred Cody, *A History of Old Testament Priesthood* (Rome: Pontifical Biblical Institute, 1969). The student can consult the section "Religious Institutions" in Roland de Vaux, *Ancient Israel: Its Life and Institutions* (London: Darton, Longman & Todd, 1961), 271–518, but should be aware that differences of opinion exist at almost every point. Menahem Haran, *Temples and Temple Service in Ancient Israel* (Winona Lake, Ind.: Eisenbrauns, 1985), brings together studies written over several decades, many of which reflect what might be called the

Israeli point of view on several issues, for example, the date of the Priestly source. See also Gary A. Anderson, *Sacrifices and Offerings in Ancient Israel* (Atlanta: Scholars Press, 1987), and G. A. Anderson and Saul M. Olyan, eds., *Priesthood and Cult in Ancient Israel* (Sheffield, England: Sheffield Academic Press, 1991).

Prophet

For the history and phenomenology of prophecy in general, see Klaus Koch, *The Prophets*, vols. 1 and 2 (Philadelphia: Fortress Press, 1982, 1984), and Joseph Blenkinsopp, *A History of Prophecy in Israel from the Settlement in the Land to the Hellenistic Period* (Philadelphia: Westminster Press, 1983). A valuable collection of essays, including the notable contribution of Max Weber, has been put together by David L. Petersen, *Prophecy in Israel* (Philadelphia: Fortress Press, 1987), whose *The Roles of Israel's Prophets* (Sheffield, England: JSOT Press, 1981) should also be read. Different aspects of prophetic traditioning are covered in Richard Coggins, Anthony Phillips, and Michael Knibb, eds., *Israel's Prophetic Tradition* (Cambridge: Cambridge University Press, 1982), and, concentrating on Isaiah, Peter R. Ackroyd, *Studies in the Religious Tradition of the Old Testament* (London: SCM Press, 1987). Robert R. Wilson, *Prophecy and Society in Ancient Israel* (Philadelphia: Fortress Press, 1980), a major contribution to the "social world" of the prophets, is critically reviewed by Robert P. Carroll, "Prophecy and Society," in Clements, ed., *World of Ancient Israel,* 203–25.

INDEX OF ANCIENT SOURCES

PRINCIPAL BIBLICAL TEXTS CITED

INDEX OF SELECTED SUBJECTS